LSP Teacher Training
Summer School

Peter Lang

Bruxelles · Bern · Berlin · New York · Oxford · Wien

Marie-Anne Chateaureynaud and Peter John (eds.)

LSP Teacher Training Summer School

The TRAILs project

Champs didactiques plurilingues
Vol. 13

INSPE Université de Bordeaux
This book is the result of research carried out in the project "Teacher Training
Summer School (TRAILs)", co-funded by the Erasmus+ programme of the European
Union (Re: 2018-1-FR01-KA203-048085).

This publication has been peer reviewed.

© P.I.E. PETER LANG S.A.
    Éditions scientifiques internationales
    Bruxelles, 2023
    1 avenue Maurice, B-1050 Bruxelles, Belgique
    www.peterlang.com ; brussels@peterlang.com

ISSN 2593-6972
ISBN 978-2-8076-1864-0
ePDF 978-2-8076-1865-7
ePub 978-2-8076-1866-4
DOI 10.3726/b20096
D/2022/5678/50

Bibliographic Information published by the Deutsche Nationalbibliothek
fte Deutsche Nationalbibliothek lists this publication in the Deutsche Nationalbibliografie;
detailed bibliographic data is available online at http://dnb.d-nb.de.

Table of Contents

Part 2: Identification of LSP Teacher Needs

Part 3: Definition of Training Outcomes Based on Identified Gaps Between LSP Provision in Europe and LSP Teacher Needs

Part 4: Innovative LSP Teacher Training Curriculum

List of Figures

List of Tables

Abbreviations

CEFR	Common European Framework of Reference for Languages
CLIL	Content and Language Integrated Learning
ECTS	European Credit Transfer System
EHEA	European Higher Education Area
ELT	English Language Learning
EMP	English for Medical Purposes
ESP	English for Specific Purposes
FLD	Foreign Language Didactics
ICT	Information and Communications Technology
LSP	Language for Specific Purposes
LSPTT	LSP Teacher Training
PBL	Problem-Based Learning
PjBL	Project-Based Learning
SDL	Self-Directed Learning
SLA	Second Language Acquisition
SLD	Speciality Language Didactics
SSP	Spanish for Specific Purposes
TBLT	Task-Based Language Teaching
VLS	Vocabulary Learning Strategies

Acknowledgements

The TRAILs project, "LSP Teacher Training Summer School (TRAILs)" was co-funded by the European Commission (Erasmus+ project no. 2018-1-FR01-KA203-048085).

Foreword by the editors

1. A few words about linguistic policy in the European context

Multilingualism has become a major issue at European level, especially since the early 2000s. This trend has been reflected in the political guidelines and directives given to the member countries.

This book is the result of a collaboration and partnership between eight European universities. It was carried out within the framework of an Erasmus+ project and it is therefore worthwhile to start by referring to the specificity of the European context.

1.1. Overview of policy orientations for the promotion of multilingualism

The Council Resolution of 14 February 2002 (CoE, 2002) represents a step towards a strategy of multilingualism by considering that knowledge of languages is one of the basic skills that every citizen needs to participate effectively in the European knowledge society. This measure aims to facilitate both integration into society and social cohesion (p. 2).

This strategic direction is reinforced by the Council in 2008: the Member States of the Commission are invited to provide from the earliest age up to higher education a diversified and high-quality offer of linguistic and cultural education options and to enable mastery of at least two foreign languages. This request is presented as "a factor of integration into a knowledge-based society" (CoE, 2008, p. 2). In the set of recommended actions for the promotion of multilingualism, the themes of employability and mobility are highlighted: emphasis is placed on better promotion of multilingualism as a factor in the competitiveness of the European economy and the mobility and employability of people (ibid).

1.2. Language learning and employability

The issue of employability in relation to language skills has been documented in EU actions and texts. For illustration, the Commission set up a Business Platform for Multilingualism in 2007, which led to the publication of a brochure entitled Languages Mean Business which advocates a strategic language dimension that can be supported by partnerships to help companies and individuals improve their job performance through language policy (p. 13) EC (2008). Another noteworthy example is the Commission staff working document (EC, 2012) entitled Language competences for employability, mobility and growth which makes clear the close links between language skills and employability, in terms of mobility and growth and which calls on Member States' education systems to better respond to the learning and professional needs of students and to "work more closely with employers, chambers of commerce and other stakeholders, linking language teaching to the creation of EU-level career paths" (p. 2).

1.3. A European perspective on language teaching in HE

To clarify how the project fits in with European policy, let's refer to the Commission's communication on a renewed agenda for higher education (EC, 2017) which shows the Commission's interest in higher education to facilitate progress in the implementation of the European project. This communication states that it is difficult to meet the increasingly important and specific training needs in higher education: "Higher education plays a unique role. Demand for highly skilled, socially engaged people is both increasing and changing. High-level skills gaps already exist." (p. 2).

Therefore, actions are recommended to meet the challenges to tackle skills mismatches and promote excellence in skills development. The expected initiative relates, on the one hand, to the quality of the programmes intended for students, since "Well-designed higher education programmes and curricula, centred on students' learning needs, are crucial for effective skills development" (EC, 2017, p. 4). The need for good teachers is stressed:

"Good teachers are crucial. Too many higher education teachers have received little or no pedagogical training and systematic investment in teachers' continuous professional development remains the exception." (ibid, p. 5)

This lack of training for teachers of higher education has been corroborated by observations in most countries of the European Union, as Trowler and Bamber (2005) highlighted.

However, compulsory training for teaching in higher education is beginning to be implemented frequently in various European countries. In France, for example, before 2017 there wasn't any formal training for senior lecturers. This situation is therefore evolving to guarantee a better quality of teaching and therefore of training for students. If this is the case in most subjects, it is even more so in the teaching of specialised languages, which requires specific knowledge. Teachers in higher education were previously specialised in their field but had no training to teach.

In the case of LSP, beginning teachers are specialised in the language, but not necessarily in language teaching and very rarely in the specialised area they are expected to teach (legal English, business Spanish, etc).

Thus, one might consider that there may be a double lack of training.

2. LSP as a field of study in higher institutions

The need for specialised languages has grown strongly over the 20th century and higher education has had to adapt to the demand for training. Thus, for several decades, European universities have been offering training and degrees in specialised languages. These courses have also become fruitful research issues, and have allowed the development of a specific field, that of LSP.

2.1. Why this perspective on LSP in relation to language policies in higher education?

It is our choice to talk about specialised languages in terms of LSP (languages for specific purposes) and not ESP (English for Specific Purposes), in order not to limit the scope to the English language, despite the historical roots of specialisation and the vast majority of English-speaking authors who have created the interest in specialised language. Dealing with LSP allows catering for all language training offers in speciality areas. The fields represented in the LSPs are multiple and constantly evolving; specialities are generally made necessary by economic and cultural needs, anchored in evolving employment and professions, and influenced by globalisation.

2.2. Why are issues of LSP teacher education critical in this context?

LSP represents the majority of language teaching and therefore of the positions to be filled in LSP for the recruitment of specialist language teachers.

Indeed, despite an increasingly strong demand for the delivery of LSP courses, there is a blatant lack of qualified LSP teachers which affects vocational education and training institutions in European contexts and beyond.

While job offers targeting language for specific purposes (LSP) teachers are proliferating, many among those vacancies tend not to be filled, due to a mismatch between the profiles of the job-seekers and the skills which are needed (Taillefer, 2008). This could be explained by the lack of recognition in research, lack of academic recognition of research and therefore of teacher-researchers in LSP.

The impact is felt on the language policy of institutions, with unfilled positions and therefore untrained generalists who teach these courses. It is also felt in the training offer which is limited to ESP. As a consequence, a loss of linguistic diversity is observed and a phenomenon of outsourcing of language training (language centres or even service providers).

2.3. Questions related to the training of teachers to deliver LSP

The issue has been much debated: do LSP teachers actually need training? Improvisation could be enough according to Dudley Evans.

It is however acknowledged that LSP teachers generally face an array of work needs, all of which require knowledge and skills and presumably some form of teacher education.

The training is highly context-specific and time-bound and, thus, should be designed on the basis of the needs of the teachers under focus.

Yet, confrontation with teachers' experiences proves that difficulties are encountered because of the quasi absence of specific training in the European context.

3. The TRAILs project

The starting point of the project is the fact that there are almost no formal/substantial teacher education courses for LSP in the EU and there is a mismatch between foreign/second language teachers for general or specific purposes who do not have sufficient professional knowledge and/ or professional competences related to their LSP teaching in various disciplines, and their actual job-demands as LSP teachers. Topics for LSP teacher education have been previously suggested by several authors. Yet, these have never before been derived from solid empirical data on LSP teacher needs (Basturkmen, 2014; Hüttner et al., 2009). Today's digital technologies provide unprecedented opportunities for digitally supported learning and teaching of LSP. Yet, the digital skills of LSP teachers seem to be insufficiently developed to effectively incorporate modern technologies into LSP teaching. By constructing an LSP teacher education programme based on solid empirical data, digital skills, and personalised learning in small groups, we will be able to cater for the needs of a modern LSP teacher.

3.1. The project's partner institutions

The ESPE d'Aquitaine of the University of Bordeaux in France (renamed INSPE in 2019) is involved not only in the continuing education of language teachers but also in their lifelong professional development, offering other training in the fields of education and training, including a focus on computer skills.

The Faculty of Maritime and Logistics Studies at Jade University of Applied Sciences in Germany has been involved in a number of international projects focusing on pedagogical designs and foreign language study (e.g., the International Maritime Management Distance Learning Course, and an online learning and assessment package).

The Department of French and English Philology and the Institute of Applied Linguistics Research of the University of Cádiz, Spain, focus on research in languages applied to academic and professional communication. Thanks to their academic experience, the project team members have good relations with national and international associations, and sister associations in Europe through specific collaborations and research networks.

One of the main priorities of the Faculty of Modern Languages and Literatures at Adam Mickiewicz University in Poland is high-quality language teaching, through the integration of professional and research objectives, and the promotion of the use of innovative solutions, including new media in language teaching.

The Faculty of Arts at the University of Ljubljana is the Slovenian institution with the longest tradition of teacher training and language teaching. All the researchers involved in the project have a Ph.D. in linguistics, mainly in language teaching methodology. They deal with three different foreign languages (English, German and Italian) and teach PSL at different faculties of the University of Ljubljana.

The Faculty of Mechanical Engineering and Naval Architecture of the University of Zagreb provides LSP courses, namely technical and business foreign languages (English and German). Professional activities and research are carried out in methods of teaching technical foreign languages, terminology and characteristics of technical texts in the foreign language, the development of LSP teaching and learning materials and textbook writing, language acquisition and the development of students' communication skills.

Arcola Research in the UK has extensive experience in applying a wide range of innovative assessment methods and tools in different modes of assessment, including "ex ante", "formative" and "summative" assessments, combining quantitative and qualitative methods. They place particular emphasis on "summative," combining quantitative and qualitative methods. They place particular emphasis on "learning through evaluation" and have developed approaches, methods, and tools for applying evaluation data to "scaling up" project results, for example, using "replication analysis".

The long tradition of CERLIS, the research center of the University of Bergamo in Italy, its international reputation and its specific interest in specialised discourse can provide expertise on how domain-specific knowledge is mediated/negotiated/delivered in various specialised communicative environments and thus contribute to the development of language teaching, high competence and new literacies from a pedagogical perspective.

3.2. Presentation of the purpose and progress of the project

The Erasmus+ TRAILs project focused on the preparation, design, and implementation of an innovative and robust Europe-wide teacher training programme for teachers of languages for specific purposes (now LSP) in response to the finding that most higher education teachers in this field have not received specific training, which is worrying, given that languages are essential in this context to ensure mobility and employability. To respond to the challenge posed by the extremely specific context of LSP, the eight partners adopted a transnational and collaborative approach: based on a study of the real situation in the field, carried out in synergy with the possibilities offered by research, the work was divided and organised in several interdependent phases (outputs), from preparation to implementation and evaluation.

The first step was to review the supply of LSP teacher training programmes in the European Higher Education Area: they were found to be scarce and heterogeneous (output 1).

Following this exploration of the institutional side, a field research (surveys and interviews) identified the needs of LSP teachers in higher education and their expectations in terms of training (output 2).

The gaps detected between existing training provision and the training required for these teachers were used to define relevant and applicable teaching-learning objectives (output 3) and then to design a LSP teacher training programme to support the development of the skills of the target audience: in-service participants and students.

The resulting lesson planning (output 4) was divided into teaching modules that alternate between interactive plenary sessions and group work.

Conducted online from 22 to 26 February 2021, the course comprises 11 modules addressing the needs of future and current LSP teachers in terms of teaching methodology, with reference to the use of ICT. Participants were also provided with the technical support of an accompanying document to scaffold the activity and extend the process of reflection. It was noted in the assessment (output 5) that all the training sessions were clearly appreciated by the participants who showed real commitment and managed, together with the trainers, to create an atmosphere favourable to learning and friendly collaboration. The results obtained were made known to the stakeholders through the organisation of dissemination events which gave rise to debates and made it possible to strengthen cooperation with networks working in a similar field, such as the Erasmus+ CATAPULT project. A booklet was produced and translated into each of the partners' languages to complement the presentation. The final conference allowed the approach to be further consolidated. The work was also presented at conferences and workshops. Among the writings on the project, we should mention the forthcoming publication by partners of a collective work "LSP Teacher Training Summer School. The TRAILs project"; the book is expected to contribute to the dissemination of the LSP teacher training programme, evaluation methods and tools. And finally, building on the work of TRAILs, the Erasmus+ LSP-TEOC. Pro project, which started in September 2020, aims to develop a multilingual online course for LSP teaching.

4. Presentation of the different chapters of the book

The first part is focused on: *LSP Teacher Training programmes in the European Higher Education Area.* Identification and analysis of LSP teacher training programmes in Europe are explored in the first chapter by Peter John, Russell Greenwood, Violeta Jurković, Snježana Kereković, and Joanna Kic-Drgas. Marie-Anne Châteaureynaud and Marie-Christine Deyrich present Professional Development of LSP Teachers as a Key Issue in European Higher Education. The two following chapters illustrate these remarks with specific examples of teacher training in Europe: Marcelo Tano presents *The professional development of teachers of Spanish for Special Purposes* and Pascaline Faure focuses on *English for Medical Purposes: from linguistics to didactics.*

The second part entitled *Identification of LSP teacher needs* deals with an analysis of LSP teacher training needs based on the TRAILs Project in four articles, one by Marie-Christine Deyrich who gives a survey of the TRAILs experience. The issue is further studied in terms of identity by Patrizia Anesa, Marie-Christine Deyrich, with a quantitative focus by Ana Bocanegra-Valle and M. Dolores Perea Barberá and, also with a qualitative focus by Paloma López-Zurita and María Vázquez-Amador.

In the third part, Definition of training outcomes is proposed. Joanna Kic-Drgas and Joanna Woźniak who base their research on the identification of gaps between LSP provision in Europe and LSP teacher needs.

The second chapter, written by Snježana Kereković, Brankica Bošnjak Terzić and Olinka Breka, addresses the issue of teaching language skills in LSP in contrast with teaching language skills in a general foreign language (GFL).

The fourth part focuses on different processes and techniques for materials adaptation in LSP, teaching and learning LSP vocabulary as well as on various aspects of three innovative approaches to LSP teaching: *Materials adaptation in LSP: processes and techniques*, by Patrizia Anesa, Katharine Sherwood, Cailean Dooge, *Teaching vocabulary in LSP* by Brankica Bošnjak Terzić, Olinka Breka, Snježana Kereković and *Task-/problem-/project-based and multimodal learning and teaching in LSP*, Olinka Breka, Snježana Kereković, Brankica Bošnjak Terzić.

Part 1

LSP TEACHER TRAINING PROGRAMMES IN THE EUROPEAN HIGHER EDUCATION AREA

1.1

Identification and Analysis of LSP Teacher Training Programmes in Europe

PETER JOHN, RUSSELL GREENWOOD,
VIOLETA JURKOVIĆ, SNJEŽANA KEREKOVIĆ,
JOANNA KIC-DRGAS

1.1.1. Introduction

In the European Higher Education Area (EHEA), quality teaching has become an issue of importance, but learning to teach in higher education has still received insufficient attention. A Communication from the Commission on a Renewed Agenda for Higher Education (European Commission, 2017) mentions the disturbing fact that "too many higher education teachers have received little or no pedagogical training". This is a matter of particular concern for teachers and learners of Languages for Specific Purposes (LSP) in higher education institutions which offer programmes that do not lead to degrees in languages. At these institutions, language teaching is narrower in focus than in general language courses and is centred on the learners' present or future specific professional needs instead of general interests. Therefore, LSP teaching also involves the analysis of written and spoken genres that learners will encounter in their present or future working situations (Basturkmen, 2010). This is a clear indication that the knowledge that LSP teachers need significantly depends on their teaching situation (Deyrich & Stunnel, 2014). Importantly, the specific language skills that learners acquire through LSP teaching are expected to enhance their employability and mobility (Grosse & Voght, 2012; Knezović, 2016).

Demand for language instruction directly relevant to professional domains has increased steadily with the aim of enhancing employment in today's typically international and global professional contexts (Bárcena, Read, & Arús, 2014; Grosse & Voght, 2012; Marra, 2013). As a result, the demand for qualified LSP teachers has risen significantly. Paradoxically, however, most LSP job offers tend not to be filled by qualified teachers that have taken systematic training in LSP teaching. The lack of university training focused on LSP teaching seems to be the most valid explanation for this mismatch. In fact, most LSP teachers have been assigned to teach LSP courses without any initial training. Another element to be considered is that language teachers who accept an LSP position or lecture within an LSP context have to overcome the complexity of the context and assume a wide variety of roles, without any previous training or present support (Paltridge, 2013). Since teacher education is vital in such a specific context, the problems raised should be dealt with in a constructive and inclusive way (Basturkmen, 2014; Majhanovich & Deyrich, 2017).

Based on these premises, the primary focus of the Erasmus+ "LSP Teacher Training Summer School" (TRAILs) (Re: 2018-1-FR01-KA203-048085) project is on LSP teacher training (LSPTT) and skills development to promote high-quality and innovative LSP teaching. In general terms, eight project partners have adopted a customised quantitative and qualitative methodology to explore the current provision of LSP teacher training in the EHEA and the needs of in-service LSP teachers. The gap between the current LSP teacher training provision and the identified needs of LSP teachers provided a basis for the definition of the training objectives, topic areas, and learning outcomes of an LSP teacher training summer school that will be held in Zagreb, Croatia, in September 2020.

The main expected result after the completion of the project is an innovative curriculum for the training of LSP teachers, applicable throughout the EHEA. In this curriculum, LSP teacher training will be linked to the needs of future and current LSP teachers in terms of teaching methodology, with particular reference to the use of information and communications technology (ICT) and blended learning and teaching. Importantly, teacher trainee employability, and teacher trainee and LSP teacher professional self-confidence and competence, will be enhanced through the acquired knowledge and skills. Last but not least, the language, digital and intercultural skills of all involved project team members and training participants will be improved, along with their awareness of the importance of continuous evaluation.

Several intellectual outputs will be produced during the course of the project: the analysis and identification of LSP teacher training programmes in the EHEA, the identification of LSP teacher needs, the definition of training objectives and outcomes, the LSP teacher training curriculum, and the evaluation model and tools. The present paper presents the adopted methodological approach for data collection and some results of the analysis of LSP teacher training programmes present in the EHEA.

The findings of this project are based on a sample of LSP teacher training programmes provided in the EHEA and will be used to develop an LSP teacher training summer school curriculum.

1.1.2. Setting guidelines for the collection of data on LSP teacher training programmes

The identification of the current LSP teacher training offer in the EHEA (courses, contents, qualifications) was based on the analysis of LSP teacher programmes in the EHEA.

In order to capture the quantitative and qualitative data, the project members developed a standardised questionnaire that was either completed on the basis of available online information (syllabi) or sent to higher education institutions providing courses on LSP teacher training in their curricula with a request for completion. The guidelines for the collection of data were defined by all project partners.

The questions guiding the planned study covered two main areas: basic information and outcomes of a module or of a complete course. The introductory questions covered information about the surveyed institution (faculty, department) and the name of the LSP teacher training provided by the institution. They helped to identify the offer of training courses provided by higher education institutions in the selected countries. To gain a holistic view of the LSP teacher training offer in the EHEA, both complete courses and modules offered within curricula were analysed. Thus, the main focus of the core part of the study was on the structure, methods used and expected outcomes of the programmes offered. The questions reflected the researched areas and referred to the study cycles of the respective programmes, the number of ECTS points delivered, entry requirements for the training, general contents of the syllabi as well as learning outcomes and teaching/learning methods used. Of interest were also the assessment methods taught within the course and used to evaluate the course. Considering the fact that the research concerned LSP, and not solely English for Specific Purposes (ESP) teacher training, the TRAILs team members decided to identify the language used for instruction during LSP teacher training. Additionally, two questions in the survey related to the ICT taught in the training and used as part of LSP teacher training as an important phenomenon supporting the training process. In order to compile a list of useful references from the field, the questionnaire also included questions about the materials and books used in LSP teacher training and/or recommended in this field. Moreover, the forms of practical training included in the course or module offered were also taken into consideration in the survey to check whether the theory is reflected in practice. The final inquiry referred to the target participants (General Language Teachers, LSP Scholars/Researchers, LSP Teachers) of the LSP training.

1.1.3. Collection of relevant information about LSP teacher training programmes in the EHEA by means of surveys

Between them, the TRAILs partners checked over 1,000 tertiary educational establishments, such as universities, for LSP teacher training in 25 EHEA member states (out of a total of 48 EHEA member states). The states surveyed were Austria, Belarus, Belgium, Bosnia and Herzegovina, Croatia, Estonia, Finland, France, Germany, Hungary, Italy, Latvia, Lithuania, Macedonia, Montenegro, Netherlands, Poland, Portugal, Serbia, Slovakia, Slovenia, Spain, Ukraine, United Kingdom and Vatican City. These surveyed countries represent roughly 60 % of the EHEA countries' population. For the data collection, fifty online, form-based surveys were set up, two for each country. Each partner was provided with an internal and an external survey for their countries of research. The internal survey was completed by the research teams themselves with information gleaned from their web-based research. The external surveys were forwarded to representatives of higher education institutions to fill out when additional information was required, for example when information gathered by the research team was sparse or incomplete. Typically, the internal surveys were created in and filled out in English, whereas the external surveys were created in and filled out in either English or the native languages of the countries checked.

1.1.4. Collection of relevant information by means of Web-based research

The research teams began by assembling a list of accredited higher education institutions in their respective countries of research, sourced from governments, departments of education and reputable online databases. The research teams then used Google Advanced Search (GAS) to search every webpage, document, subdomain and resource comprising part of the establishments' websites for key phrases such as "Language for Specific Purposes teaching" in the UK, or "Fachsprachendidaktik" in Germany and Austria, for instance. GAS was chosen during a trial period, where it was compared to and found to be more effective than other search engines and the manual checking of web domains. In instances in which the GAS Search Engine Results Page (SERP) returned results which clearly showed an LSP teacher training course, this information was entered into the country's internal survey. Such useful results typically comprised detailed module guides as pdf files. Not all GAS SERPs were equally useful, however. Some, such as web pages outlining course features for prospective students, indicated that an LSP teacher training course might exist, but the information provided was incomplete or insufficient for the internal survey. In such cases, further searches were conducted to identify the person responsible for the course, or the relevant head of the department, who was then emailed with a request to fill out the external survey. It was found that such emails were answered approximately 37 % of the time (11 times out of 30) in Germany and Austria, as an example. Of those who answered, approximately 27 % (3 out of 11) were found to have LSP teacher training courses. GAS was supplemented by the use of web archives and web caches to find deleted web content where necessary. GAS SERPs, for example, would sometimes return search results which, once clicked, would lead to a 404 (page not found) error, as the page had been moved or deleted from the location listed on the SERPs; by using web caches such as web.archive. org, these web resources were able to be restored. In instances where GAS SERPs showed that there were no results for the keywords anywhere on an establishment's website, this was taken as evidence that no LSP teacher training course existed, due to the extensive nature of GAS.

1.1.5. Assembling an LSP teacher training database

Once the partners had worked through the entirety of their lists of accredited higher education establishments, and entered the data gathered into their internal surveys and directed others to fill out the external surveys, it was necessary to generate data from the surveys for statistical purposes. First, the partners used the features of the TRAILs project's common data storage site to download the survey responses as spreadsheets. The spreadsheets were then checked for errors, such as unintelligible responses, and the responses were translated into English. This approach generated a series of identically laid-out spreadsheets, which were sorted by country.

1.1.6. Analysis of collected data on LSP teacher training programmes in the EHEA

Upon completion of the data collection by means of Web-based research and online surveys, it was found that out of the 25 surveyed EHEA countries, only 14 countries provide LSP teacher training at a tertiary education level. Together, these countries provide a total of 88 LSP teacher training formats.

When comparing the 14 EHEA countries providing LSP teacher training, it was found that they differed significantly in the scope and content of their programmes. Fig. 1.1.1 provides an overview of those countries providing LSP teacher training in higher education institutions. Given that the countries' populations range widely from roughly 2 to 83 million inhabitants, the number of higher education institutions was standardised to a proportion of LSP teacher training programmes per one million inhabitants. Without this standardisation, the population sizes of countries such as Slovenia and Germany would lead to a rather distorted impression as to the scope of their LSP teacher training provisions.

The studied countries do not only differ significantly regarding the number of LSP teacher training programmes they provide, but also regarding the format of their programmes, which can be classified into the categories of complete courses (26 in total), parts of a course (e.g. a module; 52 in total), subjects (7 in total) and others (3 in total). The term "subject" refers to smaller teaching units offered within modules. For comparison purposes, the different formats are given again as proportions per one million inhabitants (see *Fig. 1.1.1. Higher LSPTT education per 1 million inhabitants*).

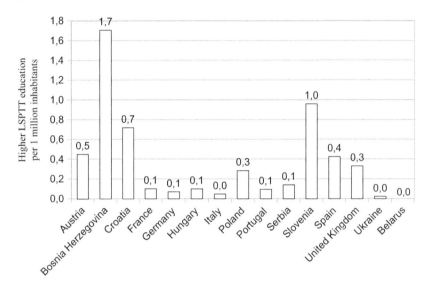

Fig. 1.1.1. Higher LSPTT education per 1 million inhabitants

Of the 62 LSP teacher training programmes not offered as full courses, 58 % (36 in total) are offered as elective modules and 34 % (21 total) as compulsory modules. The remaining 8 % (5 in total) did not specify whether the module, subject or other LSP teacher training provision was compulsory or elective. LSP courses have not been considered here as they have been deemed to be just that: LSP courses and not LSPTT courses.

The survey conducted also shows interesting results with regard to the languages for specific purposes students are trained to teach and the languages of instruction. As anticipated, English is found to be the predominant LSP that students of foreign languages are trained to teach. It accounts for more than half (52 %) of all LSP courses, modules, etc., offered to future teachers of foreign languages, and English is employed as the language of instruction in 42 % of all LSP teacher training formats.

English as the predominant language is followed by German (16 and 18 %), Spanish (17 and 17 %), French (6 and 4 %) and Russian (4 and

4 %) as the languages students are trained to teach and as the languages of instruction, respectively *(see Fig. 1.1.2. Number of participants).*

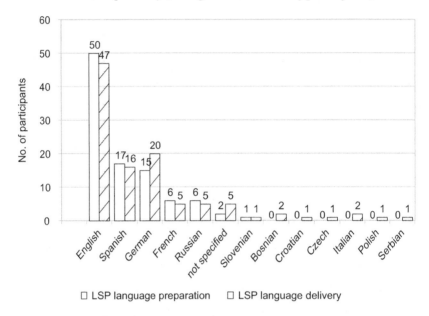

Fig. 1.1.2. Number of participants

In Slovenia, training is provided to teach Slovenian to non-native speakers (a form of LSPTT), while for the remaining languages no LSP teacher training is available, although other Languages for Specific Purposes are taught in these languages. The discrepancies between the numbers given in Fig. 1.1.2 are based on the fact that some LSP teacher training provisions are instructed in more than one language, e.g. in English and in Italian.

Other topics of particular interest in this survey are entry requirements for LSP teacher training, the degrees students obtain upon the successful completion of their studies and the number of credit points awarded on completion of the training, i.e. obtaining the degree.

A variety of entry requirements are defined for students to take on an LSP teacher training course, module or subject. The most common prerequisites relate to language ability according to the Common European Framework of Reference for Languages (CEFR). Here, competence levels range from B1 (1 instance ≈ 1 %) to B2 (7 instances ≈ 8 %) and to C1 (10 instances ≈ 9 %).

Apart from formal prerequisites, such as a completed Bachelor's degree in order to be able to enrol in a Master's course, other forms of completion of previous courses, modules or subjects were stated nine times (5 %). Additionally, some LSP teacher training programmes ask for knowledge of a specific methodology or other experience, such as knowledge of communicative teaching, specific training sessions, work experience, general didactics, pedagogy, to name but a few. The range of these more informal prerequisites is so varied that a sensible classification is hardly possible.

Of the 88 analysed LSP teacher training programmes, 11 lead to a Bachelor's degree (12 %), 60 to a Master's degree (68 %), 10 programmes result in an academic certification or diploma (9 %) and 5 do not lead to an academic degree (6 %). For the remaining two LSP teacher training programmes, the academic achievement could not be identified.

Another highly relevant aspect, that of whether the offered LSP teacher training formally contributes towards obtaining a teacher qualification, has also been scrutinised. It is found that 56 % of all programmes contribute fully (37 provisions) or partially (12 provisions) towards achieving an LSP teacher degree, while 40 % (35 provisions) do not contribute towards this objective. In four cases, no information was available as to a formal contribution towards a teacher qualification.

Once the courses, modules, subjects or other types of training are successfully completed, students will obtain the following number of credit points as defined in the European Credit Transfer System (ECTS):

Tab. 1.1.1. Awarded ECTS

Format	Minimum credit	Median credit	Maximum credit
Complete course	1	10	120
Part of a course	2.5	6	90
Subject	1	4	6

The identified credit points listed the Tab. 1.1.1. must be considered incongruent, as the ECTS clearly defines the scope of credit points granted for complete courses, modules and others. The reason why the stated values differ rather starkly from those expected were studied as the TRAILs project progressed further.

The studied LSP teacher training programmes employ a wide range of teaching and learning methods, including: lecture-style (frontal teaching), group work, individual work, eclectic style of teaching aimed at acquiring different language skills, grammar-translation methods, structural global audio-visual methods, analysing language exchanges in the professional activity, criticism on teaching/learning, lectures, text analysis, pronunciation practice, group animation techniques (pedagogical differentiation, class outside the walls), communicative-intercultural foreign language didactics, corpus-based teaching, problem methods, expression and impression methods, graphic recording methods, and many more. As in the case of the entry qualifications stated above, no prevalent methodologies could be discerned, which makes a classification of these methodologies nearly impossible.

ICT is widely employed in LSP teacher training, with the 27 most used ICT media alone being mentioned 693 times. Fig. 1.1.3. depicts these common ICT media by means of a column chart.

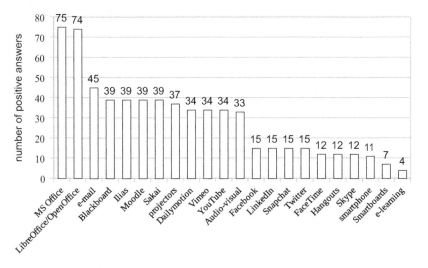

Fig. 1.1.3. ICT media used in LSPTT

1.1.7. Synthesis of the results

The survey, which covered 25 member states of the EHEA, revealed that LSP teacher training is provided by higher education institutions in 14 countries: Austria, Bosnia and Herzegovina, Croatia, France, Germany, Hungary, Italy, Poland, Portugal, Serbia, Slovenia, Spain,

United Kingdom and Ukraine. The number of higher education institutions in each country was standardised to a proportion of LSP teacher training institutions per one million inhabitants to obtain comparable results. In descending order, the countries that offer the largest number of LSP teacher training programmes are Bosnia and Herzegovina, Croatia, Slovenia and Serbia, which can be explained by the fact that these countries share a common educational tradition including firmly established LSP courses offered at higher education institutions.

LSP teacher training is provided in two predominant formats: a module or a part of a course dedicated to LSP issues (52 modules identified by the survey) and a complete course dealing with LSP issues (26 complete courses). In both formats the LSP content is offered either as an elective course (most often the case) or as a compulsory course.

The most important and at the same time the commonest entry requirement for LSP teacher training is language ability as described by the CEFR, ranging from B1 to C1. In some cases, some specific knowledge was required that students should possess, such as knowledge related to teaching methods or pedagogy in general, as well as some work experience.

The majority of ESP teacher training programmes are included in the master's programmes or in the bachelor's programmes, although there are some programmes that result in some sort of academic certification and in one case the ESP teacher training is included in the doctoral study programme.

The survey also examined the teaching and learning methods that are employed by LSP teacher trainers and students. The results show that the methods range from the traditional teaching methods, such as the lecture method and the grammar-translation method, to progressive methods, such as the intercultural approach to foreign language teaching or teaching strategies that promote critical thinking. The survey also revealed that ICT tools are frequently used in LSP teacher training.

1.1.8. Conclusion

Although in this first stage of the TRAILs project it was not possible to collect data for all 48 EHEA member countries, the sample of 25 EHEA member countries can be considered representative of the LSP teacher training programmes offered in the EHEA, as both more and less developed European countries have been surveyed. The collected data reflect differences between the higher education institutions that offer LSP teacher training programmes, but some research findings are also common to many programmes. It can be concluded that LSP teacher training programmes are diverse both in their form and scope in the EHEA.

The collected data including the information about the learning outcomes of the courses/modules that deal with LSP issues in particular, as well as the data on the needs of in-service LSP teachers, to be established in the second stage of the project, will be used as a basis for developing a novel LSP teacher training curriculum.

The initial survey conducted by team members reveals that at present, LSP teacher training programmes in the EHEA are offered in a huge variety of different formats which are far from being standardised.

1.2

Professional Development of LSP Teachers as a Key Issue in European Higher Education

Marie-Anne Châteaureynaud,
Marie-Christine Deyrich

1.2.1. Introduction

Every year, universities advertise public positions for language teachers, more than 70 % of which are intended for law, medicine, science, economics, etc. However, this exponential demand has not changed the training of future language teachers and many candidates do not have the required profile (Faure, 2014). This observation sums up very clearly the situation of training for specialist language teachers (LSP) in France, but as the TRAILs project has been able to show, it is also a widespread situation in other European countries. As a matter of fact, the generalist training that is provided prepares teachers very little for the specialities of the professional context that they will have to transmit, as the authors of the previous article have shown.

The comments expressed on the current situation of LSP teaching imply two things: pre-service training is of course useful, but in-service training should be considered as a necessity, since the vast majority of LSP teachers in post have training needs. We will therefore focus here on the needs for in-service training of LSP teachers in higher education, from a lifelong learning perspective.

After having outlined the importance of in-service training, we will discuss the specificities of this training for LSP teachers. Then, on the basis of the interviews conducted as part of the TRAILs project research, we will analyse a selection of teacher statements to provide an indication of the extent of unmet needs.

1.2.2. The importance of in-service training

Life-long learning is often defined as the process of acquiring knowledge or skills throughout life via education, training, work and general life experiences. Most of the time, the process is considered to be mainly intended for a public that did not complete their studies. However, at the university level, in higher education, many teachers in post would also like to continue with their training because of personal and professional issues.

UNESCO has been promoting a lifelong learning policy for more than four decades, and in 1996 the Ministers of Education of the European Union adopted the document entitled "A Strategy for Lifelong Learning", stating that lifelong learning holds the potential to change the public's entire understanding of education, providing an awareness that education and training are continuing processes (Coolahan, 2002).

Yang, Schneller and Roche (2015) highlight that lifelong learning – "both as a concept and in its many practical manifestations – is becoming a staple of education policy discourse around the globe". We have noted, however, that understandings of lifelong learning can differ widely, not only between countries, but also across the sub-sectors of education systems.

Continuous training is part of the lifelong learning process. It may be informal, but we contend here that institutional in-service training can deliver benefits at two levels:

- For the person being trained:
- In addition to the link to knowledge and personal development, it enables the acquisition of new skills and, where appropriate, a new certification, which may lead to other professional opportunities or to a progression in the career already begun.

  In this way, in-service training is above all a means of professional development. For the structure that trains its staff:

  Continuous training can represent a key element in the development of the structure: it raises the level of qualification of the staff, improves a form of productivity, and makes it possible to update knowledge, to adapt to technological transformations and, by offering career development prospects, to keep its staff competent.

  When dealing with teacher preparation, two distinct areas are often considered in their training: the disciplinary area, in our case languages, and the didactic area that will enable them to enter into a teaching approach:

- As regards the level of practice and knowledge of the language taught, updating is necessary throughout the teaching career and is usually done informally once the initial qualifications have been acquired.
- In higher education, on the other hand, little didactic training is provided, as the vast majority of teacher-researchers who enter professional life by passing their competitive examination do not receive training to learn how to teach.

As a result, universities are beginning to become aware of these needs and in France in 2017 a decree required institutions to offer training (sometimes very brief) for new lecturers.

"A policy of support and training for teacher-researchers and teachers has been implemented, which makes it possible to support them in their professional career, in their teaching activity (particularly in relation to the steps to improve training), in the case of reorientation of their research, or in support of their investment in other missions."(Hcéres, 2017).

C. Lison (2018) devoted a seminar to these questions, organised at the University of Bordeaux, stressing the importance of the pedagogical development of teacher-researchers.

If the institution does take the measure of training needs in higher education, for the time being it focuses on initial training. In-service training remains to be built.

1.2.3. In-service training and languages of specialisation in higher education

As many researchers have pointed out, language teachers recruited for the teaching of LSP in France do not, in most cases, have any specific training. Certified in language and often also in language teaching, most of them have no knowledge of the professional context related to the language of specialisation they will be teaching.

This is also one of the lessons of the TRAILs project, which confirmed what H. Basturkmen (2010) declared: "most LSP teachers teach LSP courses without any initial training". The author focused on the same problem in 2017, pointing out that although several European universities offer some training courses, there is a wide variety of types of training; there is no harmonisation and no programme really built from an analysis of needs in the field.

Out of the 500 surveys in the TRAILs Project, 294 responded and 75.9 % had not received any training. With regard to in-service training for the speciality language teachers surveyed, 290 had not received any in-service training, compared with only 74 who said they had received it. Responses about the content of this in-service training show that it is sometimes informal and provided by colleagues, but also takes other forms such as workshops, seminars, certification, etc. This continuing education is not systematic. It has also been observed that in most European countries, each teacher has managed to continue training in this field as best he or she can.

55.2 % of the teachers surveyed think that "LSPTT programmes should be necessary to qualify as an LSP teacher". Comments included the following: "But let me say this again – formal professional development and perhaps training sessions would help …. You know, training sessions where you can see and discuss best practices with other LSP teachers … that could be useful…. anything … my own work would benefit from such events."

Moreover, the training courses offered often involve language training in English or business English.

However, continuing training in higher education would enable universities to develop real added value. Indeed, universities would gain added value by providing more training for their teachers and promoting qualified and innovative teaching.

The three main areas of linguistic, didactic/pedagogical competence and the speciality linked to the professional field would be of benefit to students and their own learning.

1.2.4. Training needs

In the main, the project should encompass professional development and competence development, specifically the development of communication in a foreign language and of digital competence, in relation to European and regional priorities and owing to the specificity of the area of LSP teaching and learning in higher education (Mackiewicz, 2002).

The needs for continuing education as identified by our project appear to be as follows:

Analysis of target and learner needs, LSP vocabulary teaching, Materials design and development Course design and development, Disciplinary context awareness, Task-based teaching.

These needs expressed by the teachers surveyed have little to do with the level of language because, as we saw earlier, their initial training provides this level.

The needs expressed can be classified into two main areas: specialisation, with specialised vocabulary and also/professional context, and didactics.

1.2.5. The professional context

The professional context that teachers need to know more about was described by P. Faure (2014) as "multi-referential and multidimensional". Her focus was particularly on medical French.

She explains that in the necessary interview with patients, medical language implies a mastery of cultural codes and knowledge of the linguistic domains related to all aspects of the patient's life.

Speciality language teacher(s) must educate learners about the diversity of professional practices, with their cultural varieties. Training in interculturality is also necessary. Some universities, such as those in Finland, provide LSP courses with an intercutural content (e.g. Laurea University Business management dep.).

Educating learners in "foreign" professional cultures is necessary. Indeed, teachers must enable students to take ownership of the specificities of the target professional contexts.

Teacher training is therefore just as necessary in order to be able to transmit this language and this specific context in turn.

The University of Paris Sorbonne, which provides training in medical French, has offered internships in a medical environment to future LSP teachers to allow them to acculturate themselves (see next chapters for further information).

It is this training that is still sometimes lacking for many existing teachers. One of the respondents said, "There is no training for teachers.

Everyone is trained on the job". Another: "I discovered legal Spanish when I had to teach it, I had not studied law".

The professional context and its specialised lexicon evolve over the course of an LSP teaching career, and so this evolution should be taken into account and universities could regularly offer refresher courses for their teachers to update their knowledge and skills. In the rapidly changing field of technology, the renewal of knowledge is necessary and this phenomenon is so well known that some websites use as a marketing argument the fact that their courses are designed by specialists who are certified to teach the foreign language and not by language teachers who know nothing about the subject.

1.2.6. Pedagogical issues

It is certain that pedagogical competence is a central factor of being able to teach any subject.

The expression of these needs shows that in higher education, teacher training is still too absent in spite of the evolution mentioned above. Since 2017, there has been an awareness that training has not yet proved to be efficient: "It is therefore fundamental to have competent teachers. Too many higher education teachers have little or no pedagogical training and systematic investment in in-service teacher training remains the exception" (European Commission, 2017).

A pedagogical transformation must also occur in the context of in-service training, as peer support should not be underestimated. Pedagogical practices already in place at universities can influence new teachers, although the reverse is perhaps less common.

Current LSP teachers have had little or no teacher training. Here is what a respondent to the TRAILs survey said: "I confess my ignorance of the various pedagogical currents, of the various teaching and learning methods, I do what I can." or "they talk to me about different pedagogical approaches but I have no training, I would need a real internship".

Another Erasmus+ Project, Catapult, which is a project coordinated by Cédric Sarré from INSPÉ, Paris, mentions the "Pedagogical isolation" of LSP teachers. This survey also showed the pedagogical needs of many LSP teachers. They would like training on methodology and pedagogy. Just under a third (30 %) of respondents do not master the specific subjects and lack the methodological and pedagogical skills required to teach languages to students of different disciplines and language proficiency levels.

Given the evolution of educational strategies and types of pedagogy, in-service training is necessary to adapt to new educational challenges.

I. Resources:

As well as respondents mentioning resources, during an interview a teacher from a Romanian university explained that she had started to produce a specific textbook because she did not have resources that were properly adapted to her course and to her students.

"I couldn't find any textbook that was really suitable for my students, who were learning medical Spanish. One of the books was for doctors and my students did not yet have this level. The medical references were too complex. I had to start producing my own course materials." This was from an LSP teacher from a French university.

Another French teacher explains: "I trained with my colleagues and we didn't have any materials, we had to produce everything ourselves."

Moreover, as Garcia Romeu (2006) ELEFEC : "the ELEFEC (Spanish for specific purposes) materials are analysed, it must be concluded that the ELEFEC manuals currently available on the market are mostly reprints of manuals published in the 1990s (…) Therefore, as the vast majority of ELEFEC materials have been on the market for at least ten years, it is impossible for them to take into account recent changes in the international business scenario."

In the Catapult Project, over half (52 %) of respondents said that they prepared their own tailor-made materials to customise their lessons, while just over a quarter (27 %) use existing ready-made materials such as textbooks available on the market. They consistently report struggling to find the appropriate language teaching material and adapting it to different disciplines.

II. Course design

In the requests expressed by all respondents to our TRAILs survey, it seems that planning is what teachers lack, since they ask for training in order to properly target learning objectives, learner needs, programming, etc. Other issues raised by the TRAILs surveys include evaluation.

However, course design seems to be the most important need.

The TRAILs project and the surveys carried out point to this lack, as a few quotes emhasise: "I didn't learn how to design a course over the year, I just manage." "I'm struggling with progression and evaluation." "It's difficult to design all the TDS in advance." "I don't know how to design a course for the year."

This issue had already been identified as central a few years ago, for example at the University of Antwerp (Stes and Van Petegem, 2013).

According to R. Goigoux (2015), there are five main elements of the teacher's activity: regulation, explanation, motivation, differentiation and, as the central element, planning.

The overall planning or design of the course takes into account programming, strategies, resources, and evaluations, firstly a diagnostic evaluation to find out the students' audience and evaluate their needs and their difficulties, then, during the course, a formative evaluation which makes it possible to see whether some of the objectives of the course have been achieved, then a summative or even certification evaluation to graduate the student.

An essential element of this planning is temporality. The first assessment to build the planning is important. Some LSP researchers have shown the value of a properly conducted diagnostic assessment to build a course, such as Garcia Romeu (2005): "The first step should be a questionnaire covering the students' personal data, their relationship with Spanish, the importance of Spanish in their profession, how they feel about learning Spanish and what their learning references are." This survey serves to negotiate the objectives and plans of the course.

This diagnostic is also important from a pedagogical point of view: at the beginning of the academic year the students receive the course structure and the planning, and this type of evaluation allows them to be actors of their learning, to invest more easily by knowing how the course will unfold and by catching up on courses they may have missed. This allows teachers to structure the space of the course over the year, and to anticipate the organisation of student work. It is thus important to set the objectives and to ensure that the students understand them.

According to Talbot and Arrieu Mutel (2012), effective teachers "have a very clear idea of what they want to do and accomplish. They carefully plan their teaching activity, identify and work towards the achievement of short, medium and long-term academic goals. They modify their strategies according to their students' progress or learning difficulties."

III. Collaborative work

Finally, teachers would like to work more collaboratively and see the value of sharing and exchanging with their fellow teachers at LSP.

A respondent from Romania said, "I enjoy working with my colleagues, we exchange our practices but it would take more time to do so on a regular basis."

In-service training should be offered to LSP teachers as a team so that they can develop collaborative skills and have time to do so.

1.2.7. Conclusion

Lifelong learning is a challenge for education and professional development, focused on the improvement of professional skills and self-development. This remark also applies to the teaching of LSP in higher education.

In higher education, the lack of solid teaching proficiency among teachers has become a matter of concern for universities. They are beginning to measure these needs but still too often direct their training efforts towards initial training.

The survey conducted in the framework of the TRAILs Project on the teaching of languages of specialisation shows that the in-service training of these teachers remains rare: respondents stress their needs. It differs from other types of university teaching in terms of its specific content but is similar in terms of specific pedagogical needs. The main result of the survey on lifelong learning could be that as well as the professional context and specific resources they would like for in-service training on pedagogy, teachers are especially interested in course design.

The quality of LSP teaching, and consequently the quality of student learning, their level of qualification and their professionalisation also depend on this necessary continuing education. It is a virtuous circle, and a real challenge for universities and the quality of training.

1.3

The Professional Development of Teachers of Spanish for Special Purposes

Marcelo Tano

1.3.1. Introductory remarks

In this contribution, we would like to offer some comments on the situation in the university environment of the Spanish teacher who decides to integrate communication in specialised Spanish into his or her practice. It is clear that, for the vast majority of teachers who choose to teach Spanish for Special Purposes (SSP/ESP in French and Spanish),[1] initial training to teach this demanding and multidisciplinary subject is almost non-existent.

While training in foreign language didactics (FLD) has existed for many decades, this is not the case for Speciality Language Didactics (SLD) and, even less so for SSP, which is an emerging discipline in scientific terms. Its relatively new character leads us to try to define it in the broadest possible way. Thus, Tano (2017a: 600) circumscribes the concept of SSP as follows: "Branch of Hispanistics[2] that deals with the

---

[1] This acronym was gradually promoted in France by GERES in the early 2010s and emerged as an imitation of the acronym ESP (English for Special Purposes) created in the late 1970s by the Research group of ESP (GERAS). It should be remembered that, throughout this time, the Anglo-Saxon scientific community has analysed languages by focusing on specific usages, whereas the French scientific community has done so by focusing on specialities. It can be seen that, while the object of study is the same, the approach to analysis may vary. We draw the reader's attention to the importance of not confusing SSP, which originated in the French-speaking world and has also been adopted in the Spanish-speaking world, with the acronym SSP (English for Specific Purposes) commonly used by English-speaking researchers.

[2] A branch of Romance linguistics or Romance philology concerned with the study of the Spanish language and its associated cultures (Tano, 2017a: 601).

language, discourse and culture of Spanish-speaking professional communities and specialised social groups as well as the teaching of this subject".

It should be noted that the emergence of SSP coincides with a widespread interest in languages for professional purposes in an international context where the use of English alone seems to have shown its limitations. At the beginning of the 21st century, the usefulness and profitability of linguistic tools is being openly displayed as one of the levers for the professional integration of executives. In terms of training, this trend reminds us that times have changed and that learners want to make practical use of foreign languages: "Students have become users, internationalisation and global geographical mobility have taken hold and, as a result, learners are now [...] utilitarian about everything related to foreign language acquisition" (Porcher, 2004: 33). From the perspective of "human capital", a notion widely developed by the OECD,[3] Keeley (2007: 68) points out that the effective use of language tools enables interaction with people from different cultures and backgrounds, which, in a globalised economic environment, is a capacity that facilitates intercultural communication, the latter now being a guarantee of career development.

Moreover, since the Bologna Process, which advocates better intra-European employability thanks to the establishment in 2010 of the European Higher Education Area, the teaching sector that French research calls Languages for Specialists in Other Disciplines (LANSAD)[4] is expanding rapidly. Thus, in France, in order to cope with demand, the Ministry of Higher Education, Research and Innovation (MESRI) publishes each year teaching positions in LANSAD, most of which are intended mainly for the fields of science, law, economics, management, medicine and engineering. These posts are increasingly profiled as LANSAD, i.e. requiring a profile of candidates who not only know the particularities of a PSL (that of their target audience) but above all know how to teach that language in all its specificity.

---

[3]   Organisation for Economic Co-operation and Development.

[4]   "Expression referring to the foreign language teaching sector in French universities aimed at all non-language specialist students. The LANSAD sector is growing rapidly and Spanish is the second most taught foreign language" (Tano, 2017a: 602).

However, despite the gradual and obvious progress of LSPs in higher education, the findings of the scientific community are alarming. For Causa and Derivry-Plard (2013: 55), there is a paradox in LE teaching at university as we are witnessing a diversification of courses for students and a total lack of appropriate training for teachers. Tano (2016: 110) observes that Foreign Language teachers who apply for LANSAD positions overwhelmingly have classical training where PSL and its didactics are often absent. This author also notes (Tano, 2013: 127) that as a general rule, LSPs in French higher education have a complex operation that is not exempt from abuses. One of them consists in setting up language courses that are not linked to the didactics specific to these specialities. Spanish is no exception to this trend, with a proliferation of courses based on general content. This is not without consequences for the state of research in SSP which, despite efforts, remains marginal and dispersed.

Even though in French higher education Spanish is very generally the second most represented FL after English in terms of job vacancies, there is a discrepancy between the training received by teachers and the concrete needs stated in the job descriptions, so much so that Lagarde (2013: 14) asks, "In what way has Hispanism dealt with the needs in LEA[5] or LANSAD, if not, often, by delegating these teachings to LLCE[6] specialist colleagues in sub-service, to ATERs[7] or to monitors or temporary workers of any kind, poorly trained and motivated by default?". This is all the more true since DLE, a discipline which is becoming the keystone of SSP teachers in higher education, has always been a secondary issue in French Hispanism, which leads this researcher to ask again (Id.), "In what way has Spanish didactics been considered from the point of view of research, if not as applied research or action research, as the poor relation of science?".

All these observations led us to question the ins and outs of the training of Spanish teachers in higher education who, by motivation or

---

[5]　"Applied Foreign Languages", a course of study in French universities which began in the 1970s and has developed considerably to the point where most university students studying languages are now enrolled in it.

[6]　"Foreign Languages, Literatures and Cultures", a classic course in French universities.

[7]　In France, a temporary teaching and research associate is a temporary teacher-researcher employed on a fixed-term contract.

necessity, work with SSP in the classroom. This theme has therefore been the subject of a multi-year research project, which we seek to summarise in this article, after a brief theoretical framework on the training of SSP teachers, before ending with some proposals by way of conclusion.

1.3.2. Theoretical framework for the training of teachers of Spanish as a speciality

In this second part, we will draw on the main notions which, in our opinion, will allow a better understanding of the state of training of professionals who find themselves in a situation where they have to teach ESP. In order to do this, we will start with a brief reminder of the general training of foreign language teachers and then move on to the teaching skills required of any teacher of a specialised language. Finally, we will consider some elements concerning the role of the ESP teacher.

1.3.2.1. The professionalisation of foreign language teachers

As the teaching of foreign languages has become considerably more complex, some studies predict that the evolution of initial teacher training will lead to a higher level of requirements and greater professionalisation (Algan, 2021: 55). Indeed, we observe that the level is increasing not only in terms of the qualifications required but also in terms of the pedagogical and practical experience that is now required of teachers (Id.: 56). These trends lead Richer (2011: 63) to outline a reconfiguration of the LE teaching profession, a teacher who "redefines himself as a language professional".

Following Verdía Lleó (2011: 5), it seems to us that teachers' professional competence is composed of various interrelated factors: knowledge, skills and attitudes. By knowledge, we mean the knowledge that is the subject of the teaching; in this case, it refers to the formal system of the specialised Spanish language as well as the cultural aspects associated with it.

But there is also knowledge of the characteristics of the environment in which the teaching-learning process will take place and which will necessarily reveal specific needs. For this reason, another relevant aspect that should be part of the knowledge is that of the didactics specific to the teaching object. At the same time, all teachers need to develop skills to function in the classroom, in the workplace and in the wider professional community. These skills are more directly related to the tasks that the teacher performs inside and outside the classroom and are reflected in pedagogical skills, communicative skills and intercultural mediation skills. Since a teacher's attitude towards the teaching-learning process is a combination of what he or she knows, believes and feels (about himself or herself, about the profession, about students, about colleagues, about the institution he or she works for), his or her attitudes predispose him or her to act in a certain way. According to Richards and Lockhart (1998: 34), three interrelated dimensions are involved in attitudes towards teaching: the affective dimension (feelings and preferences), the cognitive dimension (opinions and beliefs) and the behavioural dimension (overt actions and statements of intention).

This view of FL teacher education sometimes comes up against contradictory realities. In the 1980s, Nunan (1988: 1–2) already noted the tendency to lend importance only to the linguistic aspects of the profession. 20 years later, Martín Peris (2009: 168) came to the same conclusions and warned us about the consequences of this situation: (i) the propensity to consider oneself as "teachers of LANGUAGES" rather than "TEACHERS of languages"; and (ii) the emphasis is placed on the analysis of "products"[8], that is, the linguistic knowledge that will have to be obtained from an objective, a programme and an evaluation, to the detriment of the analysis of "processes",[9] in other words, the linguistic competences that have to be developed, firstly through individual activity of a cognitive and emotional nature and, secondly, through cooperative interpersonal relations.

In the field of FL, the performance of the teaching task thus requires an awareness of specific needs in terms of teacher qualification. For Mateva et al. (2013: 9), FL teachers need to be aware of the range of

---

[8] The "product-oriented" curriculum "[…] gives priority to the final outcome that is achieved through its application and which takes the form of an assessable oral or written production. This type of programme focuses on language knowledge" (Tano, 2017a: 604).

[9] The process-oriented programme "[…] gives priority to the transferable cognitive operations that enable learning. The final result or product is less important than the validation of the acquisitions made throughout the planned activities. This type of programme focuses on language skills" (Tano, 2017a: 604).

competences to be acquired or consolidated, particularly in relation to the teaching methods, learning styles and pedagogical strategies best suited to each training context. In this sense, the EPG[10] competency grid (North et al., 2011: 1–5) divides the competencies of LE teachers into four main categories: (i) training and qualifications (language competence, training to teach, assessment of teaching practice, teaching experience); (ii) key pedagogical skills (methodology, lesson and sequence planning, interaction, classroom monitoring and control, assessment); (iii) cross-curricular skills (intercultural sensitivity, language sensitivity, use of information and communication technologies for teaching); and (iv) professionalism (professional conduct, task administration).

After these initial findings, we agree with Cestero Mancera (2011: 43) when she states that the widespread idea that knowledge of an FL allows it to be taught should be overcome because, as in any professional field, the FL teacher must have specialised training to teach. This training will enable him/her to carry out pedagogical experiences not only from his/her disciplinary knowledge but also from his/her didactic knowledge. In fact, these experiences are also marked by beliefs about how an FL should be learned and how it should be taught. These perceptions determine the teacher's behaviour in the classroom. Paraphrasing Barros García (2008: 274), we can say that if a teacher considers grammar and correctness to be priority objectives of teaching, he or she will design syllabi and tasks of a structural nature with special emphasis on knowledge of the language system. If, on the other hand, the teacher focuses on the use of FL as a communicative tool, he or she will organise the programmes from a functional point of view and plan interactive tasks.

In this way, the training of FL teachers should be based on contents that would become a kind of keystone for the exercise of the profession. In the case of the Spanish language, Gutiérrez Araus (2008: 83) sees three groups of teaching: (i) a first group would include subjects concerning the theoretical foundations of Spanish language teaching, such as applied linguistics and methodology; (ii) a second group of subjects would be used to give an explicit description of the language from the phonetic, grammatical, lexical, discourse and pragmatic point of view; and (iii) a third group of subjects would be centred on the study of the different variations in the use of the Spanish language, in a dual diastasis

---

10   European Profiling Grid.

and diatopic perspective. It is worth noting that it is among this third group that this author (Id.: 84) situates the SSP.

Clearly, the notions of "training" and "qualification" become the cornerstone on which all the competences linked to the professionalisation of the act of teaching an LE are progressively built. If we transpose these notions to the teaching-learning of SSP, it is clear that, in terms of language competence, if the teacher is not a native speaker, obtaining a university degree certifying an official C2 level in the target language should be the norm. In terms of training itself, a Master's degree or equivalent, attesting to at least an introduction to FLD, would seem to be the threshold below which it would be risky to venture into teaching a PSL. With regard to the latter, North et al. (2011: 1) point to the need for further training in specialist areas, among which these authors cite languages for specific purposes. Moreover, the community of trainers is unanimous in its demand that all teachers of foreign languages should have carried out professional practices during their training which have been observed, evaluated and received favourable feedback.[11] From a practical point of view, it is therefore essential that future LE teachers first observe experienced teachers in order to verify in situ what a classroom is like, how it works and what is done in it (De Santiago Guervós, 2008: 106).

While the training needs of LE teachers are met unevenly depending on the training culture of their institutions or countries, efforts to professionalise the profession are verifiable. Nowadays, for example, there is a renewed interest in the strictly didactic aspects that are at the heart of the teaching profession, i.e. those that target training in the most advanced classroom techniques and activities. This is, at least, the wish expressed by the European Profile for Language Teacher Education – A Frame of Reference' guide when it specifies the training strategy regarding knowledge and skills (Kelly et al., 2004: 48): trainee teachers critically study the different methodologies for teaching foreign languages, which they can then use to achieve their learning objectives. With regard to Spanish teachers, Moreno Fernández's study (2011: 25) states that the aspect most clearly valued by the teachers (62 % of respondents) are the characteristics centred on teaching, among which they place, first and foremost, the fact of having "good training". This training must develop professional

---

[11] This need is all the more obvious as LSP, as a polymorphous teaching object, covers plural and rather complex knowledge.

skills because the aim is to train actors in the field who are capable of managing the teaching-learning process of LE in all its complexity. The model of key competences for teachers of second and foreign languages proposed by the Instituto Cervantes (2012: 11), which includes eight major competences, mentions first of all the competence of being able to organise learning situations.

The question of the professionalisation of teachers of foreign languages is often an argument between "knowledge" and "pedagogy". However, the act of teaching a foreign language should be analysed in all its complexity by articulating teacher training around two main types of knowledge: disciplinary and didactic. Admittedly, initial teacher training is essentially based on disciplinary preparation but, since the 1990s, "[…] different approaches to teaching have taken into consideration research on the didactic transposition of knowledge, that is, the transformation of academic knowledge into teachable knowledge" (Gaussel, 2021: 1). While it is absolutely true that there can be no teaching without scientific disciplinary knowledge (the "what" of the teaching-learning process), this is not sufficient for the exercise of a profession which, going forward, also requires a certain technicality regarding the way in which FL can be taught (the "how" of the teaching-learning process).

1.3.2.2. LSP teacher: A profession with a high didactic technicality

Theorists agree that teaching an SFL well is a complex and demanding art (Vez, 1998: 79), all the more so in the case of an LSP, which we can define as an instrument for transmitting specialised knowledge and for carrying out the tasks of each profession (Tano, 2021b: 12). When defining PSL teaching as an act of transmitting specialised language knowledge, Pujol Berché (2003: 8) states that "[…] any didactic act takes as its starting point the contextualisation of the teaching both in relation to the institution […] and in relation to the LSP in question […] in order to adapt the contents and methodology to the needs of the learning public".

According to Aguirre Beltrán, (2012: 14), teaching Spanish for academic and professional communication is a multidisciplinary activity that requires a rigorous approach to the elements that make up this process so as to enable the teacher to create the appropriate conditions for learning to take place, i.e. to help learners acquire and improve a certain communicative competence in a certain area of specialisation. For Rodríguez-Piñeiro Alcalá and García Antuña (2009: 923), in the organisation of the teaching-learning process of specialised communication, it is necessary to prepare an action plan that includes programming and sequencing of the contents to be developed, which must be flexible enough to adapt to the real needs and learning rhythms of the group.

In relation to the contents of curricula, Sabater (2000: 189) advises us to avoid making the mistake of transforming the ESP course into a session in which knowledge about the speciality is transmitted instead of working on the PSL. In other words, the ESP teacher is not an expert on the students' speciality but an expert on how this specialised knowledge can be used to learn PSL. This advice is all the more timely as procedural knowledge, which guides the action of teaching, guarantees a form of efficiency in dealing with specific teaching situations.

According to Tano (2021a: 15), there are key competences for teaching SSP, among which, in addition to a good command of the formal system of the language, there is knowledge of the specific uses of the language as well as of the subjects that structure the students' future profession. In addition, there is the ability to carry out a prior analysis of needs, knowledge of active teaching methods and mastery of the recurrent textual typology of the speciality being taught (Tano, 2017a). Gómez de Enterría (2015: 58) also advocates a methodology centred on activities rooted in professional reality, so that the interaction that the learner develops reproduces as closely as possible the interactions of the world of work. We can see that teaching a PSL requires expertise in training engineering, which is compulsory in the typical profile of teachers who are involved in this type of course.

1.3.2.3. Exploring the role of the SSP teacher

The role assigned to SSP teachers stems from the value that the contemporary world attributes to the communicative skills of professionals of all kinds for whom the Spanish language can become a differentiating element in a multilingual and multicentric world. The increased importance of these teachers is due to the fact that they teach a so-called opening discipline which develops transversal skills and which can facilitate the employability and career development of their students and future professionals.

While it is true that not all SSP teachers are alike, it must be admitted that, like all FL teachers, they are key actors in the development of societies through the openness to the world that their teaching provides (Dumbrăvescu & Merino Mañueco, 2013: 368). Like all teachers, [...] "Some are good, some are bad; some are well trained, some are not; and there are also potentially excellent teachers who struggle to do their best" (Keeley, 2007: 73). Observers agree that the quality of teaching is the most important factor affecting student outcomes, with some authors (Id.) attributing to teachers "a crucial role". This decisive role is due to the fact that they "[...] guide students towards their goals and shape their perceptions" (European Commission, 2015: 3). According to the conclusions of the highest European authorities (Consejo Europeo, 2007: 7), teacher education is becoming a sine qua non for improving the quality of teaching, and an essential element in the modernisation of European education systems. This implies the presence of a qualified and, in this case, highly specialised teaching staff.

According to Pizarro (2013: 166), the interest of researchers was initially focused on FL, the curriculum and the student as a central actor in the teaching-learning process. However, nowadays, research in DFL is moving towards exploring the role of the teacher as a subject involved in this process. If this didactics initially attached great importance to aspects related to the "way of learning" (Id.: 168), it can be said that there is now a growing interest in addressing issues related to the "way of teaching". Marrero (2010: 23) states that this trend is driven by the need to recover the figure of the teacher in order to discuss how to increase teaching skills with the aim of improving the level of efficiency in the management of the act of teaching.

It should be remembered that in the approaches currently in use, namely the communicative method and the action perspective (Tano, 2018: 18), it is indeed the teacher who has to create the right conditions for the learning of FL to take place in a meaningful way. The application of these approaches requires well-trained, flexible, dynamic, active teachers who know how to use different methods and adapt their teaching style to particular contexts (Pizarro, 2013: 172). We add the requirement that these better equipped teachers should not be afraid of integrating innovation and research into their own action. This primordial role attributed to the FL teacher is recalled in the Common European Framework of Reference for Languages (Consejo de Europa, 2002: 139–140), which emphasises the decisive function of the teacher in taking into account, on the one hand, the specific circumstances of the environment in which the pedagogical activity[12] develops and, on the other hand, the best way in which students can identify, analyse and solve their learning problems.

In their study, Hálasz et al. (2018: 3) place initial and in-service teacher training among the key measures to be taken into account to develop the quality of teaching. It seems to us that the recommendations of this study could be perfectly adapted to the training of SSP teachers, particularly in the consideration of the four stages proposed by these authors (Id. 9): (i) a first stage of elaboration of a support system for professional development throughout the career and in the context of continuing education; (ii) a second stage of improvement of initial training in relation to the repositories of professional competences in the SSP, which would, moreover, remain to be defined; (iii) a third stage of professionalisation of assistance to beginning teachers; and iv) support for networks[13] and partnerships for individual and collective professional development.

However, if we wish to promote a logic that genuinely leads to a qualitative transformation of SSP teacher education, the notion of "change" (Esteve, 2004: 9) should be incorporated. It would therefore be necessary to adopt a model based on the teacher's experiences and the reality of his or her professional future; a model, in short, that is not based on theoretical knowledge alone. This approach would be based on reflective learning of the profession, which could become a general principle of training. In this perspective (Id.: 10), training would clearly be based on practice and its central axis would be training that would start from the act of teaching and be achieved through reflection. In this paradigm, the notion of "reflective practitioner", initially proposed in the process of learning as described by Schön (1994), consists of the teacher's own awareness of the teaching process. Detailed reflection would therefore be the driving force for achieving knowledge of the profession. For Pizarro (2013: 173), the concept of reflective teaching practice starts from a constructivist vision of learning whose methodological approaches link praxis and theory. Applied to the field of DFL, this approach is based on

---

[12] Although the CEFR refers quite often to the specific circumstances of intervention, it is regrettable that the framework does not sufficiently integrate the specialised dimensions of the language and of the teaching action.

[13] In France, the emergence and development of GERES, as a federating network of associations in SSP, remains a model example in this respect.

the analysis of teachers' practices, attitudes and beliefs through a critical reflection of their conceptions and teachings in order to improve them.

Improving practice in SSP is only possible if the teacher is truly aware of how the teaching-learning process takes place and is aware of the strategies and routines they adopt. From this perspective, while it is true that theory and practice feed off each other, González and Atienza (2010: 40) explain that reflective pedagogical practice is the opposite of what is traditionally envisaged: it is the teacher who seeks in the theory and not the theory that seeks to influence the teacher. We note that while these perspectives are currently informing the reflections of SSP practitioners, they are not yet always visible among SSP teachers.

1.3.3. The opinions of specialised Spanish teachers concerning their training

We wished to verify in the field to what extent the notions developed in the previous theoretical framework are part of the concerns of teaching staff who intend to teach SSP. In order to do so, we conducted two surveys which we present in the following sections and which attempt to find answers to, among others, some key questions: What was the initial preparation received for teaching SSP? In what context did it take place? Were there elements of professionalisation? What priority contents should be part of this type of specific training? What concrete measures would favour the continuous training of these teachers? What changes do they want and expect in the field of specialist language training?

1.3.3.1. Overview of the field surveys

In 2015, we conducted a first survey among SSP teachers in French engineering schools on the topic of competences for the professionalisation of teachers. Due to the fact that Spanish language is taught in almost all engineering schools in France (more than 200 listed by the MESRI), we thought it appropriate to target SSP teachers working in this specific context. In Tab. 1.3.1., we describe in a concise but detailed way the main characteristics of this survey.

Tab. 1.3.1. Description of the survey "The skills of Spanish teachers in French engineering courses"

Public	SSP teachers in French engineering schools
Objective	To know the type of training received to teach SSP in a technological and technical field
Type of survey	Quantitative and qualitative
Type of questionnaire	Anonymous and directive
Topics covered in teacher education	Initial preparation received for teaching Spanish Context in which the training to teach Spanish took place Professional training to teach SSP Prior training to teach SSP applied to engineering Content on which this specific training should focus
Support	Online, on a dedicated site, with automated data collection
Period	3 months (March to May 2015)
Method of distribution	E-mail sent to: (i) the director of studies and the language department of the 154 engineering schools officially registered in 2015 with the Conférence des Grandes Écoles; (ii) Hispanists working in engineering schools and members of the Union des Professeurs de Langues Étrangères des Grandes Écoles et des Établissements Supérieurs Scientifiques
Target population	Unknown (statistics not available)
Number of respondents	42
Sample analysed	All respondents
Sampling	Empirical
Indicators	For ease of use, percentages are rounded up or down to the mean
Response rate	Not calculable in empirical sampling
Estimated margin of error	Not calculable in empirical sampling
Probative value	Results partially generalisable to the whole reference population due to the small number of participants but considered as verifiable trends for the purpose of this research work

In 2020, a second survey aimed at taking stock of the situation of the PHS at the international level was carried out for the first time. While it is true that a first attempt at a state-of-the-art survey of PHC had been carried out in France before (Tano, 2017b), the 2020 survey had the advantage of including the topic at hand, namely the professional development of these teachers. In Tab. 1.3.2, we describe in summary form the particularities of the survey whose results will be examined.

Tab. 1.3.2. Description of the survey "The profile of university teachers involved in the field of specialised Spanish"

Public	ESP teachers working in any country where the subject is taught
Objective	To know the profile of SSP teachers working in higher education
Type of survey	Quantitative and qualitative
Type of questionnaire	Anonymous and semi-structured
Topics covered in teacher education	Speciality targeted by the teaching of ESP Type of specific training received for teaching ESP Concrete measures that would promote the in-service training of ESP teachers Expected changes in teaching ESP
Support	Online, on a dedicated site, with automated data collection
Period	4 months (March to April 2020)
Method of distribution	Email to 78 associations (Spanish teachers and Hispanists), 7 ELE portals, 6878 subscribers to the GERES mailing list and 1191 ELE teachers in faculties, departments, centres and university institutes worldwide
Target population	Unknown (statistics not available)
Number of respondents	151
Sample analysed	All respondents
Sampling	Empirical
Indicators	For ease of use, percentages are rounded up or down to the mean
Response rate	Not calculable in empirical sampling
Estimated margin of error	Not calculable in empirical sampling
Probative value	Results partially generalisable to the whole reference population (due to the small number of respondents) but qualitatively useful to develop the profile of the individuals surveyed SSP teachers in French engineering schools

1.3.3.2. Analysis of the results

In this third part, we will analyse the results of the ad hoc surveys referred to in the previous section. Specifically, we will identify the trends that can be observed from the indicators collected concerning, firstly, the training of ESP teachers in France and, secondly, that of ESP teachers in twenty-five other countries.

1.3.3.2.1. Trends in the training of SSP teachers in French higher education

The data concerning the training received by SSP teachers working in French higher education come from survey 1 above, which concerns only Spanish teachers working in a French engineering course. Insofar as this is a LANSAD type course and since this sector is the one that is developing most, we consider that these data can be extrapolated, proportionately, to all French university courses that respond to this teaching dynamic.

With regard to the results of this survey (Tano, 2016: 105), an analysis of the training pathways of practising SSP teachers reveals that the vast majority of respondents (81 %) received initial training to teach the general language and that more than half (57 %) received professional training (of the bachelor's or master's type). A good third of the respondents (33 %) stated that they had not received this training in France but in a foreign institution. It can be seen that very few teachers (14 %) had access to doctoral training, which may explain the lack of interest in research among this type of teacher and its corollary: the lack of research in the group studied. Although they were trained to teach Spanish as a general language, the vast majority of respondents (88 %) had not been trained specifically to teach SSP. When asked whether a Spanish teacher working in a technological and technical field should receive specific training beforehand in order to work in this context, more than half of the respondents (57 %) stated that this was not a compelling necessity.

However, if specific training were to be required, many (64 %) thought that it should focus on the linguistic, cultural and methodological aspects of teaching an LSP.

1.3.3.2.2. Trends in university ESP teacher training at the international level

On the basis of the data collected in 26 countries and 5 continents, a kind of profile of SSP teachers in higher education was developed. The geographical origin of the data (Tano, 2020: 5–9) reveals that half (49 %) of the SSP teachers are in Europe and almost half (44 %) are in one of the countries of the vast American continent. This study shows that the language taught is overwhelmingly (81 %) a hybrid between general Spanish and SSP. However, the titles of the subjects taught reveal either a specialised field, such as Business Spanish (24 %), Medical

Spanish (14 %), Legal Spanish (10 %), Engineering Spanish (10 %) and Economic Spanish (8 %), or specific objectives, such as Spanish for Professional Purposes (15 %) or Spanish for Specific Purposes (10 %).

These teachers, the majority of whom were native speakers (74 %), considered that a good SSP teacher should have general knowledge of the specialisation of his or her students (64 %), without being an expert in that specialisation himself or herself, but rather an expert in the LSP. In this sense and unlike in France, they have received initial training to teach SSP (58 %). A good part of the respondents report that they have learned to teach SSP not only thanks to the skills acquired during in-service training (42 %) but also thanks to self-directed training (39 %), probably due to the non-existence of institutionalised training that adapts to their needs. This self-directed training, which can take several forms, would be favoured by certain measures such as attending scientific events related to the ESP such as congresses, colloquia, study days, meetings (77 %), enrolling in a master's or doctoral programme (75 %), participating in workshops (71 %) or in teaching projects (64 %), communicating in events (64 %), or writing articles (58 %).

At all events, they were aware that certain developments were desirable in the teaching of SSP. Among their very diverse responses, three attract our attention in particular: improving didactic preparation in the initial training of SSP teachers (11 %), reforming teacher training programmes to include SSP (3 %), and ending intrusiveness by requiring a diploma to teach SSP (2 %).

1.3.4. Proposals for conclusion

The results of the two surveys of ESP teachers show that pre-service training to teach such a demanding subject is not systematic. While such training may exist in some countries, in others it is conspicuous by its absence. However, the demand for this type of teacher profile has been growing for at least two decades.

If we take France as a framework for analysis, the situation of SSP teachers is a concrete example proving the lack of measures adapted to the unavoidable prerequisites that should be required of the LSP teacher practising in specific contexts. It is true that the SSP teacher, who does not practice this profession by default, will use his initiative and creativity to train himself in order to meet the demands of his target audience. But this effort will require a considerable amount of time and energy which would be better invested in initial training, in line with the requirements of a changing environment which increasingly sees LSPs as instruments of socio-professional integration.

Clearly, the deficit or lack of adequate training to teach SSP is palpable in universities and, in general, in all countries. The current system of training needs to be reconsidered as a matter of international urgency, as the evidence is overwhelming: the generalist nature of current teacher training for LSP teachers, which still focuses on literature, grammar and translation, seems to have reached its limits. In order to adapt to the demands of the 21st century in terms of teaching and learning foreign languages for professional and/or academic use, it is necessary to train future actors in this field in the two central aspects of the profession, i.e. knowledge of the PSL and its didactics.

It also emerges from this study that the Spanish taught is never totally specialised, but rather a balanced mix of general language and LSP. This trend needs to be integrated into teacher training. Teachers can continue to self-train to teach SSP because, in any case, lifelong learning is part of their professional DNA. We believe, however, that initial training that includes the challenges of learning LSP for a university audience would enable teachers to be better equipped to deal with the demands of this kind of teaching.

An institutional shift towards taking the real needs of teacher training into account should gradually emerge in the university environment. In order to achieve this, it would be necessary to: (i) become aware that Spanish is an instrument of international communication valued in the professional environment and that its teaching should be based on the language practices actually observed in the work context; (ii) find theoretical alternatives to promote new epistemological and pedagogical paradigms specific to LSP; and (iii) come out of isolation and make contact with national and international networks of experienced SSP teachers.

It seems to us that strategic actions, based on concrete measures, would allow SSP to emerge from its state of emergent discipline and onto the path of its deployment. Thus, a realistic and immediate solution would be to require candidates to have teaching experience in SSP when the position to be filled is so profiled. In parallel, an ambitious and short-term solution could be to create a better trained teacher status in order to meet the now better identified needs of the university public. Secondly, the theoretical and practical training received by FL teachers would benefit from being underpinned by the contributions of a didactic approach that is more in tune with the specificities of LSP.

Our study has highlighted that changes are expected as the need to provide SSP teachers with better preparation becomes more and more pressing. In this sense, we conclude that it is important to pay attention to the issues that relate to the core of the profession, i.e. the professional development of SSP teachers, since, in view of all the above, there is no doubt that this is a key element for the success of students.

1.4

English for Medical Purposes: From Linguistics to Didactics

Pascaline Faure

1.4.1. Introduction: The importance of "speaking" medical English

In recent decades, learning medical English has become a major issue for medical students and physicians that are not native speakers of English, while the very particular period we are currently going through with the COVID-19 pandemic reminds us, if need be, of the importance for medical professionals to master the English language of medicine. Indeed, as we see on a daily basis, all important studies on new therapeutic protocols, all information on the progress of work on vaccines, and all notifications of new symptoms are first and foremost published in English. To miss out would be to run the risk of not offering the best possible care to the patient.

In this chapter, therefore, we propose to address issues related to the linguistic and didactic aspects of English for medical purposes (EMP).

After a brief history of medical English as a lingua franca of medicine, we will, in the first part, propose an overview of the characteristics of the language used by medical doctors and highlight the professional cultures into which this language is embedded with a view to showing how difficult, not to say impossible, it will be for a language teacher to teach EMP without a solid prior education.

In the second part, we will focus on the didactic aspects of the teaching-learning of EMP by reviewing the different actors and contexts, while underlining the necessity to conduct proper needs analysis and develop close cooperation with content teachers and healthcare professionals.

In the third part, we will suggest possible avenues for setting up an education program for EMP teachers, with a view to making proposals that can be adapted to other specialised languages.

1.4.2. A brief history of English as Lingua Franca of medicine

The hegemonic position of English in the language of medicine has not always been so. Before English, French and German alternately occupied a preponderant place, and traces of this can still be found in the vocabulary of obstetrics ("accouchement", "bougie", "fourchette", etc.) and clinical medicine ("bruit", "rales", etc.) for French (Faure, 2018), and in the vocabulary of psychiatry ("angst", "witzelsucht", etc.) and infectious diseases ("Ehrlichia", "Escherichia coli", "Neisseria", "Rinderpest", etc.) for German. The hegemony of English, and more precisely of North American English, dates back to the Second World War. Buoyed by their victory and taking advantage of the debacle of the European countries, North American researchers began to occupy the forefront of the medical scene (e.g. the first open-heart operation by Blalock at the Johns Hopkins Hospital in Baltimore in 1944, an operation that paved the way to modern cardiac surgery, and the first kidney transplant by Murray and Harrison in Boston in 1954). Since then, English has continued to permeate European medical languages, notably through borrowings ("bypass", "screening", "shunt", "flutter", "burn-out", etc.) (Faure, 2010).

But this hegemony is not only linguistic. It has in fact led to cultural and scientific hegemony (for example, it was under Anglo-Saxon influence that "evidence-based medicine" took precedence over "patient-based medicine"). It is therefore the vision of medicine (and medical practice) as a whole that has become "americanized".

In addition to medical language and culture, this hegemonic position of North American English has other consequences. For example, non-native researchers and health professionals have limited and often delayed access to research, which is essentially published in English.

The hegemonic position of North American English also has an impact on national scientific journals, whose quality of publications is diminished. For example, Egger and al. (1997) showed that German scientists tend to publish their significant results in English-language journals and their non-significant results in German-language journals.

Over the last forty years, scientists have been under considerable pressure from their supervisors to publish their research results in scientific journals. This pressure can be summarised by the expression "publish or perish", to which one must add "in English".

The sums allocated to research laboratories and the promotions granted to researchers depend on the number of publications and the impact factor of the journals in which these publications appear . In medicine, the journals with a high impact factor are all Anglo-Saxon (*New England Journal of Medicine, The Lancet, Nature, JAMA, British Medical Journal*, etc.). To give an idea of the extent of the impact factors of leading medical journals as compared with those of prominent journals in other fields of research, *NEJM's* impact factor is 74,699, while *ESP*, one of the most salient journals in the field of English for specific purposes, is 2,612.

Another edifying figure is the percentage of world medical publications between 2005 and 2015 for the four main languages: publications in French accounted for 0.13 %, behind English (99.44 %), but ahead of Chinese (0.11 %) and Spanish (0.08 %).

The fact that learning medical English has become a major issue in French and European medical schools (excluding English-speaking countries) is thus easy to understand.

1.4.3. Medical English

Having listed and discussed some of the 21st-century skills, we naturally should ask ourselves how to purposefully and explicitly teach these skills in LSP contexts. In the subsequent sections we will discuss task-based language learning, problem-based learning and project-based learning in an attempt to address the question of whether these teaching and learning methods can cater to the needs of 21st-century learners in LSP settings, and to what extent.

1.4.3.1. A specialised language

Despite the great number of definitions for specialised languages (SLs) over the years, we retained one which we think accounts for their complexity, namely that proposed by Vander Yeught (2016). For him, a specialised language (e.g. the medical language) is constructed around its community's intentionality (e.g. curing the sick), and in return the community (e.g. healthcare professionals) constructs itself around its specialised language (e.g. medical English) within a specialised domain (e.g. Western medicine) that has its own history:

> An SL is an "intentionalised" form of a natural language that puts its communicative function at the service of the purpose of the domain among specialised communities. [...] Specialised languages need not be highly technical or abstruse to qualify as such, the major criterion is that their communicative capacities are not deployed for communication's sake, but are harnessed to the service of the purpose of the domain. (Van der Yeught 2016:52)

Within a specialised domain (e.g. medicine), a specialised language (e.g. the language of medicine) divides into different space- and time-depending languages (e.g. the modern English language of medicine) which are spoken by politically-structured national communities (e.g. British doctors) and which are culture-bound (e.g. evidence-based medicine).

Within an SL, the lexicon conveys "a lot about the directness of the domain, its intentionality, its objects and their aspectual shapes and its related background abilities" (Van der Yeught, 2016: 54). Hence, a word like "theatre", used in British medical English, summons the history of 18th-century European surgery, where medical amphitheatres permitted the viewing of surgical operations performed on live patients, and draws its specialised meaning ("a place where surgeries are performed") from the context of its utterance (e.g. a medical context). Therefore, the specialised lexicon will only be properly interpreted within the framework of its specialised domain.

1.4.3.2. The lexicon

When we analyse the lexicon of modern medical English from a synchronic perspective, we observe two main types of intentionality: concision and privacy. Indeed, in modern Western medicine, looking after the sick demands that the healthcare professional be both efficient and thoughtful. To meet either need, the language of medicine resorts to abbreviations. For instance, OR for "Operating Room" in American

English serves the purpose of concision. By being difficult to decipher, Hi5 to designate an HIV-positive patient serves the purpose of privacy. But when we study the lexicon from a diachronic perspective, we notice that what characterises medical English first and foremost is loanwords.

Like any specialised language, the language of medicine has been constructed according to the needs of the medical profession. From the need to name body parts, diseases, techniques and instruments as precisely as possible to avoid ambiguity and misinterpretation, to the obligation to express oneself quickly and to get to the point in order to save lives, medicine has developed linguistic tools to serve its cause in accordance with scientific progress and recommendations in professional practice.

Today, the lexicon of the English medical language has a number of characteristics, such as:

- truncation and, within truncation, apheresis ("scope" instead of "endoscope"), syncope ("appy" for "appendicectomy") or apocope ("onc" for "oncologist")
- amalgam ("urinalysis" for "urine analysis")
- the ellipse of whole words ("a physical" for "a physical examination")
- initialism (ENT for "ear nose throat") and acronym (CABG for "coronary artery bypass grafting"), which can be derived ("she ODed" for "she overdosed")
- encoding (B_x for biopsy – the indexed $_x$ would be a remnant of the Jupiter symbol)(Dirckx, 1983)
- hypallage ("a perforated IUD1" meaning "an IUD that has perforated the uterus")
- encryption ("acute lead poisoning" for "gunshot wound")
- euphemism ("a child with special needs" to refer to a mentally handicapped child)
- anthroponym (Cushing disease)
- toponym (Lujo, merger of Lusaka in Zambia and Johannesburg in South Africa)
- metaphor (cytokine storm)
- metonymy ("the Pill" for "the contraceptive pill")
- or antonomasia ("Clearblue" for "pregnancy testing")

1.4.3.3. Registers

There are various registers in medical English. The register used in doctor-patient communication differs from that used in doctor-doctor communication. For example, when speaking to the patient, the doctor will opt for a common lexicon ("navel" for "umbilicus" or "heartburn" for "acid reflux") rather than a scientific lexicon.

Between physicians, we note the use of two types of lexicon: the scientific lexicon – and within this lexicon, particularly among specialists in the same discipline, the technical lexicon (called "jargon") among which there are many acronyms (e.g. GORD[1] for "acid reflux") – and the slang lexicon (e.g. "disasteroma" for "polytrauma") with, for the latter, a possible reference to television culture (e.g. "a Jack Bauer" referring to a doctor who works long hours) or "culinary" culture (e.g. "a double whopper" referring to an obese patient) (Goldman, 2014).

1.4.3.4. Genres

Each genre has specific characteristics (Swales, 1990). Among the various written genres found in medicine, the research article is probably the most prominent inasmuch as it allows researchers to publish the results of their studies. It usually follows the IMRAD format (Introduction, [Material and] Method, Results and Discussion) and tends to comprise about 10 pages on average. Medical students are trained to read research articles as early as their second year of medicine. Being able to read research articles meets various objectives, among which keeping abreast of the latest findings, getting prepared to critically appraise the validity of published medical studies, and building up a reference section for their Ph. D.

The abstract, which is a shortened version of the research article meant to be read and indexed on scientific search engines such as PubMed, usually follows the same IMRAD format (see Fig. 1.4.1).

---

[1]   Gastro-Oesophageal Reflux Disease.

The NEW ENGLAND
JOURNAL of MEDICINE

ESTABLISHED IN 1812   AUGUST 6, 2020   VOL. 383   NO. 6

A Randomized Trial of Hydroxychloroquine as Postexposure Prophylaxis for Covid-19

D.R. Boulware, M.F. Pullen, A.S. Bangdiwala, K.A. Pastick, S.M. Lofgren, E.C. Okafor, C.P. Skipper, A.A. Nascene, M.R. Nicol, M. Abassi, N.W. Engen, M.P. Cheng, D. LaBar, S.A. Lother, L.J. MacKenzie, G. Drobot, N. Marten, R. Zarychanski, L.E. Kelly, I.S. Schwartz, E.G. McDonald, R. Rajasingham, T.C. Lee, and K.H. Hullsiek

ABSTRACT

BACKGROUND
Coronavirus disease 2019 (Covid-19) occurs after exposure to severe acute respiratory syndrome coronavirus 2 (SARS-CoV-2). For persons who are exposed, the standard of care is observation and quarantine. Whether hydroxychloroquine can prevent symptomatic infection after SARS-CoV-2 exposure is unknown.

METHODS
We conducted a randomized, double-blind, placebo-controlled trial across the United States and parts of Canada testing hydroxychloroquine as postexposure prophylaxis. We enrolled adults who had household or occupational exposure to someone with confirmed Covid-19 at a distance of less than 6 ft for more than 10 minutes while wearing neither a face mask nor an eye shield (high-risk exposure) or while wearing a face mask but no eye shield (moderate-risk exposure). Within 4 days after exposure, we randomly assigned participants to receive either placebo or hydroxychloroquine (800 mg once, followed by 600 mg in 6 to 8 hours, then 600 mg daily for 4 additional days). The primary outcome was the incidence of either laboratory-confirmed Covid-19 or illness compatible with Covid-19 within 14 days.

RESULTS
We enrolled 821 asymptomatic participants. Overall, 87.6% of the participants (719 of 821) reported a high-risk exposure to a confirmed Covid-19 contact. The incidence of new illness compatible with Covid-19 did not differ significantly between participants receiving hydroxychloroquine (49 of 414 [11.8%]) or those receiving placebo (58 of 407 [14.3%]); the absolute difference was −2.4 percentage points (95% confidence interval, −7.0 to 2.2; P=0.35). Side effects were more common with hydroxychloroquine than with placebo (40.1% vs. 16.8%), but no serious adverse reactions were reported.

The authors' full names, academic degrees, and affiliations are listed in the Appendix. Address reprint requests to Dr. Boulware at the University of Minnesota, 689 23rd Ave., Minneapolis, MN 55455, or at boulw001@umn.edu.

This article was published on June 3, 2020, at NEJM.org.

N Engl J Med 2020;383:517-25.
DOI: 10.1056/NEJMoa2016638
Copyright © 2020 Massachusetts Medical Society

Fig. 1.4.1. Abstract

Likewise, the poster, designed to be displayed and discussed within the poster hall in medical conferences, tends to also follow the IMRAD format (see Fig. 1.4.2.):

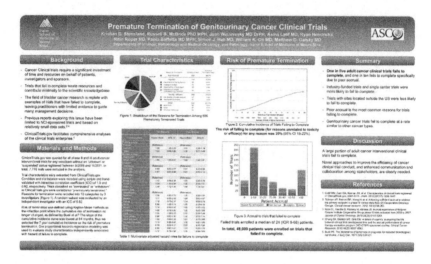

Fig. 1.4.2. Poster

Another genre which has a long-standing tradition in the medical literature is the case-report and is still presented in many medical journals. Apart from its educational value, the major merits of case reporting are to detect novelties, to allow pharmacovigilance, and to put emphasis on the narrative aspect (see Fig. 1.4.3.):

THE NATIONAL MEDICAL JOURNAL OF INDIA   VOL. 14, NO. 4, 2001
223

Clinical Case Report

A pregnant woman with recurring metastasis

SURESH CHANDRA, SANJAY A. PAI,
N. K. VENKATARAMANA

A 27-year-old woman presented to our hospital in 1996 with complaints of diminishing vision. She had been examined 3 years earlier at another hospital for headache, vomiting and visual disturbances. The CT scan showed a small hyperdense nodule with a large cystic component in the left parieto-occipital region. The material removed at parieto-occipital craniotomy was reported to be a metastatic adenocarcinoma with a differential diagnosis of gemistocytic astrocytoma. Detailed investigations failed to reveal a primary tumour. However, since the patient was pregnant, her pregnancy was terminated. This was followed by cranial irradiation (6000 Gy) and chemotherapy (vincristine and CCNU). Twenty-two months later, she returned to the same hospital with a complaint of headache. A repeat CT scan showed a picture similar to the previous one, and the tissue removed at surgery was once again interpreted as a metastatic adenocarcinoma. Investigations once again failed to disclose the primary neoplasm. When she presented to our hospital a year later, she was pregnant. Her CT scan showed a cystic lesion with a solid mass in the left parieto-occipital area. The patient underwent surgery for the third time and the tissue was sent to our laboratory. Her pregnancy was again terminated. Subsequent to this hospital admission, the patient developed a recurrence a year later (1997) in the same area for which she was re-operated.

The tumour pathology of the third surgery showed it to be composed of round to spindle-shaped cells with vesicular nuclei and numerous mitotic figures. Haemorrhage, necrosis and calcification were present. The tumour had infiltrated the meninges and glia. The neoplasm was interpreted as a meningial sarcoma. Review of the previous histopathological slides showed large cells with abundant eosinophilic cytoplasm, an eccentric nucleus with a nucleolus (Fig. 1) and globular cytoplasmic eosinophilic inclusions. Phosphotungstic acid haematoxylin (PTAH) and glial fibrillary acid protein (GFAP) stains done on all three occasions were negative, indicating that the cells were not of glial origin. The slides were interpreted as a secretory meningioma. The slides from the fourth surgical excision were similar to those of the third. The final impression was that of a secretory meningioma which had undergone malignant transformation.

Meningiomas are common, usually benign neoplasms. Because of the pluripotential nature of the arachnoid cap cells from which they arise, meningiomas can have an extremely

Manipal Hospital, 98 Rustom Bagh, Airport Road, Bangalore 560017,
Karnataka, India
SURESH CHANDRA, SANJAY A. PAI   Department of Pathology
N. K. VENKATARAMANA   Department of Neurosurgery

Correspondence to SURESH CHANDRA

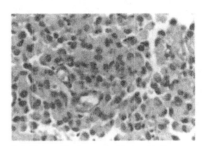

Fig 1. Haematoxylin and eosin stained section of the first tumour

diverse morphological spectrum including fibrous, clear cell, chordoid, lymphoplasmacyte-rich and secretory types.[12] Sex hormones are known to affect the rate of growth of meningiomas in pregnancy.[13]

The histological features of the neoplasm were typical of a secretory meningioma in the initial two operations and of a meningeal sarcoma in the later surgery. The sarcomatous transformation was probably not due to radiation because the histological features of the first recurrence (second surgery) were similar to those of the first excision. Secretory meningioma is known to mimic adenocarcinoma, which, like other meningiomas, is consistently negative for GFAP.[3,4] That the neoplasm was a variant of a meningioma could have been suspected at the second surgery. It is extremely unusual for a malignant tumour, particularly of unknown origin, to metastasize to the same area.

REFERENCES
1 Kleihues P, Burger PC, Scheithauer BW. The new WHO classification of brain tumours. *Brain Pathol* 1993;3:255–68.
2 Marivel JC, Sang DI. Pathology of meningiomas. In: Rosen PP, Fechner RE (eds). *Pathology Annual 1991, Part 2, Volume 26*. Connecticut: Appleton and Lange, 1991:139–93.
3 Maiuri RM, Scheithauer BW, Lacigiani G, Lombard D, Rocca A, Lossi M, *et al.* Oestrogen receptors in meningiomas. A correlative PET and immunohistochemical study. *Nucl Med Commun* 1997;18:606–15.
4 Lantos PL, VandenBerg SR, Kleihues P. Tumours of the nervous system. In: Graham DI, Lantos PL (eds). *Greenfield's neuropathology. Vol 2*, 6th ed. London: Arnold, 1997:739.

The National Medical Journal of India invites clinical case reports for publication. These should be 500–600 words with a maximum of 5 references and 1 illustration. Only reports which have a message, allow formulation of a hypothesis, help direct future research, report a new phenomenon will be considered for publication in the Journal.
—Editor

Fig. 1.4.3. Clinical case report

Other written genres used in medicine include prescriptions, medical certificates, referral letters, lab results or radiology reports. All have their own typical discourse structure, typical language and patterns.

Among spoken genres, the most prominent is the doctor-patient consultation, which follows a set structure as recommended in the *Calgary-Cambridge Guide to the Medical Interview* (Silverman, Kurtz and Draper 2013).

1.4.3.5. Professional cultures

The Anglo-Saxon professional medical culture presents many specific features often linked to the context of practice. For example, for a gynaecological examination in the United States, the practitioner is strongly advised not to be alone with a patient (he must be accompanied by what is called a "chaperone") to avoid any lawsuit.

The teaching-learning of these cultural elements is essential to avoid, like one of our colleagues, a French emergency doctor who went to work in an American hospital, from being sued for rape by one of his patients. But this implies knowing them and, as they are evolving, it implies keeping a watch. Now, when living several thousand kilometres away, it appears to be difficult, which brings us to the second part of this chapter.

1.4.4. English for medical purposes

This section is an overview of what "English for medical purposes" is. We present the various contexts in which it emerges and make suggestions as to how a proper needs analysis should be conducted to offer optimised EMP classes.

1.4.4.1. The contexts

Demand for language training in the health sector comes from two main sources: higher education (Faculties of Medicine, Faculties of Pharmacy, Faculties of Dentistry, Midwifery Schools, Veterinary Schools and Nursing Institutes) and continuing medical and paramedical education (Hospitals, Clinics, Health Centres, Pharmaceutical Laboratories and Physicians' Unions).

The requests may vary within the same source:

- in the form (intensive and extensive, face-to-face courses, lectures, guided self-study, or seminars)
- in the themes (midwifery, ENT, urology, etc.)
- in the contents (lexicon, grammar, etc.)
- and in the objectives (to give a poster presentation, to write a scientific paper, to interview a patient, etc.)

1.4.4.2. Communication situations

Before setting the objectives, it is essential to identify all the communication situations that the learner will be confronted with:

- *In what context will he or she use the foreign language? At the university? In a hospital?*
- *How much verbal interaction will he or she have in his or her professional or academic practice?*
- *Who will he or she talk to? Other health professionals? Patients? Their families? Other students? Teachers?*
- *What topics will he or she talk about? Care? Treatments?*
- *Will he or she have to read? What kind of materials? Research articles? Clinical cases? Course handouts?*
- *Will he or she have to write? What type of documents? Observations? Letters? Clinical studies?*
- *What will his or her status be? A doctor? An intern? A hospital practitioner? A researcher? A nurse? A paramedic?*
- *What is his or her speciality? Radiology? Gynaecology? Paediatrics?*

1.4.4.3. Skills

From the communication situations that the teacher will have listed, he or she will have to deduce a certain number of skills that will serve as the backbone of the course. We have categorised the skills as follows:

General pre-professional skills (higher education)

Read an article; write an abstract; do a literature search; attend a conference and take notes.

General professional skills (continuing education)

Write a research article; make an oral presentation (conference paper, observation, poster, etc.); conduct an oral interaction (interview a patient, greet the family, etc.); write a professional document (prescription, examination report, letter to a colleague, certificate, etc.); and know the health-care system and health care institutions (functioning, organisation and hierarchy).

Specific professional skills (continuing education)

Specific professional skills are as numerous as the positions, personal motivations (working in another country, obtaining a university hospital position, doing an internship abroad, being promoted, etc.) and existing specialities.

1.4.4.4. Contents

- The content will vary depending on the skills to be acquired and the source of the request. In any case, regardless of the learner's linguistic level, it is essential to integrate disciplinary content straight-away for three reasons:

- A language course that mobilises disciplinary content is necessarily more motivating for a learner already invested in a pre-professional or professional world.

- A language course in the LSP domain should be optimal since the time that the learner can devote to this learning is limited by the workload and memory load that he or she has in his or her subject area.

- The subject matter content is a reassuring basis and gives the learner a sense of "killing two birds with one stone" and learning in both languages – the second language becoming a vehicle as much as the first.

1.4.4.5. The teacher

There are two main types of EMP teachers. The first and probably the most common is the general foreign language teacher that is usually a non-native speaker of English:

[...] these courses [LSP teaching occurs in French universities, in medical, law, business and science faculties, and technical universities] are generally taught by language rather than content specialists; these instructors usually have the same initial training as their MFL [modern foreign languages] colleagues in university language departments. (Whyte 2016)

On the other hand, we do also meet healthcare professionals (mainly nurses and doctors) – generally native speakers of English – some of whom have completed a Teaching English as a Foreign Language (TEFL) course[2]. These instructors are common in private language schools and have little or no knowledge of language didactics.

The ideal situation would be to have an LSP teacher who would be both a healthcare professional – preferably a native speaker of English (although having learnt English as a second language does have some advantages in terms of empathy with the learner and second language acquisition perspective) – and a foreign language teacher.

Indeed, to build an LSP course undeniably requires from the teacher an excellent knowledge of the field (environment and communication situations related to status/position), a perfect mastery of the terminology, and an ability to choose and use relevant materials. Therefore, in addition to training engineering skills, the teacher must have sufficient knowledge of the discipline to be able to set up and conduct an LSP course (Humbley, 2001). And this is probably where the problem lies. Because while it is often said that LSP courses are a meeting of experts and that the teacher can rely on the "technical" knowledge of his or her learners, the reality is quite different.

This leads us to argue that the LSP teacher must have a minimum level of knowledge in the discipline. "A minimum" because when we think about the EMP teacher, it seems impossible for him or her to become an expert in all of the often extremely specialised specialities of medicine. However, we argue that the EMP teacher should have a basic knowledge of anatomy, physiology and semiology. These basics would enable him or her to understand and meet the terminology needed by their learners, to prepare relevant sequences, to use adapted material and to reinforce his or her legitimacy.

If any language teacher can teach a general language course, it is impossible for them to prepare different sequences without first taking

---

[2] A full-time TEFL course lasts 4 weeks or 120 hours.

a close interest in the discipline from a terminological point of view but also from a cultural point of view. These cultural constraints cannot be ignored by the teacher, who is often required to teach learners that may wish to go and practice in one of the countries of the target language.

Moreover, being a native speaker is not enough. While a native speaker who has lived in their own country can put their experience as a patient to good use, this does not mean that they can teach in all contexts. Indeed, while he or she may be familiar with the patient's terminology, medical terminology – especially in Germanic languages – differs significantly. The native teacher must therefore learn this terminology in the same way as a non-native speaker.

Our experience has shown that a teacher with a medical background who is not a didactician is not in a position to build a language course from meaningful tasks aimed at the progressive and sustainable acquisition of language skills in a non-native learner. The construction of a language course requires reflection and knowledge of pedagogy: Task-Based Language Teaching (TBLT), Content and Language Integrated Learning (CLIL), and Second Language Acquisition (SLA), and more concretely: designing exercises, choosing relevant materials, exploiting these materials, setting up evaluation, etc.

It is clear that working as an LSP teacher requires specialised training that must include several components: linguistics in the broadest sense (etymology, terminology and discourse analysis), didactics, history, culture, communication and discipline, which brings us to the third and final part of this chapter.

1.4.5. Improving EMP teacher education

In this section, we focus on the teachers that teach English for medical purposes and more precisely on how their education could be improved. Our objective when designing new programmes is to make EMP teachers more knowledgeable in their target domain but also to ensure that they have more than one string to their bow.

1.4.5.1. Developing courses

In France, most foreign language teachers that happen to teach LSP in universities hold either a CAPES[3] or an Agrégation. Both are competitive recruitment examinations designed for general language teachers that plan to teach in secondary schools for the CAPES and in high schools for the Agrégation.

Thirty years ago, due to the exponential growth of LSP teaching positions in universities held until then by Lecturers and Professors, the Ministry of Education decided to recruit secondary and high school language teachers by creating hundreds of PRCE[4] and PRAG[5] positions. Nowadays, most LSP teachers are either PRCE or PRAG, with none of them having received LSP education. To make matters worse, the number of hours they have to teach (384 hours as compared with 192 hours for a Lecturer) leaves very little time to do any research.

We therefore strongly advocate that LSP be introduced as early as possible in foreign language teacher education and that courses specifically designed for LSP teachers be developed. Therefore, in France, the idea would be to integrate LSP as an option at the Agrégation alongside with literature, linguistics and civilisation, and prior to recruitment examinations, to imagine Master's specifically designed for would-be LSP teachers.

1.4.5.2. Integrating teaching of the specialised field

Most LSP teachers have little or no knowledge of the target domain prior to taking up their position. To try to make up for this lack of specific training, it would be a good idea to integrate content teaching. This teaching, provided by specialists and professionals in the field, would offer a basis of fundamental knowledge for LSP teachers.

We could imagine EMP teachers receiving hours of classes on the six major systems: respiratory, cardiovascular, neurological, gastrointestinal, genito-urinary and locomotor, based on an introduction to anatomy, physiology and semiology.

---

[3] Certificat d'aptitude au professorat de l'enseignement du second degré.
[4] Professeur certifié.
[5] Professeur agrégé.

The program would also include instruction in the didactics of medical English, medical sociology (Anglo-Saxon healthcare systems, healthcare institutions, the pharmaceutical industry, clinical research, etc.), medical terminology (Greco-Latin roots, neologisms, metaphors, etc.) and genres (consultation, research article, clinical case-report, prescription, etc.). The second semester's internship could be organised within the various hospital departments so that the EMP teachers could carry out their observations in an authentic professional environment.

1.4.5.3. *Integrating education into professional cultures*

Whether it is a question of adapting to the professional setting *stricto sensu* (e.g. a hospital) or communicating with its actors (e.g. patients), the EMP learner would gain a lot from mastering the codes before interacting, which should save time and avoid possible failures. It is often down to the EMP teacher to transmit intercultural knowledge. Yet, the teacher is neither a professional in the specialised domain nor an ethnologist. Therefore, it would be a good idea to integrate, based on an analysis of exchanges between actors in the target environment and interviews with professionals in the specialised domain, teaching of cultures, which would highlight similarities and differences.

1.4.5.4. *Proposing multilingual and multidisciplinary training courses*

Because LSP teachers are often required to teach in several specialities, it seems important to broaden their areas of expertise.

In 2012, with our colleague Martine Derivry, we had imagined two Masters. The first called "Didactics applied to languages for medical purposes (LMP)" included a choice of 4 languages (French, English, Spanish and German).

The second called "Teaching English and French in the fields of health and science" comprised at least two languages and several specialities such as medicine, physics, chemistry, geology, biology, mathematics and computer science from which the student could choose. The multilingual dimension was aimed to allow future teachers (native or non-native speakers of one of the proposed languages) to teach outside the national framework.

The originality of these two Master's was that they integrated disciplinary teaching provided by professionals in the domain in addition to training in the didactics of specialised languages, terminology, history of science, professional cultures, phonetics, etc., and that the places of internship belonged to specialised fields (hospital, pharmaceutical laboratory, etc.).

Unfortunately, none of these Masters came about.

1.4.6. Conclusion: For an LSP teacher education

Every year for more than 20 years now, the number of PRAG/PRCE positions offered by the universities has been mainly for LSP classes. However, the education of language teachers does not allow them to be immediately operational in specialised fields. We argue that we should set up relevant courses in collaboration with professionals from the different target domains.

We should also give future teachers the desire and opportunity to continue their studies and do their Ph.D., by integrating the notion of LSP early in their curriculum. In this way, their profile would correspond to that of the positions offered as Lecturers and University Professors. We could even consider a year of study in the discipline as a prerequisite.

Furthermore, the emergence of language centres within universities that we have been seeing for more than 20 years is not in the direction of language teacher specialisation, since for the moment, LSP teachers are often involved in a dozen or so specialities that have nothing to do with each other. On the contrary, LSP teachers should be appointed on site so that they can develop networks and deepen their specialisation.

Part 2

IDENTIFICATION OF LSP TEACHER NEEDS

2.1

LSP Teaching and Teacher Needs in Focus

Marie-Christine Deyrich

2.1.1. Introduction

A quest for excellence in skills development for graduates is high on the agenda and, consequently, quality teaching has become a major issue in higher education. However, learning to teach remains a matter that has not been given enough attention in the European Higher Education Area (EHEA). As mentioned in the Renewed Agenda for Higher Education adopted by the Commission in May 2017, "Too many tertiary education teachers have little or no pedagogical training" (European Commission, 2017: 5). In the field of Languages for Specific Purposes (LSP), the situation is even worse since most higher education teachers concerned have received little or no specific training (Basturkmen, 2014). Indeed, despite increasingly strong demand for the delivery of LSP courses, there is a blatant lack of qualified LSP teachers, which affects vocational education and training institutions in European contexts and beyond (Brudermann et al., 2016). It is in this context that the 2-year TRAILs project was launched in 2018 with the objective of designing, testing and assessing innovative LSP teacher training programmes.

2.1.2. LSP teaching and teacher needs

Demand outstrips the supply of competent teachers of LSP in higher education. The high demand for LSP provision is related to academic and societal expectations, whereby the foreign language sector is considered as an asset and a springboard for higher graduates who need a relatively good level of proficiency in one or more foreign languages in order to manage in the labour market (Räsänen, 2008). The close links between language needs and the world of work must be considered in the context of the internationalisation of higher education (Deyrich et al., 2016), where language skills are expected to enhance mobility and employability. Given the high stakes, it is unsurprising that there is an ongoing worldwide increase in LSP courses for students who are non-specialists of the language, i.e., specialists in other disciplines. However, while job offers targeting LSP teachers are on the rise, many of these vacancies tend to remain unfilled in the French context (Brudermann et al., 2016), due to a mismatch between the profiles of job-seekers and the skills which are needed. The mismatch problem is also reported in many other contexts, where the lack of effective teacher-training programmes is held as the determining factor (Ghafournia, N. & Sabet, 2014). Teachers are almost never prepared to teach in this sector (O'Connell & Chaplier, 2015), which is worrying since teacher needs in the domain are multifarious, complex and interrelated, owing to the specificity of teaching a foreign language for specific/special purposes in higher education.

A systematic investigation of needs is thus considered as vital for our purpose. Much research has been conducted on needs analysis in LSP: "the means of establishing the how and what of a course" (Hyland, 2006: 73). But, as mentioned by Bocanegra-Valle and Basturkmen (2019), needs have always been approached from and for the perspective of the learner, while teacher needs are invariably overlooked in needs analysis. That is why it is critically important that teacher needs should be taken into consideration to inform decisions about topics in teacher education programmes. Basturkmen (2014) explains that the description of the needs of LSP teachers found in the literature must be deepened by means of empirical investigations to shed further light on the nature of these needs. Correspondingly, an in-depth investigation into the needs of LSP teachers is a fundamental step in the contribution this project makes towards finding solutions and tools to support skills development for LSP staff and for future LSP teachers in higher education, both at national level for each of the partners and at the European level.

2.1.3. Methodological framework

To address the challenge set in the highly specific context of LSP, a transnational and collaborative approach is being tested and evaluated in the TRAILs project. Based on input from research and good practice, the project relies on the innovative potential of ICT for communication and preparation. A customised methodology is being defined step by step and adopted in the course of all the following consecutive phases: (1) Review of existing LSP higher education teacher training programmes in different European countries and identification of good practice; (2) Identification of teachers' needs based on LSP teacher interviews; (3) Identification of gaps between the provision of LSP teacher training and teacher needs, definition of training objectives, topic areas and outcomes of the TRAILs Summer School; (4) Design of a programme for LSP teacher training, implementation (5) Organisation and evaluation of a pilot summer school for (future) LSP teachers.

The first stage of the project, namely the identification and analysis of LSP teacher training programmes in Europe, involved the setting up of preparatory guidelines for the collection of data on LSP teacher training programmes in Europe (John et al., 2019). Relevant information was then collected on LSP teacher training programmes in Europe. Two online form-based surveys, one internal and one external, were set up for each partner to then send out to the countries of research, totalling fifty surveys in all. The internal survey was completed by data collected from web-based research conducted by the project research teams. External surveys were forwarded to representatives of tertiary education institutions to fill out when additional information was required. The results of the identification of LSP teacher training programmes in the European higher education area were then synthesised and analysed.

Concerning the second stage of the project, LSP teacher needs were analysed in terms of the needs of junior/experienced LSP teachers, the required qualifications, teaching skills and methodology, materials design, use of ICT, testing and assessment, disciplinary knowledge, and so on. The identification of LSP teacher needs is based on the following key activities: (1) Setting the guidelines for the collection of data on LSP teacher needs through questionnaires and interviews; (2) Collecting the necessary information about LSP teacher needs; (3) Analysing the collected data; (4) Synthesising the results of the identification of LSP teacher needs; (5) Data analysis.

2.1.4. Preliminary Findings

Following the guidelines, TRAILs partners checked over 1,000 tertiary educational establishments for LSP teacher training in 25 EHEA member states. The summary given by John et al. (ibid) points to the very limited number of courses identified by the partners: out of the 25 surveyed EHEA countries, only 14 countries were found to provide LSP teacher training at a tertiary education level. Together, these countries provide a total of 88 LSP teacher training formats. Another point is the difference in terms of scope: a total of 26 full-length courses were found, 52 short courses, 7 classified as "subjects" or "modules" and 3 as "other". The extent to which these courses contribute towards obtaining a recognised teacher qualification was also scrutinised. It was found that 37 programmes contribute fully towards achieving an LSP teacher degree and 12 partially, while 40 % (35 provisions) do not contribute towards a recognised teacher qualification.

Interesting results were also obtained with regard to the target language selected for LSP. As anticipated, the predominant language that LSP students of foreign languages are trained to teach is English (52 % of all LSP courses). It is followed by German (17 %), Spanish (16 %), French (11 %) and Russian (5 %).

Preliminary data on LSP teacher needs have already been collected. They will be completed through interviews conducted with a selected panel of LSP language teachers ready to be interviewed. 33 countries of the EHEA were investigated for the online questionnaire. 621 responses were received and have been synthesised. Half of the respondents teach LSP at Bachelor level. 66 % are working on a full-time permanent basis; 1 % (16 respondents) have full-time fixed contracts while 11.8 % have part-time contracts; the remaining 5.6 % correspond to other situations.

Most respondents disclose that they have not received any pre-service training on LSP (469 out of 621) or any in-service training (446). Additionally, when asked whether they know of any LSP courses in their country, only 101 say they do. This is in sharp contrast to the results that indicate their beliefs regarding the necessity of teacher training programmes to qualify as an LSP teacher: 193 strongly agree, 165 agree, 175 neither agree nor disagree, 68 disagree.

It is also apparent that their needs converge in terms of priority and specificity: when asked to make a choice from a list of 43 items about knowledge and training issues which are needed to teach LSP, the first five issues selected by the interviewees as "very important" were (in order of importance): (1) Analysis of target and learner needs; (2) Materials design and development; (3) Course design and development; (4) General principles of LSP; (5) Task-based teaching. The specificity of their needs sometimes goes further than skills development: When asked to insert any additional relevant comments into the questionnaire, answers tend to highlight the specificity of their needs in terms of professional recognition, as expressed by one of the respondents: "LSP teachers' knowledge, competences and efforts are not appreciated enough at our higher and secondary institutions. Our colleagues know almost nothing about LSP. For them you just teach English/Italian/German....".

2.1.5. Implications/Discussion

The TRAILs project addresses an issue that is generally left by the wayside: the issue of teacher education and skills development in the field of languages for specific purposes. Although LSP represent most language courses at university, research and projects on teacher needs and teacher education in this specific field are rare or fragmented. It is expected that TRAILs will contribute to high-quality and innovative teaching in the field and that the work done will also contribute to promoting LSP in language teaching.

It is hoped that the transnational collaborative approach adopted will be influential in terms of methodology. The project is successfully advancing step by step towards its overall objective: the investigation of needs and gaps will serve as a basis for a definition of training outcomes, and a curriculum for an LSP teacher training programme which be tested through the TRAILs Summer School. At this stage, it is envisaged that the transferability potential of the adopted methodology based on the guidelines will provide the basis for the analysis of the provision of training in any discipline.

2.1.6. Conclusions

The co-construction methodology in the TRAILs project is based on a collaborative approach to foster high-quality teaching (which in turn will impact the learning experience and achievements of students) in order to overcome a skills mismatch in HE language teaching. The project is moving forward thanks to the complementarity of the partners involved in the project (High LSP specialists, Teacher Training Institutions) and their drive to put into perspective current practice and needs with a view to designing and implementing an innovative programme to meet the challenges and needs identified. The collaborative process will also apply in the synergies offered to those attending the TRAILs summer school, both students and LSP teachers. It is anticipated that this collaborative approach will also involve stakeholders (sectoral associations, scholarly institutions and policymakers) as they will be invited to contribute to the discussion.

2.2

Responding to LSP Teacher Needs: Evolving Challenges and New Paradigms[1]

PATRIZIA ANESA, MARIE-CHRISTINE DEYRICH

2.2.1. Introduction

This chapter investigates the teaching of Languages for Specific Purposes (LSP) and the needs of its teachers in the light of teacher identity issues. It stems from the acknowledgement that quality teaching in LSP can be successfully fostered by taking into account not only the learner's needs but also the demands expressed by the teachers involved. This constitutes a paradigmatic shift from a one-dimensional approach (focusing almost exclusively on one of the categories involved in the learning process, i.e. the students) to a multidimensional perspective, which aims to respond to teacher needs as well. In particular, this study aims to investigate how the numerous roles that LSP teachers assume result in a variety of (often unaddressed) needs and in the coexistence of different professional identities, which are often ignored and whose management can be problematic. Along these lines, it also explores the education and training gaps which may affect the quality of teaching in this field.

---

[1] A part of this study was presented at *ISATT 2019 "Education Beyond the Crisis: New Skills, Children's Rights and Teaching Contexts"* (Addressing LSP Teaching and Teacher Needs: The TRAILs Project, by Marie-Christine Deyrich, Norah Leroy, and Marie-Anne Châteaureynaud; see in particular Sections 3, 4, 5, and 6). Although this paper has been conceived, planned and written jointly, Patrizia Anesa is responsible for Sections 1, 2, and 7, while Marie-Christine Deyrich is responsible for Sections 3, 4, 5, and 6.

In this respect, European institutions have set out to establish a link between quality teaching and student learning outcomes, thus implying that "effective pedagogical skills" are essential for student achievement (European Commission, 2013). Accordingly, teacher effectiveness has rapidly become of major consideration in the education policy agenda. To meet the teaching challenges posed by higher learning expectations, teacher preparation and development are recognised as "key building blocks in developing effective teachers" (Darling-Hammond, 2017). However, teacher training remains a matter that has not been given enough attention in the 48 countries of the European Higher Education Area (EHEA). As mentioned in the *Renewed Agenda for Higher Education* adopted by the European Commission in May 2017, "[t]oo many tertiary education teachers have little or no pedagogical training" (European Commission, 2017: 5).

In the field of Languages for Specific Purposes (LSP), the situation is even more significant since most tertiary education teachers concerned have received little or no specific training (Basturkmen, 2014). Indeed, despite increased demand for the delivery of LSP courses, there is an obvious lack of qualified LSP teachers, which affects vocational education and training institutions in European contexts and beyond (Brudermann et al., 2016). It is in this context that the two-year TRAILs project was launched in 2018 with the objective of designing, testing, and assessing innovative LSP teacher-training programmes. This project originates from the assumption that the quality of language learning in tertiary education has to be ensured not only through efficient planning and implementation, but also by guaranteeing adequate education and training for LSP teachers.

The need for further development of LSP teaching, both in terms of programme design and teacher education, has been pointed out in several reports, especially with regard to developing countries (Kırkgöz, 2018), but European institutions are also remarkably affected by this tendency. With the objective of offering new theoretical and pedagogical insights for LSP practitioners, the TRAILs project aims to go beyond the mere description of existing LSP programmes; rather, it considers strong research-based studies and empirical data in order to suggest how to implement new tools and strategies which may respond more adequately to the needs of LSP teachers across Europe.

This chapter offers some insights into the current situation of LSP teaching and, in particular, of teacher training across European tertiary education institutions. Firstly, the notion of LSP teacher identity is discussed in order to present some of the theoretical foundations upon which this study is based. This premise is followed by a reflection on the current gaps existing in LSP teacher education across Europe. Subsequently, the methodological framework in which the first stages of this project are situated is described, and the preliminary findings of the research surveys are presented. The final sections offer a discussion of the implications that these findings may have for the development of innovative teacher-training programmes and presents future activities to be implemented.

2.2.2. LSP Teacher Identities

In order to better understand the motivations and needs of LSP teachers in the particular world of specialised languages at university, it is necessary to examine what characterises this teaching body. To do this, we suggest investigating their role in the light of the notion of identity.

2.2.2.1. The notion of identity

Teacher identity has become a key construct in educational research in that it inevitably shapes teachers' own beliefs and practices (Schutz et al., 2018). While in everyday parlance "teacher identity" can be conceived as a single attribute related purely to an occupational dimension – a person is either a teacher or is not – this construct is intrinsically dynamic, responsive to contextual factors, and multidimensional.

The notion of teacher identity is to a large extent elusive and often debated. We embrace the idea that it is part of an ongoing process (Beijaard, Meijer, & Verloop, 2004), one which is fluid and dynamic. As Sachs (2005) aptly stresses, identity "is negotiated through experience and the sense that is made of that experience" (2005: 15). Along the same lines, Kelchtermans points out that identity can be defined as an "ongoing process of making sense of one's experiences and their impact on the 'self'" (2009: 261). The concept of identity is fundamentally systemic and depends on the strong interrelation between a series of elements, such as self-reflection, emotions, agency, stories, discourses, and context (Beauchamp & Thomas, 2009). Consequently, the concept also displays a strong situational character (Wenger, 2007).

The notion of identity has important implications for understanding teachers' needs and motivations, and for mapping how such needs and motivations develop in given workplace cultures according to political, institutional, and social forces (Richardson & Watt, 2018). In particular, teachers experience an ongoing tension between the need to renegotiate their identities and that of preserving their current conceptualisations; the choice of which of these two aspects has to be privileged often depends on the level of agency that teachers display, especially in relation to a given community (Ruohotie-Lyhty, 2016).

Beyond the several models available in terms of teacher identities, we feel that the LSP teacher's multifaceted identity is determined, inter alia, by four main aspects, namely:

- Language (and related culture)
- Discipline
- Institution
- School of thought (in terms of language acquisition theories and teaching methods).

These aspects inevitably interact, creating multiple, complex identities, and sub-identities. Indeed, the professional identity of LSP teachers may also be seen as the result of multiple sub-identities which are often hierarchically positioned. For instance, the notions of English teacher, ESP teacher, Business English teacher, Business English teacher teaching at a Business School, etc., can be seen as coexisting sub-identities. However, the relation between these forms of identity is not intended here as purely vertical, but rather circular, in that each sub-identification inevitably shapes (and in turn is shaped by) the others.

An LSP teacher may have to assume a variety of work roles, which include instructor, counsellor, teacher, course designer, materials designer, examiner, researcher, and CLIL advisor (Deyrich & Leroy, 2017; Taillefer, 2013), amongst others. Inevitably, the needs arising from each activity may be different, as is also true for the competences required to carry out the various tasks effectively, which vary according to the specific occupational context and evolve over time. As a corollary, teachers often have to deal with the negotiation of multiple identities, both at an individual and a societal level (Bukor, 2015). The tension arising from the negotiation of identities is remarkably evident in the case of LSP teachers, who often experience the feeling of belonging to multiple communities of practice at the same time, without a precise positioning. Consequently, this may lead to a sense of detachment from a clear disciplinary belonging. However, this awareness has not led to the systemic development of training programmes which take into account the multifaceted nature of the LSP teaching profession and the related heterogeneous needs expressed by teachers.

2.2.2.2. Facing changes

LSP teachers' professional practices in tertiary education in Europe have been profoundly impacted by reforms such as the Bologna Process (Fortanet-Gómez & Räisänen, 2008), as well as by significant shifts in education priorities, including the internationalisation of programmes. These changes inevitably generate the need for LSP teachers to be able to constantly respond to new challenges at a personal and professional level (Campion, 2016), and this process concerns both junior and experienced teachers (Kubanyiova & Crookes, 2016). Not only do teachers need to develop new skills, to acquire novel teaching methods, to create original syllabi or to integrate new technology and its affordance into their teaching practices, but they are also faced with the necessity to regularly reshape their professional identity (Tao & Gao, 2018). Indeed, when changes occur, they may have an impact on how teachers perceive themselves within the educational context in which they operate. In particular, changes require a continuous adaptation in terms of perception and expression of one's identity (Kanno & Stuart, 2011), which may be problematic to manage. For instance, the evolving landscape of LSP teaching at the university level leads to expectations that LSP teachers should provide instruction in a wide range of LSP fields, which may vary considerably from their primary area of expertise. Furthermore, their role may be criticised by professionals working in a specific field (Tao & Gao, 2017), who may question the subject-matter knowledge displayed by the LSP instructors.

On a final note, one key aspect to be included in teacher-training programmes concerns the development of digital skills. Thus, starting from the gaps in training related to the use of ICT in education, the TRAILs project also delineates the digital skills development that is desirable to foster innovative and participatory practices in the design and implementation of LSP training activities. Indeed, being sufficiently trained to integrate ICT usage into teaching processes is the *sine qua non* for transforming teaching practices in the digital era. The activities are thus aimed at providing teachers with the appropriate support which is essential to promote involvement and autonomy. This will allow teachers to be part of a participatory ICT-enhanced collaboration which provides opportunities for sharing innovative pedagogical practices. With the aim of creating technology-assisted LSP courses tailored to students' specific needs, instructors have to acquire a wide range of skills which go beyond basic digital literacy or "web literacy" (Chapelle & Hegelheimer, 2004). Rather, they are required to develop a meta-technological ability to actively select, adapt, and produce materials and activities within a technology-assisted approach which considers the specificities of a given learning environment. This means not only using an existing technology, but actively appropriating it so that it can fit a given pedagogical design.

2.2.2.3. Developing standardised and specific competences

The TRAILs project has as its main priority the development of high-quality skills and competences for teachers of LSP courses in tertiary education. On a clarifying note, it should be pointed out that in this study the focus is specifically on LSP teaching, which we conceptualise as those courses with predominantly language learning outcomes. Thus, related conceptualisations such as CLIL (Content and Language Integrated Learning) and EMI (English Medium Instruction) do not represent the main object of this investigation, although they are inevitably strongly interrelated. This is because EMI courses tend to focus on content learning results and specifically concern subjects taught in English[2] and CLIL courses are generally placed at the crossroads somewhere between EMI and LSP courses (Airey, 2016). Although often disregarded, these differences have important epistemological implications in that the competences required change profoundly according to the learning outcomes which are envisaged. LSP courses are thus intended to improve the language competence which enables the learning of the specific content (Kırkgöz, 2018).

Operationally, the objectives of the TRAILs project are not pursued by taking into account exclusively pre-conceived theories about teacher training, but mainly by focusing on the actual needs expressed by the

---

[2]   Instead, our study has a more inclusive focus and embraces a vast range of foreign languages (see Chapter 1, this volume).

teachers involved in the project, considering the European as well as the local contexts and the different institutional, legal, and societal priorities. The language and the specificity of the disciplinary area are also accounted for.

Although tertiary education programmes are required to foster continuous professional development, it is evident that the needs of LSP teaching are only rarely addressed. Indeed, LSP teacher training is generally limited, often lacking any standardised format (see Chapter 1, this volume), and it is to a large extent left to the individual initiative. The objective of this project is thus high-quality and innovative teaching of LSP in the EHEA. To achieve this, it concentrates on the pedagogical, communicative, and intercultural skills which are needed, and which teachers identify as being essential to their professional and personal development in the light of the professional identity issues that they may experience. The competences to be advanced are transversal and based on international and intercultural collaboration.

2.2.3. LSP teaching and teacher needs

Demand for competent teachers of LSP in tertiary education outstrips supply. The high demand for LSP provision is related to academic and societal expectations, whereby the foreign language sector is an asset and a springboard for university graduates and postgraduates who need a relatively high level of proficiency in one or more foreign languages in order to succeed in today's labour market (Räsänen, 2008). The close links between language needs and the world of work must be considered in the context of the internationalisation of tertiary education (Deyrich et al., 2016) where language skills are expected to enhance mobility and facilitate employability. Given that the stakes are so high, it is unsurprising that there is an ongoing worldwide increase in LSP courses for students who are non-specialists of the language, i.e. specialists in other disciplines. However, while job offers targeting LSP teachers are on the rise, many of these vacancies tend to remain unfilled, as in the French context (Brudermann et al., 2016), due to a mismatch between the profiles of the job-seekers and the skills which are needed. This problem of incongruity is also reported in many other contexts where the lack of effective teacher-training programmes is held as the determining factor (Ghafournia & Sabet, 2014). It has been argued that teachers are almost never prepared to teach in this sector (O'Connell & Chaplier, 2015), and this is of particular concern since the needs of teachers in the field are multifarious, complex, and interrelated, owing to the specificity of teaching LSP courses in tertiary education.

A systematic investigation of "needs" is thus considered as vital to our purpose. A significant number of studies have been conducted on the use of needs analysis in LSP: "the means of establishing the how and what of a course" (Hyland, 2006: 73). However, as mentioned by Bocanegra-Valle and Basturkmen (2019), needs have always been approached from the point of view of the learner, while teacher perspectives are invariably overlooked during the process. It is, however, critically important that teacher needs should be taken into consideration to inform decisions about topics in teacher education programmes. Basturkmen (2014) explains that the description of the needs of LSP teachers found in the literature must be deepened by means of empirical investigations in order to shed further light on the nature of these needs. Therefore, an in-depth investigation into the needs of LSP teachers is a fundamental step in the contribution this project makes towards finding solutions and tools to support skills development for LSP staff and for future LSP teachers in tertiary education, both at national level (for each of the partner countries) and at the European level.

2.2.4. Methodological framework

To address the challenge set in the highly specific context of LSP, a transnational and collaborative approach is being tested and evaluated in the TRAILs project. Based on input from research and good practice, the project relies on the innovative potential of ICT for communication and preparation. A customised methodology is being defined step by step and adopted in the course of all the following consecutive phases: (1) Review of existing LSP higher education teacher training programmes in different European countries and the identification of good practice; (2) Identification of teachers' needs according to LSP teacher questionnaires and semi-structured interviews; (3) Identification of gaps between the current provision of LSP teacher training and actual teacher needs, definition of training objectives, topic areas and outcomes of the TRAILs Summer School; (4) Design of a programme for LSP teacher training, implementation; and (5) Organisation and evaluation of a pilot Summer School for (future) LSP teachers.

This chapter has the first two phases as its focal point, and particular attention is devoted to the presentation of the preliminary results emerging from the questionnaires compiled by LSP teachers. The first stage of the project, namely the identification and analysis of LSP teacher training programmes in Europe, involved the setting up of preparatory guidelines for the collection of data on these programmes (John et al., 2019), and then the collection of the relevant information. Two online form-based surveys, one internal and the other external, were created for each partner to send out to the countries of research, totalling fifty surveys in all. The internal survey was completed with data collected from web-based research conducted by the project teams. External surveys were forwarded to tertiary education institutions for representatives to fill out when additional information was required. The results of the identification of LSP teacher-training programmes in the European tertiary education area were then synthesised and analysed.

Concerning the second stage of the project, the focus was on the identification of LSP teacher needs. Drawing on questionnaires and interviews, teacher needs were analysed in terms of the needs of junior/experienced LSP teachers, the required qualifications, teaching skills and methodology, materials design, use of ICT, testing and assessment, disciplinary knowledge, and so on. The identification of LSP teacher needs is based on the following key activities: (1) setting the guidelines for the collection of data on LSP teacher needs through questionnaires and interviews; (2) collecting the necessary information about LSP teacher needs; (3) analysing the collected data; and (4) synthesising the results of the identification of LSP teacher needs.

2.2.5. Preliminary Findings

Following the guidelines, TRAILs partners checked over 1,000 tertiary educational establishments for LSP teacher training in 25 countries in the EHEA. Data on LSP teacher needs were first collected through a questionnaire specifically designed by the research team. This process was completed through interviews undertaken with a selected panel of LSP language teachers ready to be interviewed.

More specifically, the EHEA countries sampled were: Austria, Belarus, Belgium, Bosnia and Herzegovina, Croatia, Estonia, Finland, France, Germany, Hungary, Italy, Latvia, Lithuania, North Macedonia,

Montenegro, the Netherlands, Poland, Portugal, Serbia, Slovakia, Slovenia, Spain, the United Kingdom, Ukraine and Vatican City. The 25 countries sampled (out of 48 in total) correspond to 52 % in terms of countries and 59 % in terms of population. In total, 1,024 universities were sampled and investigated by means of the online questionnaire, with 621 completed questionnaires received and synthesised.

The summary given by John et al. (*ibid*) points to the very limited number of courses identified by the partners: out of the 25 EHEA countries surveyed, only 14 countries were found to provide LSP teacher training at a tertiary education level. Together, these 14 countries provided a total of 88 LSP teacher-training formats. Another point was the difference in terms of scope: a total of 26 full-length courses were found, 52 short courses, 7 classified as "subjects" or "modules", and 3 as "other". The extent to which these courses contribute towards obtaining a recognised teacher qualification was also scrutinised. It was found that 37 programmes contribute fully towards achieving an LSP teacher degree and 12 partially, while 40 % (35 provisions) do not contribute towards a recognised teacher qualification.

Half of the respondents teach LSP at Bachelor level, followed by Master (33.8 %), PhD (10 %), and "other" (6.2 %). Most respondents disclosed that they have not received any pre-service training in LSP (75 %) or any in-service training (71 %). Additionally, when asked whether they had knowledge of any LSP training courses in their country, only 16 % replied in the affirmative. This was in sharp contrast to the results regarding the respondents' belief in the necessity of teacher training programmes in order to qualify as an LSP teacher: 33 % strongly agreed, 28 % agreed, 28 % neither agreed nor disagreed, and 11 % disagreed.

It is also apparent that their needs converge in terms of priority and specificity: when asked to make a choice of knowledge and training issues needed in order to successfully teach LSP, the top five issues selected by the interviewees as "very important" (from a total list of 43 items) were (in order of importance): (1) analysis of target and learner needs; (2) materials design and development; (3) course design and development; (4) general principles of LSP; and (5) task-based teaching. The specificity of their needs sometimes goes further than just skills development: when asked to add any further relevant comments to the questionnaire, answers tended to highlight the specificity of their needs in terms of professional recognition, as expressed by one of the respondents: "LSP teachers' knowledge, competences and efforts are not appreciated enough at our higher and secondary institutions. Our colleagues know almost nothing about LSP. For them you just teach English/Italian/German...."

2.2.6. Discussion

These preliminary findings from the first stages confirm that the main issue that the TRAILs project addresses is one which is generally left by the wayside: teacher training and skills development in the field of languages for specific purposes. Although LSP represents most language courses at university, research and projects on teacher needs and teacher education in this field are rare or fragmented. In this respect, TRAILs attempts to contribute to the development of high-quality and innovative teaching in the field, thanks to the personal view offered by the teachers involved.

The transnational collaborative approach adopted also aims to be influential in terms of methodology. The problematisation of LSP teacher identities and how they may affect teacher needs can serve as a solid basis for a definition of the desired training outcomes and the adequate curriculum for an LSP teacher-training programme to be tested through the TRAILs Summer School. Thus, it is envisaged that the transferability potential of the adopted methodology may provide the foundation for the definition of training objectives in other disciplines.

Moreover, the co-construction methodology which characterises this project is based on a clear collaborative approach which aims to foster high-quality teaching, which in turn will impact the learning experience and achievements of students. More specifically, this approach is made possible thanks to the complementarity of the partners involved in the project (such as LSP specialists and teacher training institutions) and their drive to put into perspective current practice and needs with a view to designing and implementing an innovative programme to meet those challenges and needs identified. The synergies emerging from this collaborative process are key for those attending the TRAILs Summer School, both students and LSP teachers. It is anticipated that this collaborative approach will also involve stakeholders (sectorial associations, scholarly institutions, and policymakers) as they will be invited to contribute to the discussion.

2.2.7. Conclusions

The TRAILs project started with the acknowledgement that LSP has become a prominent area of teaching in tertiary education around the world. The challenge remains for LSP teachers to navigate their identity not only individually but also collectively, in that a collective awareness can support them to reclaim their identity as professionals and also to face new educational and social challenges more effectively than can be done in isolation (Heck et al., 2019).

In the last few years, LSP has also undergone transformations influenced by changing trends in approaches to, and methodologies used in, language teaching. Although innovative practices in LSP teaching are certainly present, they are generally the result of personal intuition and motivation, and there remains a shortage of standardised evaluations of such initiatives, as well as of standardised training programmes across institutions.

This study also argues that the policies concerning the training of LSP teachers in tertiary education need to be investigated within a given national and local framework, but at the same time that they should also be observed from a European and an international perspective, taking into account the inevitable tension which exists between national and supranational exigencies (Deyrich, 2019).

Given the nature of the project, which draws considerably on the emic view of LSP teaching offered by practitioners, the findings derive from multiple perspectives and are determined by the diversity of experiences from different local contexts; thus, this study aims to develop teacher training curricula and tools which are standardised, but which are, at the same time, adaptable to different regional, educational contexts. It is hoped that the findings of the project can inform teachers, curriculum designers, researchers, and policymakers across Europe. In particular, despite the growing scholarly interest in the construct of teacher identity at large, as well as in its formation and development, there exists a clear need for evidence-based models of how LSP teachers author their professional identity. This awareness can, ultimately, contribute to the development of more appropriate teacher-training programmes which consider teachers' own needs and motivations, especially in the light of the complexity of their occupational identity.

Furthermore, it is hoped that teacher training centres will be encouraged to offer continuous support to tackle the issues and the gaps which have been identified in LSP teacher training, and that the outcomes of this project can be employed to this end. Consequently, national and international cooperation between centres is likely to be enhanced, thanks to a collaborative network of highly specialised centres focusing specifically on LSP teacher training.

2.3

A Quantitative Analysis of LSP Teacher Needs Across the European Higher Education Area

Ana Bocanegra-Valle,
M. Dolores Perea-Barberá

2.3.1. Needs analysis and LSP teacher needs

Results from the work developed under the TRAILs project have shown that courses for pre-service and/or in-service Languages for Specific Purposes (LSP) teachers are largely absent from language teachers' education programmes in many countries within the European Higher Education Area (EHEA). Moreover, findings have revealed that in those countries where such LSP teacher training courses are offered, they differ considerably in terms of duration, entry requirements, teaching format, content and topics addressed, or teaching/learning methods (see chapter by John et al. in this book). Against this backdrop, LSP teachers may have a variety of differing needs to be met and they may have to make up for the absence of or insufficient formal training.

What are "teacher needs"? In the context of LSP teaching/learning, "needs" has been used as an umbrella term to refer to those wants, necessities, lacks, gaps, concerns, expectations, motivations, values, desires, deficiencies or requirements that learners have for learning a foreign language with academic or occupational purposes. In this chapter, "teacher needs" refer to the knowledge and skills that LSP teachers are required to master in order to effectively teach a foreign language for academic or occupational purposes. They also refer to those professional necessities that these LSP teachers have in order to function and progress successfully in academia.

What is "needs analysis"? Needs analysis, also known as needs assessment, has been identified as a key area and a defining characteristic of LSP whose focus has evolved significantly over the past fifty years (Upton, 2012). Seminal works in preceding decades like those of Munby (1978), Hutchinson and Waters (1987), and Dudley-Evans and St John (1998) marked a watershed in the knowledge of needs assessment and its development in the field of LSP. As Flowerdew (2013: 326) puts it, need analysis "has a long history and is constantly evolving and redefining itself". Needs analysis or needs assessment has been defined as "the systematic collection and analysis of all information necessary for defining and validating a defensible curriculum" (Brown, 2016: 4) – that is, collecting and assessing information relevant to course design and establishing the how and what of the course (Dudley-Evans & St John, 1998; Hyland, 2006). This is the basis for the design and development of an LSP teacher needs analysis within the framework of the TRAILs project: our aim has been to gather data on the needs of LSP teachers (who will be learners in an LSP education and training course) and conduct an analysis of such needs with a view to assisting in the definition and validation of a defensible and innovative curriculum aimed at LSP teachers.

As the literature has attested, research on the needs of LSP learners abounds (e.g. Belcher & Lukkarila, 2011; Bocanegra-Valle, 2016; Brown, 2016; Flowerdew, 2013; Huhta et al., 2013; Woodrow, 2018); however, it has been argued that the literature focusing on LSP teacher education is very limited (e.g. Basturkmen, 2014, 2019; Bocanegra-Valle & Basturkmen, 2019; Ding & Bruce, 2017; Ding & Campion, 2016; Hall, 2013; Papadima-Sophocleous et al., 2019) and even scarcer in terms of proper research and empirical studies on teacher needs. As Bocanegra-Valle and Basturkmen (2019: 128) remark, "[T]eacher needs are invariably overlooked in the discussions regarding needs assessment, and this may explain the paucity of research on this matter". Recent exceptions, however, attest to an emerging interest in identifying the education and training needs of LSP teachers from differing perspectives and in diverse contexts (Alexander, 2007; Basturkmen, 2019; Bocanegra-Valle & Basturkmen, 2019; Campion, 2016; Huang, 2018; Kırkgöz, 2019; Tao & Gao, 2018).

Why investigate teacher needs? Assessing the needs of LSP teachers is appropriate for two main reasons. Hyland (2008: 113) noted that needs analysis "involves decisions based on teachers' interests, values, and beliefs about teaching, learning and language". Thus, assessing the needs of LSP teachers first helps to advance knowledge about the LSP teacher as a relevant figure in higher education, and about their necessities, views and concerns regarding their own teaching practice. In addition, it has been observed that "the community that ESP professionals know the least about is their own" (Belcher, 2013: 544), and also, that "[f]ew links have been made in the ESP literature between ESP teacher learning and the wider literature on language teacher education" (Basturkmen, 2019: 320). Therefore, studies which delve into LSP teachers and their knowledge, education and training needs are highly relevant in the LSP field, mainly because they will help us to understand and extend our knowledge about the roles and challenges that LSP teachers have in the teaching profession in general, and the language teaching profession in particular.

A second and key reason is that needs analysis has been identified as the backbone of course design, as the cornerstone that "leads to a very focused course" (Dudley-Evans & St John, 1998: 122) and as the first step in the design of LSP courses and programmes (Anthony, 2018; Basturkmen, 2010; Bocanegra-Valle, 2016; Brown, 2016; Dudley-Evans & St John, 1998; Flowerdew, 2013; Huhta et al., 2013; Hutchinson & Waters, 1987; Hyland, 2006; Upton, 2012; Woodrow, 2018). It has been argued that "[i]n every genuine ESP course, needs assessment is obligatory, and in many programs, an ongoing needs assessment is integral to curriculum design and evaluation" (Johns & Price-Machado, 2001: 49); hence, if a defensible curriculum that satisfies LSP teachers is going to be designed and developed, it should be based on the needs of LSP teachers, as previously identified by an appropriate assessment. These needs, as Woodrow (2018: 29) reminds us, should then be "translated into course objectives and teaching aims through a series of steps". This has also been attained in the TRAILs project with the development of the LSP teacher school (see later contributions in Part 3 of this book).

The final aim of this chapter is to determine the needs of LSP teachers across the EHEA. Therefore, it sets out to provide the results of the quantitative analysis of LSP teacher needs that has been conducted in the framework of the TRAILs project. It first explains the methodology that has been implemented and one of the instruments (a questionnaire survey) that has been used for the gathering of data – in this case, quantitative data. Then it provides details about the participants in this assessment process. Results and main findings are discussed in the last section.

2.3.2. Methodology and data collection

This section addresses the methodological framework adopted for this study and focuses on the way data was gathered by means of a questionnaire survey as well as the main features of this data-collection instrument. It also provides an overview of the participants in this study.

2.3.2.1. *Methodological framework*

Needs-analysis data may be collected in a number of ways (text analysis, language audits, ethnography, diaries or target-situation observations, to name a few). For the full needs analysis conducted under the TRAILs project, a mixed-methods approach (Dörnyei, 2016) has been adopted because it combines the collection of data by means of questionnaires (quantitative data) and semi-structured interviews (qualitative data). This chapter focuses on the quantitative approach to this data analysis (for the qualitative analysis, please see chapter by López-Zurita & Vázquez-Amador in this book).

Using questionnaires and interviews in needs analysis has been found to be a reliable and appropriate data selection technique: "[i]t is not uncommon for needs analysis projects to include both questionnaires and interviews, often interviewing a subset of respondents who completed a questionnaire, or developing a set of questionnaire items from information collected in interviews" (Basturkmen, 2010: 31). The needs analysis in this chapter makes use of the former instrument. It began with some groundwork which included a detailed review of the literature. This led first to the design, development and generation of a needs-analysis questionnaire (that is, the first data-collection instrument used). Once the questionnaire was completed, and data were gathered and analysed, an interview was developed with the aim of making up for potential disadvantages derived from the sole use of questionnaires, exploring unfamiliar fields, and identifying areas for further research.[1]

---

[1]   Following Brown (2001) and Dörney (2003, 2007), some of the limitations of using questionnaires in needs assessment are: their rigidity and impersonality, the simplicity and superficiality of answers, the limitation of data to be gathered, little or no opportunity to correct respondents' mistakes, tendency to agree with sentences respondents are unsure or feel ambivalent about, respondents with literacy problems, fatigue effect if the questionnaire is too long, or high simplicity of questions.

The interviews were also designed to help to delve into weak or inconsistent replies to statements in the questionnaire so that the combination of both instruments would contribute to building a more accurate understanding of the contexts in which LSP teachers develop their knowledge and to nurturing the LSP teaching profession across the EHEA. The combination of these two instruments and, therefore, the multiplicity of perspectives that both instruments provided on the needs of LSP teachers were expected to enhance the outcomes and findings of this analysis. This chapter focuses on the quantitative data gathered by means of the questionnaire survey. For the qualitative data analysis, please refer to the chapter by López-Zurita and Vázquez-Amador in this book.

The following subsections provide details about the quantitative data-collection instrument, how it was designed and developed, its content, and the way questionnaires were distributed. They also give a profile of the questionnaire participants.

2.3.2.2. Data-collection instrument

A questionnaire was developed after a thorough review of the existing literature on LSP teacher education, training and needs. It also took into consideration the foreign language (FL) and LSP teaching experience of the partners involved in the TRAILs project. The term questionnaire refers here to "any written instrument that presents respondents with a series of questions or statements to which they are to react either by writing out their answers or selecting from among existing answers" (Brown, 2001: 6).

An initial questionnaire draft was designed and piloted twice at the initial stage of its development – by the designing team first (internal piloting) and then by all TRAILs members (external piloting). Thanks to these trial runs the designing team could (i) collect feedback about how the instrument worked and whether it performed the job it had been designed for; and (ii) make alterations and fine-tune the final version on the basis of the collected feedback (Dörnyei, 2003). Throughout this piloting stage the clarity of instructions was checked, the overall layout of the questionnaire was analysed, wording was corrected, problematic statements were reworded and improved, omissions, duplications and irregularities were identified, and internal consistency was improved.

Fig. 2.3.1. Screenshots of English (left) and Croatian (right) versions of the questionnaire as developed on Google Forms and circulated online

The questionnaire was initially designed in English – as this was the common working language for TRAILs. Once a final version was completed, it was translated into the remaining seven languages of the participating countries in the project (that is, Croatian, French, German, Italian, Polish, Slovenian and Spanish). Fig. 2.3.1 illustrates the front page of the English and Croatian versions as distributed online via Google Forms.

The project's aim was to obtain a representative sample of the whole population of LSP teachers working in the EHEA and, therefore, "snowball sampling" (Dörnyei, 2003: 72) was found to be a suitable procedure for administering the questionnaire – that is, a few LSP teachers and LSP teaching hubs were identified, and they were asked to circulate the questionnaire among other LSP teacher colleagues or hubs they could identify. The eight versions of the online questionnaire were circulated among target LSP teachers across EHEA countries via national and international associations (e.g. the British Association of Lecturers in English for Academic Purposes in the United Kingdom, the European Association of Languages for Specific Purposes in Spain, or the Slovene Association of LSP teachers in Slovenia), national and international online resources (e.g. Linguist List), personal contacts, email messages addressed to higher education departments, and invitations posted on academic social media (e.g. ResearchGate) and TRAILs website.

The questionnaire was divided into four parts (see English version in Annex). It contained 32 questions preceded by a short introduction to the aims of the TRAILs project that also encouraged participation. It offered seven combined types of questions, namely:

   i. open questions offering open-response items (e.g. Q28 or Q30);

   ii. open questions containing statements that participants had to complete (e.g. Q6 or Q7);

   iii. closed-response items offering existing possibilities to be ticked as appropriate (e.g. Q12 or Q14);

   iv. biodata items that asked participants for personal information (e.g. Q1 or Q2);

   v. opinion items that asked participants for their views or opinions (e.g. Q23 or Q24);

   vi. Q-sort items or items that asked the participants to rank or prioritise a particular aspect (e.g. Q27); or

   vii. judgemental ratings that sought participants' feedback on a particular aspect (e.g. Q25 or Q26).

Part 1 (Q1–Q16) aimed at profiling the LSP teachers participating in the questionnaire. Here, participants were asked to provide information about their age, EHEA working country, FL taught, LSP-related discipline, or FL versus LSP teaching experience.

Part 2 (Q17–Q23) aimed at gathering information pertaining to the participants' teacher education and training experience. It also aimed at furthering the results obtained in previous work (see chapter by John et al. in this book). A key question here is Q23, in which participants were asked to agree or disagree (on a scale of 1 to 5) with the necessity of LSP teacher training programmes for the qualification of LSP teachers.

Part 3 (Q24–Q29) focused on teacher needs and opened with a question (Q24) that tried to gauge participants' awareness of the similarities or dissimilarities in needs among FL and LSP teachers. Following this key question, participants were asked to tick from a list of 43 prompts those knowledge and training needs which they found to be very important, important, fairly important, slightly important or unimportant (Q27). Another list in Q29 contained 17 prompts and aimed at identifying other needs (different from knowledge and training needs) that respondents might have experienced in the course of their careers. For both lists, participants were given the opportunity to add comments or any other needs that had not been anticipated in the list and were deemed relevant.

Lastly, Part 4 completed the questionnaire by asking for further comments and suggestions, and thanking participants.

The eight versions of the questionnaire were available online for three weeks. Upon closing, results were gathered from the English version first (which provided the highest number of replies as a whole). Thanks to this significant number of replies (61.8 % as shall be detailed in the next subsection) it was possible to get a first picture of the general trend of LSP teacher needs. Later on, replies provided in the other languages were translated into English and added to the English data for the complete quantification and analysis of LSP teacher needs. The eight data sets were merged into an English-only file, missing data was rebuilt and duplicated data removed, labels were standardised and the whole set of data was reanalysed with a view to final results. Replies to all questions and to all questionnaire versions were uploaded to Google Drive so that they could be accessed by all TRAILs members.

2.3.2.2. Profile of participants

The questionnaire reached a high participant response rate. 621 replies were gathered from all versions: 22 Croatian, 384 English, 41 French, 15 Italian, 48 Polish, 27 Slovene, and 75 Spanish. The English and Spanish versions returned the highest response rates (61.8 % and 12.1 %, respectively). Replies came from 33 EHEA countries and 3 non-EHEA countries. The highest response rate was returned from Spain (n = 133), Italy (n = 69), France (n = 65) Croatia (n = 50), Poland (n = 50), Serbia (n = 43), Slovenia (n = 30), the United Kingdom (n = 28) or Belgium (n = 20). Other countries contributing to the questionnaire were (in alphabetic order) Austria (n = 7), Bosnia-Herzegovina (n = 8), Bulgaria (n = 2), Czech Republic (n = 1), Denmark (n = 1), Estonia (n = 3), Finland (n = 12), Georgia (n = 1), Germany (n = 14), Greece (n = 6), Hungary (n = 17), Ireland (n = 1), Latvia (n = 1), Lithuania (n = 7), Luxembourg (n = 1), Macedonia (n = 3), Montenegro (n = 2), Portugal (n = 3), Romania (n = 15), Russia (n = 2), Slovakia (n = 8), Sweden (n = 10), Turkey (n = 2), and Ukraine (n = 3). These 621 participants worked in over a hundred different higher education institutions across the EHEA.

Tab. 2.3.1 sums up the main details regarding the profile of participants in the questionnaire as gathered from the replies provided to questions in Part 1 (see Annex). From these results, it can be concluded that the average questionnaire participant is a female LSP teacher, between 41 and 50 years old who works under a full-time permanent contract, has a doctoral degree and also has relevant teaching qualifications but not LSP-related pre-service or in-service training, who is non-Anglophone (that is, with a first language different from English), and teaches English for academic, business or engineering purposes at Bachelor's-degree level; this average participant has 15–20 years' teaching experience in higher education and previous experience in teaching languages for general purposes at different educational levels.

Tab. 2.3.1. Profile of questionnaire participants (Q1–Q16)

Detail	Results
Gender	Female (78.9 %), male (19.6 %), other (1 %), would rather not say (0.5 %)
Age group	21–30 (3.7 %), 31–40 (17.6 %), 41–50 (35.8 %), 51–60 (31.5 %), 61–70 (9.9 %), 71+ (1.5 %)
Employment status	Full time permanent (64.7 %), part time permanent (5.5 %), full time fixed (16.4 %), part time fixed (7.2 %), retired (0.9 %), emeritus (0.5 %), freelance (1.6 %), other (3.2 %)
Highest qualification	PhD (56.8 %), MA (29.1 %), MSc (5.1 %), BA (5.6 %), other (2.4 %), no answer (1 %)
Teaching qualification	PhD (17.4 %), MA (24.2 %), MSc (1.6 %), BA (2.3 %), other (31.6 %), no answer (22.9 %)
HE teaching experience	1–5 years (14.2 %), 6–10 years (16.7 %), 11–15 years (18.4 %), 16–20 years (18.2 %), 21–25 years (14.3 %), 26–30 years (10.6 %), 30+ (6.6 %), no answer (1 %)
LSP training	Yes (19.6 %), no (75.6 %), not sure (4.8 %)
First language	English (13.3 %), non-Anglophone (86.7 %)
LSP language	English (71.5 %), German (10.1 %), Spanish (5.8), French (5.2 %), Italian (2.8 %), other (4.6 %)
Teaching degrees	Bachelor (50 %), Master (33.8 %), PhD (10 %), other (6.2 %)
LSP-related discipline	Academic (17.7 %), Business (17.4 %), Engineering (11.3 %), Hard sciences (3.4 %), Humanities (9.5 %), Language teacher education (11 %), Law (3 %), Marketing (5.7 %), Medicine (7 %), Natural sciences (4.1 %), Transportation (2.2 %), Tourism (7 %), Military (0.7 %)
Prior FL teacher	Yes (58 %), no (42 %)
Reasons for becoming an LSP teacher	An opening (18.8 %), better salary (5.8 %), career opportunities (24.9 %), change of institution (15.5 %), intrinsic motivation (21.1 %), no other option (3.9 %), personal reasons (9.1 %), flexibility (0.9 %)

2.3.3. Results and discussion

Part 2 of the questionnaire (Q17–Q23) focused on LSP teacher training and was aimed at supporting and furthering the findings from the previous study on LSP training in Europe (see John et al. in this book). As shown in Tab. 2.3.2, replies to questions 17–20 revealed that most teachers had not received any LSP-related training either before (75.5 %) or during (71.8 %) their teaching careers.

Tab. 2.3.2. **Have you received any pre- or in-service training on LSP? (Q17–Q20)**

Answer	Pre-service (n/%)	In-service (n/%)
Yes	122 (19.6 %)	143 (23.1 %)
No	469 (75.5 %)	446 (71.8 %)
Not sure	30 (4.9 %)	30 (4.8 %)
No answer	-----	2 (0.3 %)

Additionally, 514 respondents (82.8 %) were not aware of the existence of LSP teacher training courses in their countries (see Q21). When asked to provide details about those courses they claimed to have completed (Q18 and Q20) or were aware of (Q22), replies were very diverse and did not always refer to LSP teacher training programmes, but to courses of all kinds on or about LSP – that is, summer courses, workshops, modules that were part of larger courses on FL teaching, TESOL courses, Cambridge exams, or even conferences. By way of example:

- Master in Secondary Teaching 60 credits, 1 Year (October to July), 2 months practice in a public school, Final Master Project.
- Many IATEFL, BALEAP, BAAL workshops.
- CELTA/Diploma in TESOL.
- Teaching English for Business 10 days intensive course London Chamber of Commerce and Industry organised by Inside Word Language School, Hungary.
- Institutional in-service courses + workshops arranged by a national network.
- Edinburgh University 2-week course in EMP, British Council courses in LSP.
- National University Programme in Finland PILC, 1 year, multilingual, distance studies + seminar weeks (4).

Replies to Part 2 of this questionnaire concurred with the main findings on current training programmes (see chapter by John et al. in this book); namely, that LSP teacher training programmes in the EHEA are not firmly established at higher education institutions and, in those existing cases, they are far from being standardised as regards formats, duration, or resulting certification. They also concurred with the finding that English is the predominant LSP that the students are trained to teach or the predominant language of instruction.

Q23 asked respondents to say whether they agreed or disagreed with the statement "LSP teacher training programmes should be necessary to qualify as an LSP teacher". As Fig. 2.3.2 shows, the tendency of this group of LSP teachers was to agree strongly (n = 193; 31.1 %) or somehow (n = 165; 26.6 %) with this statement, or else they could not tell whether they agreed or not (but certainly did not disagree) – in this case 175 participants (28.2 %) neither agreed nor disagreed with the statement. Replies to this question were key for the selection of interviewees in a later stage of the study (see López-Zurita & Vázquez-Amador in this book for details).

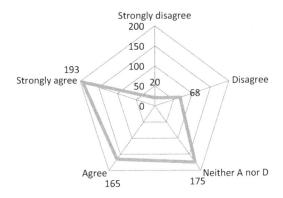

Fig. 2.3.2. LSP teacher training programmes should be necessary to qualify as an LSP teacher (Q23)

Teacher needs were the object of Part 3 (Q24–Q29) of the questionnaire. A key question here (Q24) pointed at potential differences or similarities faced by LSP teachers as compared to FL or general language (GL) teachers and, together with Q23, was also central to the selection of interviewees. Data in Fig. 2.3.3 reveal that for most participants (n = 316; 50.9 %) LSP and GL teachers did not share the same needs, and that these needs were somehow different (n = 243; 39.1 %) or very different (n = 73; 11.8 %). For 102 (16.4 %) participants, however, LSP and GL teachers shared very similar (n = 23; 3.7 %) or somehow similar (n = 79; 12.7 %) needs. And yet, 202 (32.5 %) participants could not tell whether LSP and GL did or did not share the same needs.

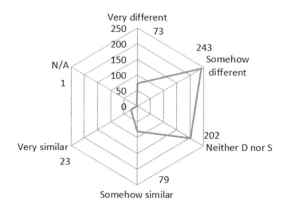

Fig. 2.3.3. Does an LSP teacher have similar or different needs to a GL teacher? (Q24)

Q25 and Q26 provided participants with the opportunity to explain why they felt teacher needs were different or similar in both teaching contexts. Comments were useful at this stage in that they helped to confirm the inventory of needs in Q27 and Q29. Some of these comments were:

➤ Students are there for a professional and specific purpose, changing the dynamics between the student and teacher.

➤ It is fundamental to know the skills the students should master for their jobs.

➤ Resources; specific vocabulary which is work-related.

➤ Interest in the target domain, specialised knowledge, openness to difference.

➤ Domain, needs analyses, understanding the concept of "specific" in LSP (areas, activities, skills, discourse community, genres, etc.).

➤ We need to focus on our students' discipline needs. The teacher must be up-to-date on the new trends in the students' field of studies, understand them and must try to teach students the vocabulary they would need in their studies and future jobs.

Q27, Q28 and Q29 aimed at obtaining a final list of LSP teacher needs based on the participants' experience and preferences. Needs listed in Q27 pertained to knowledge and training, and needs listed in Q29 pertained to other needs that could not be specifically related to knowledge and training. An initial inventory of 43 knowledge- and training-related needs was identified from the literature review and the questionnaire designers' experience. Needs were presented in alphabetic order and individually. They were not grouped under common themes or sub-themes so as to clearly pinpoint individual statements and avoid their passing unnoticed under group labels. Participants were asked to rate each need as very important, important, fairly important, slightly important, or unimportant. For the quantification and ordering of needs, each rating item was given from five (very important) to one point (unimportant), including four points (important), three points (fairly important), and two points (slightly important).

The results yielded a final inventory of knowledge- and training-related needs, listed in order of relevance, and matching the participants' priorities according to the labels given (see Tab. 2.3.3): "Analysis of target and learner needs", "LSP vocabulary teaching", "Materials design and development", "Disciplinary context awareness", "Course design and development", "Lesson planning", "General principles of LSP", "Disciplinary genres", "Task-based teaching", and "Materials evaluation" were rated as the ten most relevant needs (and therefore, those that should be prioritised in the design and development of any LSP teacher training programme); and "EHEA/EU educational policies", "Form-based teaching", "Learners with specific physical disabilities", "Learners with specific cognitive disabilities", "Quality management", "English as a Medium of Instruction (EMI)", "Corpus-based teaching", "Teacher talk of LSP teachers", "Research methods", and "Disciplinary pedagogies" were rated as the least relevant.

Ratings ranged between 3321 points for the most relevant need ("Analysis of target and learner needs") and 2314 points for the least relevant need ("EHEA/EU education policies"). It should be noted, however, that even though this list of needs showed some sort of prioritised perceptions, views and concerns, participant teachers perceived all these needs as relevant for them and the LSP profession; that is, the difference between the most and least relevant needs does not fall below half the identified range (3321–2314 points), and nearly all needs fall within the first quartile of the list (ranged from 3321 to 2490 points). Therefore, relevance differences among the identified needs have not been found significant.[2]

When participants were asked to add any other LSP teacher need they might find relevant for them in particular, or for the whole profession (see Q28), two new knowledge- and training-related needs emerged: (i) interculturality and internationalisation (i.e., intercultural competence, intercultural behaviour, intercultural communication, international classrooms, global communication); and (ii) English as a Lingua Franca (ELF). Given that these two aspects have been claimed to be recurrent themes that go hand-in-hand in needs analyses accounts (Flowerdew, 2013; Johns & Price-Machado, 2001; Nickerson, 2013), both interculturality/internationalisation and ELF have been integrated into the final list of LSP teacher needs.

---

[2]   Quartiles have been identified as: Quartile 1 = 3321–2491 points; Quartile 2 = 2490–1661 points; Quartile 3 = 1660–831 points; Quartile 4 = 830–0 points. The two needs that fall outside Quartile 1 are "Form-based teaching" and "EHEA/EU education policies" but they are positioned high in Quartile 2.

Tab. 2.3.3. Knowledge- and training-related needs (Q27–Q28)

LSP teacher needs (in order of relevance) (*Rating points*)			
Needs	*Rating*	*Needs*	*Rating*
1. Analysis of target and learner needs	3321	23. Testing practices	2992
2. LSP vocabulary teaching	3295	24. LSP communities of practice	2981
3. Materials design and development	3239	25. Classroom management and practice	2955
4. Disciplinary context awareness	3213	26. Content & Language Integrated Learning (CLIL)	2939
5. Course design and development	3211	27. LSP research opportunities	2928
6. Lesson planning	3135	28. Academic discourse	2919
7. General principles about LSP	3131	29. Group work and group management	2908
8. Disciplinary genres	3120	30. Adult teaching	2869
9. Task-based teaching	3113	31. Pronunciation teaching	2839
10. Materials evaluation	3098	32. Negotiation skills and time management	2744
11. Teacher and student motivation	3097	33. General pedagogy	2743
12. Skills teaching	3091	34. Disciplinary pedagogies	2700
13. Assessment methods	3081	35. Research methods	2675
14. LSP challenges, opportunities and constraints	3081	36. Teacher talk of LSP teachers	2647
15. Syllabus design and development	3072	37. Corpus-based teaching	2643
16. Learning strategies	3070	38. English as a Medium of Instruction (EMI)	2623
17. Teaching methodologies	3062	39. Quality management	2623
18. Disciplinary knowledge and training	3048	40. Learners with specific cognitive disabilities	2518
19. Content-Based Training (CBT)	3026	41. Learners with specific physical disabilities	2508

(*Continued*)

Tab. 2.3.3. Continued

20.	Information & Communication Technologies (ICTs)	3023	42.	Form-based teaching	2411
21.	Autonomous and self-directed learning	3019	43.	EHEA/EU educational policies	2314
22.	Self-study, critical thinking and student autonomy	2992		*New needs:*	
			44.	Interculturality/internationalisation	
			45.	English as a lingua franca	

Together with this first resulting list of needs, 17 additional needs were identified as different from knowledge and training (see Tab. 2.3.4). On the one hand, "Content and language teacher collaboration", "Critical reflection on own practice", "Formal professional development opportunities", "LSP peer collaboration", and "Participation in international groups" were found to be the most relevant needs; on the other hand, "Mentoring", "Teacher support", "Credibility in the disciplinary community", and "Engagement in the disciplinary community" were found to be the least relevant. In contrast to the first list, no other needs were reported besides the 17 above. As is the case with the knowledge- and training-related needs, all these needs were valued as highly relevant among participants, and relevance differences were not found to be significant given that, with the exception of "Mentoring" in the third quartile, most needs fell within the first or second quartiles (ranged 397–299 and 298–199 points, respectively), and rating point differences were minimal among some needs (e.g. compare needs no. 3, 4 and 5, or needs no. 9, 10 and 11 in Tab. 2.3.4).[3]

---

[3] For these other needs, rating quartiles have been identified as: Quartile 1 = 397–299 points; Quartile 2 = 298–199 points; Quartile 3 = 198–100 points; Quartile 4 = 99–0 points.

Tab. 2.3.4. Other LSP teacher needs (Q29)

LSP teacher needs (in order of relevance) (*Rating points*)			
Needs	*Rating*	*Needs*	*Rating*
1. Content and language teacher collaboration	397	10. Refresher courses	262
2. Critical reflection on own practice	370	11. Team work	261
3. Formal professional development	329	12. Mobility programmes	241
4. LSP peer collaboration	329	13. Informal professional development opportunities	239
5. Participation in international groups	322	14. Engagement in the disciplinary community	236
6. Links with professionals and industry	305	15. Credibility in the disciplinary community	229
7. Research opportunities	285	16. Teacher support	228
8. Participation in national groups	275	17. Mentoring	167
9. Innovation opportunities	263		

2.3.4. Concluding remarks

Upton (2012: 26) reminded us that the field of LSP has matured and grown in significance in the past five decades because "[o]ur understanding of what students' needs are has evolved and expanded; how we analyse, describe and teach language is much richer; and our view of the contexts and purposes of language is much more complex". Needs analysis has been, and still is, central to LSP, but as the field has evolved, so LSP teachers have developed and changed their roles and needs to meet new teaching challenges and professional demands. Yet this reality has not been sufficiently covered in LSP research or the scholarly literature.

The whole needs analysis developed for the TRAILs project has integrated quantitative and qualitative data gathered from 621 LSP teachers with varying levels of experience in 33 EHEA countries. The use of questionnaires and interviews has aggregated the advantages of both data-collection instruments and their strengths have been used to the best advantage of one single study. This chapter, however, delves into the quantitative analysis of LSP teacher needs (for the qualitative analysis, see the chapter by López-Zurita & Vázquez-Amador in this book). In addition to revealing 62 LSP teacher needs (45 knowledge- and training-related, and 17 professional development needs), the results from the questionnaire data have also revealed education and training gaps that concur with some of the findings noted in the preceding identification and analysis of LSP teacher training programmes in Europe (see chapter by John et al. in this book). Thus, as the TRAILs project moved forward, the sharing of these needs analysis results was intended to contribute first to the definition of LSP training objectives, modules and methodologies that were realistic in the EHEA context, and then to the design and development of an innovative LSP teacher training curriculum. It was also intended to raise awareness of the challenges faced by LSP teachers with the aim of opening a constructive and engaging dialogue about the LSP profession (education, training and professional development) in Europe.

The findings in this chapter only reflect a single stakeholder perspective (that of LSP teachers) and might therefore be understood to "lead to no more than a partial sketch of the professional context" (Huhta et al., 2013: 16); however, the high number of respondents (that is, 621), the number of participating countries (33 in the EHEA and 3 outside), the diversity of participants' backgrounds, the representativeness of the sampled population, the depth of the questionnaire, and the additional feedback and details gathered thanks to the interviews have provided this needs analysis with sufficient reliability and validity for the design of a sensible curriculum aimed at the development and implementation of the innovative LSP teacher training programme that eventually completed this TRAILs project.

Annex: Questionnaire on LSP teacher needs (English abridged version)

Part 1. LSP teacher details

Q1. Which option describes you?

Q2. Which age group describes you?

Q3. Which country of the European Higher Education Area do you work in?

Q4. What is the name of the university or higher education institution you work at?

Q5. What is your current employment status?

Q6. What is your highest qualification?

Q7. Do you hold any relevant teaching and/or LSP teaching qualifications?

Q8. How long have you been teaching LSP in higher education institutions?

Q9. What is your first language?

Q10. What foreign language/s do you teach in your LSP courses?

Q11. At what levels do you teach LSP?

Q12. What field or discipline is your LSP teaching related to? Please, tick all disciplines that apply to your former and present LSP teaching experience

Q13. Are you a general foreign/second language teacher with previous experience in primary, secondary or tertiary education who has moved into LSP?

Q14. If yes, could you briefly explain why you moved from general FL/L2 to LSP teaching?

Q15. Have you taught LSP courses outside higher education institutions?

Q16. If yes, please specify course title and type, organising institution, duration, training language, etc in as much detail as possible

Part 2. LSP teacher training

Q17. Have you received any specific pre-service training on LSP?

Q18. If yes, please specify course title and type, organising institution, duration, training language, etc. in as much detail as possible

Q19. Have you received any specific in-service training on LSP?

Q20. If yes, please specify course title and type, organising institution, duration, training language, etc. in as much detail as possible

Q21. Do you know of any specific LSP teacher training courses that are offered in your country?

Q22. If yes, please specify course title and type, organising institution, duration, training language, etc. in as much detail as possible

Q23. On a scale of 1–5, do you agree with the following statement: "LSP teacher training programmes should be necessary to qualify as an LSP teacher".

Part 3. Teacher needs

Q24. In your view, does an LSP teacher have similar or different needs to a general foreign language teacher?

Q25. If "somehow similar" (4) or "very similar" (5), where does such similarity lie? (Please, explain briefly)

Q26. If "somehow different" (2) or "very different" (1), where does such difference lie? (Please, explain briefly)

Q27. In your view, an LSP teacher needs knowledge and training on the following issues: (Please, tick all that apply) Very important – Important – Fairly important – Slightly important – Unimportant – Not sure [Note: for the list of needs, see the resulting list on Tab. 2.3.3 of this chapter]

Q28. Besides all those above, an LSP teacher needs knowledge and training in … Please, specify.

Q29. Besides those LSP teacher knowledge and training needs identified above, what other needs do you, as an LSP teacher, currently have or have experienced at any point along your career? (Please, tick all that apply) [Note: for the list of needs, see the resulting list on Tab. 2.3.4 of this chapter]

Part 4. Final

Q30. Please, use the box below to insert any additional comments you find relevant and would like to add to this questionnaire

Q31. The TRAILs team is working on an interview to be conducted to supplement and narrow down the data gathered on this questionnaire. May we contact you for a follow-up interview?

Q32. If yes, please provide us with your email address or either email us via lsptrails@gmail.com, and we shall contact you in due course

Once again, thanks very much for your feedback and time!

2.4

A Qualitative Analysis of LSP Teacher Needs Across the European Higher Education Area

Paloma López-Zurita, María Vázquez-Amador

2.4.1. Introduction

A Language for Specific Purposes (LSP) teacher's roles are quite challenging. LSP teachers need to be experts not only in specific language teaching, but also in acquiring specific knowledge, providing materials, designing syllabuses, collaborating with subject specialists, researching and evaluating the course and the students (Ahmed, 2014; Basturkmen, 2010, 2014; Belcher, 2006; Dudley-Evans & St. John, 1998; Górska-Poręcka, 2013; Hall, 2013). Despite all these challenges, LSP teacher education and development is a rather underexplored area (Bocanegra-Valle & Basturkmen, 2019; Kakoulli Constantinou, Papadima-Sophocleous, & Souleles, 2019). The LSP literature has focused on the learner's needs rather than on those of the teacher (Basturkmen, 2014; Bocanegra-Valle, 2016; Kennedy, 1983).

However, there are some studies that focus on different aspects of LSP teacher needs. Zavašnik (2007) investigated LSP teacher training needs in Slovenia. Chostelidou, Griva & Tsakiridou (2009) identified the training needs of English for Specific Purposes (ESP) teachers in Greece. Constantinou, Papadima-Sophocleous and Souleles (2019) studied the profiles of ESP practitioners in tertiary education and their needs in terms of ESP Teacher Education. Bocanegra-Valle and Basturkmen (2019) explored the teacher education needs of experienced ESP instructors in two Spanish universities. Kırkgöz (2019) designed an innovative ESP teacher education course in Turkey in order to address the teacher's needs. Alebaid (2020) documented the training needs of ESP teachers working in Kuwait.

Several research methods are used to gather information about needs analysis, such as observation, interviews, questionnaires, language tests, etc. (Vandermeeren, 2005). Interviews are the most frequently used strategies in qualitative research. "The interview is a key data-gathering tool in many branches of the social sciences, most notably in anthropology and linguistics fieldwork" (Long, 2005: 35). In applied linguistics, interview research has increased, particularly in qualitative studies that investigate "participants' identities, experiences, beliefs, and orientations toward a range of phenomena" (Talmy, 2010: 111). Interviews are employed to obtain information which may otherwise be very difficult to gather (Codó, 2008) and may not be accessible using questionnaires (Blaxter, Hughes &Tight, 2006, cited in Alshenqeeti, 2014).

Questionnaires and interviews can supplement each other in order to obtain data. They are among the main instruments used in the mixed method approach, defined as "research in which the investigator collects and analyses data, integrates the findings, and draws inferences using both qualitative and quantitative approaches or methods in a single study or program of inquiry" (Tashakkori & Creswell, 2007: 4, cited in Gollin-Kies, 2014). The use of mixed methods can improve the validity and reliability of the data (Zohrabi, 2013). Validity in quantitative research concerns the degree to which a study reflects the specific concepts investigated and reliability refers to the extent to which a research instrument provides the same results on repeated trials (Alshenqeeti, 2014).

In this scenario, this chapter is part of a larger project, the European "LSP Teacher Training Summer School" project (TRAILs), which addresses the issue of teacher education and skills development to promote high-quality and innovative teaching in the field of Language for Specific Purposes. Identifying LSP teacher needs is an essential part of the project and the identification of these needs was the first step in this research. In order to do so, a questionnaire and an interview were designed and conducted. This chapter employs a qualitative approach in order to supplement the quantitative analysis of LSP teacher needs reported in the preceding chapter of this book, by Bocanegra-Valle and Perea-Barberá.

The interview was developed with the aim of making up for the potential disadvantages of using questionnaires only, exploring unfamiliar fields, and identifying areas for further research. It was intended that interviews would also help to delve into weak or inconsistent replies to statements in the questionnaire and that the combination of both instruments would contribute to building a more accurate understanding of the contexts in which LSP teachers develop their knowledge and nurture the LSP teaching profession across the European Higher Education Area.

2.4.2. Methodology

This section describes the data collection instrument, namely the interviews. It gives information about the number of interviewees, the conditions to be met for their selection, the language of the interviews, the length and mode of the interviews and the interviewing procedure.

As already mentioned, the main aim of supplementing questionnaires with interview data was initially to further knowledge on teacher needs by eliciting respondents' perceptions and trying to identify gaps or information which might have passed unnoticed during the design and development of the questionnaire. However, some replies to the questionnaire were key to the identification of LSP teacher needs and helped to define the focus of the interview, its organisation and content, as well as the target interviewees. The interview thus aimed at yielding in-depth data that reinforced and enhanced questionnaire findings as well as at probing emerging new issues within the same coverage domain.

2.4.2.1. Data-collection instrument: Interviews

Before reaching the final design of the interview, the following research questions arose:

i. Number of interviewees: How many interviews in all? How many per country?

The questionnaire gathered 621 responses; around half of the questionnaire participants provided their emails for a follow-up interview as per each version: 14 Croatian, 192 English, 23 French, 6 German, 5 Italian, 20 Polish, 12 Slovene, and 31 Spanish. Out of these 303 potential interviewees, 46 were found to comply with conditions (a) and (b) below and were initially selected. Due to a number of invitation refusals or interviewee unavailability, a total of 29 interviews were eventually conducted,

27 in English and 2 in Polish. The distribution of potential interviewees per partner responded to the assignment criteria of proximity, the native or second language and a common average number per partner. The final distribution of accepted interviews was: Adam Mickiewickz University (Poland), 4; Arcola Group (United Kingdom), 3 (1 interview and 2 transcriptions of interviews conducted by the Spanish team - University of Cádiz), 3; Bergamo University (Italy), 4; Bordeaux University (France), 5; Jade University (Germany), 5; Ljubljana University (Slovenia,) 4 and Zagreb University (Croatia), 4.

ii. Interviewees: Who should we interview? What criteria selection should be implemented?

For the selection of the subset of LSP teachers to be interviewed, two conditions had to be met:

➤ participants had accepted to be interviewed by providing their email addresses in the questionnaire (Q31–32); and

➤ participants met five previously agreed-on criteria, namely:

- participants agreed or disagreed with the statement "LSP teacher training programmes should be necessary to qualify as an LSP teacher" (Q23) in the questionnaire;
- participants had replied that LSP teachers had similar or very similar needs to general language teachers (Q24) in the questionnaire;
- participants had received or had not received LSP teacher training;
- participants were either experienced or novice LSP teachers; and,
- participants had been LSP teachers only for their whole career or had come from teaching languages for general purposes.

These five criteria were identified and it was agreed by all TRAILs partners that they embodied inconsistencies across questionnaire replies and, therefore, that these selected interviewees were expected to lead to the modification of questionnaire findings, provide additional support, add other knowledge- and training-related needs and, if possible, become useful for case-study investigation. The profile of interviewees corresponded to LSP teachers who worked in the following EHEA countries: Belgium (1), Finland (1), France (5), Germany (2), Hungary (2), Croatia (3), Italy (3), Poland (2), Romania (2), Serbia (1), Slovenia (1), Spain (4) and the UK (1).

iii. Language: In what language should the interviews be conducted?

As it was the lingua franca and common language among the members of the TRAILs group, interviews were conducted in English with the exception of two cases which used Polish instead.

iv. Length and mode: How long should interviews be? Which interviewing mode should we implement?

The average recording time was 15 minutes and the mode depended on the availability and proximity of respondents: face to face in those cases where it was possible, by telephone conversation, via Skype or videoconferencing.

v. Method: Which interviewing and data-gathering procedure should we follow?

The interview was semi-structured in design, and contained eight open-ended questions that varied depending on the context of the interviewees and their replies in the questionnaire (see Annex). These specific open questions were expected to help to gather factual information that could be easily coded or summarised, while at the same time allowing for a flexible approach. Most questions were divided into two options (options a and b) so that it was possible to customise and personalise the interview questions by adapting them to the particular context of each interviewee. By way of example, question 1 had two options: IQ1a was aimed at those LSP teachers who disagreed with the statement "LSP teacher training programmes should be necessary to qualify as an LSP teacher" (Q23) in the questionnaire, and IQ1B was aimed at those LSP teachers who agreed with this statement.

As shown in Tab. 2.4.1, all questions linked the interview and the questionnaire with the aim of establishing connections between replies provided to the questionnaire and filling information gaps.

This data-collection instrument proved to be highly demanding for all TRAILs members. First, it was very time-consuming as many interviewees were not as available as expected. Some interviews were also difficult to set up and conduct because interviewer and interviewee were located in different countries, with differing zone times, and varying schedules. Also, in many cases the interview needed to be conducted by previously agreed electronic means, which involved particular software capabilities and facilities on both interviewer's and interviewee's sides.

Tab. 2.4.1. Cross-reference of interview and questionnaire prompts

Interview question	Questionnaire question
IQ1a/IQ1b	Q23
IQ2	Q24
IQ3a/IQ3b	Q17, Q18, Q19, Q20
IQ4a/IQ4b	Q8
IQ5a/IQ5b	Q13, Q14
IQ6	Q27
IQ7	Q29

The 29 interviews were recorded and transcribed into written text – in the case of the Polish interviews, translation into English was also necessary. The transcriptions were uploaded to Google Drive and made available to TRAILs members.

We also provided the participants with an interview protocol which comprised the design and development of a privacy and consent form in accordance with EU General Data Protection Regulation legislation and an interview form with a set of questions. At the beginning of each interview, interviewees were asked to sign this consent form or accept its terms verbally. Thanks to the consent form, participants were informed about the goal and procedure of the interview, and their privacy and anonymity were also safeguarded.

2.4.2.2. Data Analysis

Twenty-nine LSP teachers were interviewed: 22 (75.9 %) female teachers and 7 (24.1 %) male teachers, most of them experienced LSP teachers (69 %) in the age group of 41–50 (44.8 %) followed by the 51–60 age group (31 %), 31–40 age group (13.8 %) and 61–70 age group (10.3 %). Among them:

- 55.2 % agreed with the statement that LSP teacher training programmes should be necessary to qualify as LSP teachers (20.7 % disagreed and 24.1 % did not know);
- 69 % found that general foreign language and LSP teachers have similar needs, and for 31 % these needs were very similar;

- 75.9 % reported not having received any pre-service or in-service LSP teacher training, whereas 24.1 % thought (some were not sure) they had received it;
- 56.7 % interviewees were teachers who had switched from teaching a foreign language for general purposes to teaching LSP, and 43.3 % had only been LSP teachers.

As already mentioned, all the partners conducted and transcribed the interviews. The transcriptions gathered 63,202 words (2,180 words per interview on average).

To analyse the responses and the respondents, each of the 29 LSP teacher interviews was assigned a code (R1 to R29). Results were obtained after an exhaustive semantic analysis of the transcriptions of answers. This was conducted question by question, with the extraction, where appropriate, of the most common recurring themes that would lead to the establishment of generalisations on the information obtained.

2.4.3. Results and discussion

The results and discussion are distributed according to the question they refer to.

Question 1 (IQ1): "The necessity of LSP teacher training programmes to qualify as an LSP teacher"

IQ1 asked LSP teachers whether they agree or disagree with the statement "LSP teacher training programmes should be necessary to qualify as an LSP teacher". As mentioned above, 55.2 % agreed with the statement (IQ1a). They think this training should be necessary because for them, it was non-existent and they have learnt how to teach LSP "by doing" (R13, R16). Nowadays these training courses continue to be very scarce. Using their own words, they indicated that although "what mostly matters is practising" (R12), LSP implies "different needs, different materials and different vocabulary" (R11) and consequently "LSP teachers need a training programme and a pedagogical background" (R18), as well as "training for specific terminology and strategies" (R15). Traditional teacher training in the EHEA has not included languages for specific purposes, as some interviewees complain: "teaching is a profession and teacher training should include instruction in all types of teaching contexts, and not just focus on one type" (R17). Most of them added personal remarks on the special features that have traditionally characterised LSP teaching: sound command of special terminology and speech (R11, R21), lack of specialised materials, lack of specialised training and the feeling of being isolated from other teachers, of being self-taught (R20, R22, R23, R26, R28; R29). They also think LSP training is a lifelong learning process because LSP, like the sciences from which they are derived, evolves continually ["specialised languages change, evolve; we introduce new things and for that reason, such as workshops or trainings, [sic] should take place" (R24). "At a certain level, which means either corporate or teaching adults at the university level, you need to pack formal training" (R25)]. As in the previous option, awareness arises as a key point ["training is necessary to increase awareness of the analysis of the language and the specialist content. LSP does require much more than just looking at vocabulary but also structures and also how they are used in the real world because we might think how things are used" (R29)].

For 24.1 %, the answer to IQ1 is not clear-cut: they think LSPTT may be useful but is not absolutely necessary, as one may "do it off the cuff" (R6). It helps to make teachers more confident in their performance. In general, they think experience is what gives teachers the skills to teach LSP, although having some courses would undoubtedly help.

20.7 % do not agree on this necessity (IQ1b), as they consider that LSP training is included within the general training a good teacher already must have ["Every teacher leaving University should be prepared to work with different groups of learners" (R1)]. Not only do they consider this training unnecessary but some also doubt the existence of languages for specific purposes as defined in this research ["All adult learners have specific purposes (R1)"; "I do not see the difference between language teaching in general and the teaching of specialist languages" (R5)]. Using their own words, for them LSP is just "a part of curriculum development" (R3), usually acquired through "professional experience" (R4), and "in environments where you can pick up the special language" (R2), as "the best source to learn special languages is the learners themselves" (R2). Nevertheless, with just one exception (R5), all these interviewees agree that inexperienced teachers in this field must have an awareness about teaching specific-purpose language and not general language, as well as the difficulty of this fact ["novice teachers should be more aware that they should not be afraid of teaching LSP" (R2)]. The fear of teaching

LSP is constantly commented on by the interviewers. This issue will be discussed later.

Question 2 (IQ2): "Similarities between LSP and GL teacher's needs"

IQ2 aimed to explore the similarities between the needs of LSP and general language teachers. The replies, however, did not clearly point at similarities, but rather, at different needs. The idea of LSP teaching being more demanding and more time-consuming because of the lack of published materials and the necessity to create your own is mentioned by R2, R12, R16, R17, R22, R24. By way of example, the following excerpt contains some of the comments from interviewee R2. This experienced LSP teacher began by saying that teaching the language, whether for general or specific purposes, was much the same, but soon claimed that teaching LSP was "more demanding", as it required an LSP teacher to be "more creative" and also, that it was "more time consuming"; s/he pointed to three differences but did not express any similarity:

> ... what I like to use is the Christmas metaphor that in my opinion ... so the special language or LSP is a decoration on the tree ... so you need to have very solid foundations ... this is the reason why it is not extremely different from teaching general English but I know that *there are subtle differences* I think *that LSP teaching is more demanding* because you can rely on yourself more since *the course books are not so elaborate* as in the case of general English *they are not so up-to-date as in general English* ... so your job is *more demanding* as an LSP teacher ... And I think *you have to be more creative if you teach LSP ... and it is also more time consuming.* (R2) [italics added]

Something similar occurred with interviewee R4. Again an experienced LSP teacher, s/he began by pointing out similarities between the two teaching contexts, such as classroom management or large heterogeneous student groups; then, s/he seemed to feel uncertain about the similarities and differences ["I can imagine there are" (R4)] and concluded by noting some differences which, in his/her view, were "unique to LSP":

> Yes, I do. I think a general teacher has similar... well let me phrase it this way: both classroom experiences, both for students and teacher, I think there are a number of similarities. I think there is a degree of overlap. In today's classrooms, teachers or instructors, call them what you want, have to manage diverse classroom both in terms of ethnic make-up, in terms of language proficiency. In my teaching experience all of the groups teach have widely diverse language backgrounds etc. they will also have to experience a range of expectations from students from their institutions, so I see

a number of similarities. Yes. Obviously, I can imagine *there are a number of particularities and peculiarities etc. that come with the domain of LSP.* For instance, students who think that their English is… sometimes *I see that students have strong language backgrounds, but they're not familiar with a particular register,* and *that makes them insecure, and it handicaps them,* which I think is unfair. French teachers, particularly in Belgium, *teachers of French will not experience that as much as LSP teachers.* English is such an omnipresent language in The Netherlands as compared to German, or French. *So that is, I think, unique to LSP.* (R4) [italics added]

Another difference that interviewees detected when trying to explain similarities between teaching general language and LSP was the need to have a good command of the language, a high level of grammar and teaching experience to be confident enough. Teachers indicated that "C1–C2 level of English is already quite specific" (R3); "you need this scaffolding of the grammar before you can teach the special language" (R9); "if you are trained up to a certain level as an English teacher you should be able to manage everything related to the language" (R10); "from the level B1 you must have an adapted strategy" (R14). In all these cases, although the initial purpose was a different one, they eventually stated that LSP teaching requires a high level of grammar from both students and teachers, and also experience from teachers to feel confident about a field that is not part of their original training.

Question 3 (IQ3): "LSP Teacher Training"

Q3 was again divided into two options. IQ3a was aimed at LSP teachers who had received LSP Teacher Training and IQ3b at those who had not. The first group was asked to comment on their experience, whether they would recommend this type of course, whether the course had made their teaching change and what kind of impact, if any, it had had on their professional development. The second group was asked whether they felt that completing one of these courses would have contributed to improving their teaching and enhancing their role as an LSP teacher. Only 24.1 % of interviewees identified with IQ3a. They included a wide range of training which was not LSP-specific. For instance, after answering that s/he had not taken any courses, R3 seemed to remember that s/he had attended a one-day course on LSP and that was all the specific training s/he had had in a long professional career, as s/he was an experienced teacher. In two cases (R5 and R18), the respondents emphasised that the courses had included not only content but also methodology for LSP. The rest of the answers seem to refer mainly to course content, as they mentioned Business (R1); British Culture and Politics (R20); Lexical Competence (R24); General Methodology (R25); English for Academic Purposes (R28), etc. All this shows again that the LSPTT course offering is quite scarce in Europe. This is also the main reason why the respondents in group IQ3b (75.9 %) had not attended any courses: either simply because they did not exist or because they were not offered. All of them would have liked to have received some training, as seen in the following remarks: "that would have saved me some time and a few embarrassing experiences" (R4); "it would have covered the basics of discourse analysis and register analysis to go ahead and become a better LSP teacher" (R10); "it would have helped me" (R12); "things could have been easier" (R15); "it would help to find the resources to be able to teach LSP" (R17), etc.

Generally speaking, respondents to IQ3b share four ideas:

- they would all have considered LSPTT a great help,
- they complain about their self-taught status imposed by the absence of LSPTT courses,
- they have also learnt with the help of other experienced ESP teachers, e.g.: "I was mentored by my much more experienced colleagues" (R23) and
- the development of awareness about LSP is important to gain in confidence and learn about it, e.g.: "I have many colleagues who haven't received LSP teacher training because they do not reflect on their pedagogical approach, they do not progress and face many difficulties teaching LSP". (R16). This awareness is nevertheless a common feature for all those interviewed except for one, who does not believe in the existence of ESP, as s/he says, "I would never refer to myself as a teacher of ESP, though that is what my module description claims (…) I am a good English teacher (…) I still can't imagine what benefit would be" (referring to LSPTT courses) (R6).

Question 4 (IQ4): "Previous LSP teaching experience. Main challenges"

This question also had two options: IQ4a for experienced LSP teachers and IQ4b for novices. The first group was asked about the changes they had experienced in terms of knowledge, training and professional needs over the years, if any. The second was asked about the problems they faced teaching LSP and whether they felt that their needs differed from their more experienced colleagues. All the interviewees chose the first option, as they were experienced LSP teachers. The main changes they have experienced over the years may be classified into 6 sections, in which we include the main idea by using quotations from the respondents:

(a) Students:
 - "Students *have changed*" (R27); "now the level of English in classes *is higher* than before" (R3, R4, R9, R27); "*the number of students in class has increased*" (R13). [italics added]

(b) Personal features
 - "Over the years *you enjoy teaching* more, you *feel more confident*, more *relaxed*" (R1, R9, R11, R20, R23, R24, R25); "You become more *self-reflective and eager to learn* and improve" (R4); "The *efficiency* of classes *is* much *better*" (R5). [italics added]

(c) Acquired knowledge:
 - "With experience you *need to work less* with the materials" (R1); Teachers are more *familiar with contents* (R7, R18, R27). "My knowledge has *expanded*" (R22); "you *deepen* your knowledge" (R20); "I *know more* about specialised language" (R21); "I also have *more hindsight and more specific resources* for my teaching" (R15); "I wanted to become *an expert in the same domain as my students*" (R16). [italics added]

(d) Need for continuous adaptation:
 - "Teaching LSP is a *lifelong learning process* with the necessity of being continually up-to-date, as sciences change" (R7); "One of the advantages of being an LSP teacher is that *you can't stand still* and just do what you have been doing the last 15 years" (R10); "Teaching LSP is a *constant evolution*. We change aims, assessment and contents regularly" (R14); "I mostly engage with *keeping up to date*" (R19); "*We can never stop learning*" (R25). [italics added]

(e) Technology:
 - "Technology is *the real new challenge*" (R2 + R5, R8, R12, R15, R16, R19, R26). [italics added]

(f) New approaches towards teaching:

- *"From grammar to a more holistic approach"* (R26); "from grammar *to new strategies* for self-learning" (R28); *"LSP is being replaced* by CLIL or English Medium Instruction Approach" (R29). [italics added]

We would like to highlight one of the respondents' contributions that may summarise the others: "I have to keep up with all the technology and new resources, topics but also to overcome a huge shift in their needs and learning styles" (R22). As with previous questions, R6 continues to differentiate and disagree: "Nothing has changed".

Question 5 (IQ5): "Moving from GL to LSP teaching experiences and reasons"

IQ5 made a distinction between teachers that had always taught LSP and those who had switched from general FL to LSP teaching. In the first option (IQ5a) they were asked whether their LSP teaching had been their own choice, what challenges and problems they had faced and what needs they had for this teaching. In the second (IQ5b) they were asked about the main changes, challenges and needs they had experienced when they switched from FL to LSP. Only one teacher in the first group had chosen LSP as an option for his/her professional career; in the other cases this teaching was a requirement of their departments and the general feeling about it was fairly negative: "I've learned to accept it" (R4); "it was like being thrown into deep water a bit" (R5); they also comment they do not feel confident and comfortable: "it is quite tough" (R12).

The main differences between FL and LSP that were voiced by the second group (IQ5b) mainly concern content and students. Specific content is a challenge too, as observed by the first group, and also makes them feel unconfident; on the other hand, their feeling is that students are more motivated. As interviewee R8 comments: "that was very rewarding (motivated students) and scary at the same time (content)". [brackets added for clarification]

Question 6 (IQ6): "Main LSP teacher needs (knowledge and training)"

With a view to identifying new LSP teacher needs, IQ6 asked LSP teachers to prioritise their needs on the basis of the questionnaire results and add any other needs that were crucial to them and were missing in the questionnaire list. All replies agreed with the questionnaire results.

"Target and learner needs analysis", "Specialised vocabulary teaching" and "Materials design and development" were the most relevant knowledge- and training-related needs they had, and, most importantly, they did not provide any other need that had not been previously identified in the questionnaire results. To illustrate this point:

> I would say yes I do agree with that I mean obviously you want to understand the needs of your students and when it comes to vocabulary obviously again I would concentrate of the strategies on *how to develop, how to build up your own vocabulary* and so the students obviously they need to have their own strategies to acquire relevant vocabulary. But it helps teachers if they are familiar with that vocabulary or if they have been successful learners again, that helps because they can relate to students and the *materials development*, again this is something that obviously it helps because *we can't find the relevant publications.* Obviously it's very difficult for the publishers to respond, *so yeah I would agree with that. Yeah I can't think of anything else.* (R28) [italics added]

Further analysing the results of IQ6, over half of the responses validated the importance of the three crucial needs identified in the questionnaire, without prioritising any of them (n = 15; R1, R5, R8, R9, R13, R14, R15, R16, R18, R20, R23, R24, R26, R28, R29). Nearly a quarter of the respondents chose "Materials design and development" as their first and most important need (n = 7; R2, R3, R4, R7, R10, R22), followed by a group of 5 respondents who chose "Target and learner needs analysis" (R11, R17, R19, R25, R27); only two interviewees considered "Specialised vocabulary teaching" as their most relevant need (R6 and R21). Although they did not provide any other need that had not been previously identified in the questionnaire results, some of them added valuable comments, such as the following:

> Perhaps a technical observation. *I would prioritise language awareness both on the part of the students' instructors but also management.* Language is more than the grammar and vocab. It shapes, it provides, it yields, it triggers identity performances, it allows us to make things happen in the world. Anything that has to do with performativity, idexicality, social meanings, contextualisation. These things matter as much as formal accuracy, lexical range, lexicogrammar, etc. So, the building blocks and usage. (R4) [italics added]

Question 7 (IQ7): "Other LSP teacher needs"

Lastly, IQ7 again asked interviewees to agree or disagree with other needs besides those prioritised in the questionnaire results. On this occasion they again had to prioritise "Collaboration between content and language teachers"; "Critical reflection on own practice"; and "Formal professional development opportunities". They were also asked to add other needs. Results show that most of them (n = 12; R1, R8, R9, R10, R11, R13, R15, R16, R17, R18, R20, R21) considered the three statements to be similarly important. "Collaboration between content and language teachers" was chosen by 10 respondents (R5, R12, R14, R19, R21, R23, R24, R26, R28), followed by "Critical reflection on own practice", that was very important for R2, R4, R7, R25 and R27. Only R3 and R22 considered "Formal professional development opportunities" very relevant. The responses strengthened the questionnaire findings and no further needs were identified.

Interviewees R21 and R16 are good examples:

I agree that the *cooperation with the content teacher is important* … but it is largely lacking. (…) the problem is that the results of our courses are often seen as non-essential by the other teaching staff (…) But let me say this again – *formal professional development and perhaps training sessions would help* …. You know, training sessions where you can see and discuss best practices with other LSP teachers … that could be useful… anything … my own work would benefit from such events. (R21). [italics added]

Yes, *collaboration between content and language teachers is essentia*l but it is not easy. I have lost my temper at times with certain colleagues or with the institution itself because of the lack of recognition (…). (R16) [italics added]

The respondents did not add any more tangible needs but used the interview as an opportunity to express their own ideas about what the teaching of LSP entails. Paraphrasing their answers, LSP teachers usually "suffer" from a lack of self-esteem (R2, R6, R11) that likely stems from a "lack of recognition" (R16), as "[i]t is actually our fault that we do not have that ability to sell our professionalism" (R10), and all that results in a feeling of isolation (R14, R17, R21, R22).

2.4.4. Conclusion

The interview replies were analysed qualitatively with a view to furthering knowledge on this topic and identifying new LSP teacher needs that had not emerged through the questionnaire. Finding out about the beliefs, concerns or interests of diverse LSP teachers was also a notable target of this analysis.

In general terms, most interviewees agreed that teaching LSP was more demanding than teaching general language, as it involves different elements such as special vocabulary, materials and student needs.

Most respondents had received no training in LSP teaching or had received training which was not LSP-specific. They said that they had learned through their own LSP teaching experience. As experienced teachers, they have noticed certain changes along their careers. They have gained confidence and knowledge and have adapted to new learning/teaching environments, such as Information Technology and new approaches to teaching.

The interviewees who had always been LSP teachers admitted that this was not by choice. The GL teachers who switched to LSP teaching regarded content as a challenge but, on the other hand, appreciated their students' motivation.

Regarding LSP teachers' needs, the results were consistent with the questionnaire and the interviewees stressed the importance of needs analysis, specialised vocabulary and material design.

A closer look at the transcriptions revealed some other aspects.

The richness of some participants' comments reflected their experience and expertise in LSP teaching and the profession, and concur with some of the findings in the current literature – namely, that teaching LSP is a long-term process (Campion, 2016) or that developing specialised knowledge is one of the greatest challenges (Bocanegra-Valle & Basturkmen, 2019).

Interviewees' profiles were consistent with the "discrepancies" that had been agreed upon and identified from the questionnaire replies.

These anomalies proved to be contradictory in their arguments at times, so that, rather than furthering the questionnaire results, the interviews did not help to enhance or refine the questionnaire findings – that is, they did not add any other LSP teacher need, be it knowledge- and training-related or any other.

Lastly, the discrepancies or disparities initially found between participants were not as broad as had been first anticipated and, in fact, helped to reinforce the questionnaire findings. Thus, the interview results might provide insights into wider issues if individually analysed (case study research).

All these data reinforce the need to design an LSP teacher training programme in order to promote high-quality and innovative teaching in the field of LSP.

Annex

Project title: LSP Teacher Training Summer School (TRAILs). Project reference: 2018-1-FR01-KA203-048085. Project website: http://TRAILs.espe-aquitaine.fr/

Interview. Questions

Thank you very much for meeting us/me here today. As you probably remember, you've recently completed an online questionnaire on the needs of LSP teachers. In this interview, we'll further the discussion about your needs as an LSP teacher, your professional development requirements and your views on what it is to teach a language for specific and academic purposes. This interview has eight questions and is expected to last approximately twenty minutes.

IQ1

IQ1a [*aimed at LSP teachers who disagreed with the statement in Q23*] – Question 23 of the online questionnaire asked you to rate on a scale of 1 (strongly disagree) to 5 (strongly agree) whether you agreed with the following statement: "LSP teacher training programmes should be necessary to qualify as an LSP teacher". Your reply was against, or at least not in favour of this statement. Could you elaborate on the reasons for your reply?

IQ1b [*aimed at LSP teachers who agreed with the statement in Q23*] – Question 23 of the online questionnaire asked you to rate on a scale of 1 (strongly disagree) to 5 (strongly agree) whether you agreed with the following statement: "LSP teacher training programmes should be necessary to qualify as an LSP teacher". Your reply was in favour of, or at least not against, this statement. Could you elaborate on the reasons for your reply?

IQ2 – We found that for you, an LSP teacher has similar needs to a general English teacher, which is interesting. Could you elaborate on this?

IQ3

IQ3a [*aimed at LSP teachers who have received LSPTT*] – You are one of the few LSP teachers who reported having attended LSP teacher training courses. Could you tell me/us about your experience? Would you recommend this type of courses? To what extent would you say that your teaching has changed/been modified after this course? Has this course had any impact on your professional development? If so, could you please elaborate?

IQ3b [*aimed at LSP teachers who have not received any LSPTT*] – You reported not having attended any LSP teacher training, perhaps some general courses on pedagogy or foreign language teaching, even in a particular branch of LSP (like Business English). Why haven't you received any kind of LSP teacher training? Do you feel that completing an LSP teacher training course would have contributed to improving your teaching and enhancing your role as an LSP teacher? If so, in what ways?

IQ4

IQ4a [*aimed at experienced LSP teachers*] – We/I see that you have been teaching LSP courses for some years already, so you are an experienced or highly experienced LSP teacher. Have your knowledge, training and professional needs changed over these years? If so, in what ways have they changed? Please elaborate.

IQ4b [*aimed at novice LSP teachers*] – We/I see that you are a novice LSP teacher. Could you tell us/me about your experience as a less experienced LSP teacher, about the problems and constraints you have been facing? Do you feel that your needs differ from those of your more experienced colleagues? Please explain.

IQ5

IQ5a [*aimed at LSP teachers only*] – You've always taught languages for specific purposes. Was this your own choice or were you required by your Department to become involved in LSP? What are the main challenges and problems you were faced with? What particular needs did you have for this LSP teaching?

IQ5b [*aimed at LSP teachers coming from teaching languages for general purposes*] – You switched from general FL teaching to LSP teaching. What were the main changes you experienced in this transition? What were the main challenges you were faced with? What were your main needs at that time?

IQ6 – The analysis of results from the online questionnaire has revealed that LSP teachers need knowledge and training mostly on: 1. Target and learner needs analysis; 2. specialised vocabulary teaching; and 3. Materials design and development. Do you agree? Would you prioritise other needs? What knowledge and training needs are crucial to you as an LSP teacher?

IQ7 – The analysis of results from the online questionnaire has revealed that LSP teachers have other needs, not only knowledge and training needs, and the most important of these are: 1. Collaboration between content and language teachers; 2. Critical reflection on own practice; and 3. Formal professional development opportunities. Do you agree? Would you prioritise other needs? What are the most crucial needs for you as an LSP teacher?

IQ8 – To conclude this interview, are there any additional comments you would like to add? Many thanks for your time and help in this project!

Part 3

DEFINITION OF TRAINING OUTCOMES BASED ON IDENTIFIED GAPS BETWEEN LSP PROVISION IN EUROPE AND LSP TEACHER NEEDS

3.1

Training Outcomes Based on Identified Gaps between LSP Provision in Europe and LSP Teachers' Needs

Joanna Kic-Drgas, Joanna Woźniak

3.1.1. Introduction

In the European Higher Education Area (EHEA) the quality of foreign language teaching is becoming a priority. In the Communication from 30 May 2017 on the revamped EU agenda for higher education, the European Commission stated the following:

> "Designing, building and delivering good study programmes is not easy. Good teachers are crucial. Too many higher education teachers have received little or no pedagogical training and systematic investment in teachers' continuous professional development remains the exception. National and institutional strategies to improve career opportunities and rewards for good teachers are becoming more common but are far from standard." (European Commission, 2017)

This statement also applies to LSP didactics. The growing interest in LSP has increased the number of LSP courses at universities and colleges. As a result, teachers often begin to teach LSP without any special professional preparation. The gap in teacher preparation is partly filled by the research results from the TRAILs Project. During the first project outcome, project partners analysed LSP teacher training programmes provided in the EHEA in order to determine the provision of LSP teacher professional development programmes in higher education institutions in the EHEA. The second task explored the needs of in-service LSP teachers. The results of both tasks within the first project outcome thus provide a basis for the third step of TRAILs, namely the identification of gaps between LSP teacher training provision and LSP teachers' needs. These gaps contribute further to the definition of LSP learning outcomes, modules and methodologies that are realistic within the EHEA context, and to the development of the Curriculum for the winter School. The final step of the project was the winter School and its evaluation, which was planned to take place in Zagreb.

This paper presents the methodological approach to the definition of learning objectives. It starts with the main definition of what a learning outcome is. Then, it presents the main assumptions and goals of task 3. Since the task was based on the earlier results of the first and second outcomes, the key results of the provision of LSP teacher training programmes (O1) and of the needs analysis (O2) will be recapped. The following part of the report will present a model of Bloom's taxonomy on which the outcome-setting scheme was based. Thereafter, the scheme and the methodology used to create the objectives will be provided. In the last part of the report, some statistical results concerning Outcome 3 will be presented.

3.1.2. Learning outcomes: Definition and role in the language teaching and learning process

Since a recommendation on the European Qualifications Framework was established by the Council of Europe and the European Parliament in 2008, "learning outcomes" as a term is inextricably connected with education and training policies in Europe. It is defined by the European Centre for the Development of Vocational Training (Cedefop) as:

(a) "statements of what a learner knows, understands and is able to do on completion of a learning process, which are defined in terms of knowledge, skills and competence" (Cedefop, 2014, p. 74)
(b) "learning outcomes are defined as 'sets of knowledge, skills and/or competences an individual has acquired and/or is able to demonstrate after completion of a learning process, either formal, non-formal or informal" (Cedefop, 2014, p. 73)

The learning statements about the intended knowledge, skills and competences of a learner:

"play an increasingly important role in efforts to improve the quality and relevance of education and training in Europe. [They] help to clarify programme and qualifications intentions and make it easier for those involved – learners, parents, teachers or assessors – to work towards these expectations. The increased transparency offered by learning outcomes also provides an important reference point for policy-makers, making it easier to judge the match between society's needs and the programmes and qualifications offered within education and training. Learning outcomes, however, can be written in many different ways and it is not a given that they will add value as expected." (Cedefop, 2017, p. 5)

Learning outcomes statements form an important part of curricula, which set the framework for planning learning experiences. They help teachers in the teaching process, providing them with a range of methods. They also play an informative role for learners, by showing them what they are expected to know/do and understand after a given learning activity. Learning outcomes can be general and complete when they refer to an entire programme, or detailed but limited when they focus on a specific module or its part. Learning outcomes are used for different purposes, such as (Cedefop, 2017, p. 22):

1. Qualifications frameworks and their level descriptors
2. Qualification standards
3. Curriculum development
4. Assessment and validation
5. Quality assurance
6. Teaching and training

For all these purposes, learning outcomes are described in terms of the knowledge, skills and social competences which an individual learner can achieve.

3.1.3. Definition of learning outcomes for LSP teacher training: General assumptions

The definition of training outcomes should be based on the gaps identified between the results of the analysis of LSP teacher training programmes in Europe (O1) and the identification of LSP teacher needs (Outcome 2). The questions that should be answered during the identification of the gaps in Outcome 3 are:

1. What are the gaps in the provision of practical training in LSP teaching and learning?
2. What are the gaps in the provision of conducting needs analysis in LSP teaching and learning?
3. What are the gaps in the provision of training in teaching methodology in LSP teaching and learning?
4. What are the gaps in the provision of training in materials design in LSP teaching and learning?
5. What are the gaps in the provision of training in the use of ICT in LSP teaching and learning?
6. What are the gaps in the provision of training in testing and assessment in LSP teaching and learning?
7. What are the gaps in the provision of training in research methodology in LSP teaching and learning?

The realisation of the third outcome of TRAILs is expected to contribute to the development of LSP teacher professional development in European higher education institutions. The added value and impact of the definition of training outcomes is its transnationality and innovation. The transnationality of the task means that the gaps identified in LSP teacher training provision concern firstly the national level of each project partner, and secondly the international European level. The fact that to date no research has identified the gaps between LSP teacher training provision in Europe and LSP teacher needs for which training outcomes are desired proves the innovation of Outcome 3 of the project. The identification of the gaps was also a fundamental value for the curriculum of the TRAILs winter School.

The adopted methodology is qualitative (textual analysis). It is transferable to any discipline in which the provision of training and actual needs of practitioners need to be juxtaposed in order to identify the gaps that provide the basis for the training outcomes. Specifically, the definition of training outcomes will serve as a foundation upon which curricula, syllabi and programmes for LSP teachers professional development should be prepared, designed, and supported.

A three-stage approach was adopted for preparing the definition of training outcomes based on the gaps identified between LSP provision in Europe and LSP teacher needs:

1. Adam Mickiewicz University in Poznań identified the main gaps between the provision of LSP teacher training and LSP teacher needs. These gaps were grouped thematically and divided into seven pillars.

2. Each pillar (see *Fig. 3.1.5: Seven pillars of LSP teacher training*) with the main gaps collected was assigned to a single partner. The partners were asked to formulate, in their opinion the five most crucial learning objectives concerning the pillar they were in charge of. Based on the proposals sent in, the partners from Adam Mickiewicz University in Poznań, in cooperation with the partners from the University of Ljubljana who are responsible for Outcome 4 (developing an innovative LSP teacher training curriculum), have compiled the detailed training outcomes of the TRAILs winter school and presented them to all project partners.

3. All project partners have provided feedback on the learning outcomes formulated, and Adam Mickiewicz University in Poznań has compiled the final inventory of training outcomes for the TRAILs winter School.

The gaps identified were based on the results of Outcome 1 and Outcome 2. In the next two subchapters the most important findings of LSP teacher training provision and LSP in-service teacher needs analysis will be recapped.

3.1.3.1. Main results of Outcome 1: LSP teacher training provision – as a basis for identification of gaps

Within the first task, a total of 1,024 university institutions from 25 EHEA countries were analysed. The survey shows 68 university institutions from 14 different EHEA countries, in which students are offered LSP teacher training in various forms. In some higher education institutions, not one, but several LSP teacher training courses are provided, so the total number of LSP teacher training courses in the EHEA is 88. Considering the above results, it can be concluded that LSP teacher training is treated quite marginally within the EHEA. Only 8 % of all academic institutions examined with philological fields of study have LSP teacher training in their educational offer.

Apart from a few similarities, such as the use of certain ICT tools, the LSP teacher training programmes identified demonstrate fundamental differences relating to both their formal and content-related aspects. In particular, the formal differences concern the manner in which LSP teacher training is provided, the number of teaching hours, the number of ECTS points awarded, or the qualifications provided. The differences determined at the content-related level refer to the prerequisites that allow a student to take part in the course, the learning outcomes, methods, techniques and instruments used and taught during the course, as well as the evaluation system.

Considering the total number of courses, and the lack of uniformity in the courses offered, it can also be concluded that the current status of teaching of specialised languages at European universities is relatively marginalised and insufficient, considering the current changes in, and needs of, both teachers and students.

3.1.3.2. *Main results of Outcome 2: LSP teachers' needs analysis – as a basis for identification of gaps*

The second project task combined quantitative and qualitative methods to analyse LSP teachers' needs. The results of a survey carried out among 621 LSP teachers with different levels of professional experience from 33 EHEA countries revealed significant educational and training gaps, and suggested 62 different LSP teacher needs. Moreover, the study confirmed that most teachers had not received any LSP teacher training before or during their teaching careers, and most of them were not even aware of the existence of LSP teacher training courses in their countries. Furthermore, the understanding of LSP teacher training, as confirmed in the results of needs analysis, is often misleading.

The study showed that all 43 knowledge- and training-related needs indicated in the questionnaire played an important role for LSP teachers. Moreover, the respondents also gave two further knowledge- and training-related needs. 17 additional needs were identified as different from knowledge and training. Although the differences between the most frequently mentioned needs and those slightly less frequently mentioned are small, it is necessary to indicate those areas of needs which are an absolute priority for the majority of LSP teachers, namely:

1. Analysis of target and learner needs,
2. LSP vocabulary teaching,

3. Materials design and development,
4. Disciplinary context awareness,
5. Course design and development,
6. Lesson planning,
7. General principles of LSP,
8. Disciplinary genres,
9. Task-based teaching, and
10. Materials evaluation.

Among additional needs, the most relevant were:

1. Content and language teacher collaboration,
2. Critical reflection on own practice,
3. Formal professional development opportunities,
4. LSP peer collaboration and
5. Participation in international groups.

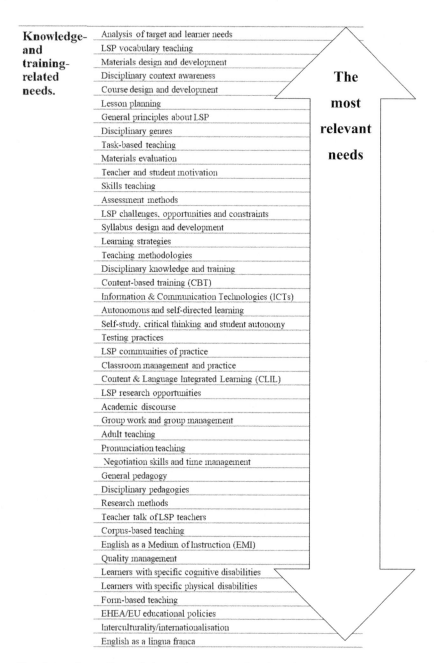

Knowledge- and training-related needs.

Analysis of target and learner needs
LSP vocabulary teaching
Materials design and development
Disciplinary context awareness
Course design and development
Lesson planning
General principles about LSP
Disciplinary genres
Task-based teaching
Materials evaluation
Teacher and student motivation
Skills teaching
Assessment methods
LSP challenges, opportunities and constraints
Syllabus design and development
Learning strategies
Teaching methodologies
Disciplinary knowledge and training
Content-based training (CBT)
Information & Communication Technologies (ICTs)
Autonomous and self-directed learning
Self-study, critical thinking and student autonomy
Testing practices
LSP communities of practice
Classroom management and practice
Content & Language Integrated Learning (CLIL)
LSP research opportunities
Academic discourse
Group work and group management
Adult teaching
Pronunciation teaching
Negotiation skills and time management
General pedagogy
Disciplinary pedagogies
Research methods
Teacher talk of LSP teachers
Corpus-based teaching
English as a Medium of Instruction (EMI)
Quality management
Learners with specific cognitive disabilities
Learners with specific physical disabilities
Form-based teaching
EHEA/EU educational policies
Interculturality/internationalisation
English as a lingua franca

The most relevant needs

Fig. 3.1.1. List of knowledge and training related teachers' needs in accordance to their priority

Other needs	Content and language teacher collaboration
	Critical reflection on own practice
	Formal professional development opportunities
	LSP peer collaboration
	Participation in international groups
	Links with professionals and industry
	Research opportunities
	Participation in national groups
	Innovation opportunities
	Refresher courses
	Team work
	Mobility opportunities
	Informal professional development opportunities
	Engagement in the disciplinary community
	Credibility in the disciplinary community
	Teacher support
	Mentoring

Fig. 3.1.2. List of other teachers' needs in accordance to their priority

The findings from O1 and O2 have proven that LSP teacher training programmes in the EHEA have not been established in higher education institutions and they are not standardised enough in terms of formats, duration, certification, content, methods, and assessment.

3.1.3.3. Identified gaps

Compiling the results of O1 and O2 the following gaps between LSP teacher training provision in Europe and LSP teachers' needs can be identified:

1. The provision of practical training in LSP teaching and learning in European higher education institutions is insufficient in relation to the identified needs of LSP teachers.

2. The provision of conducting needs analysis in LSP teaching and learning in European higher education institutions is insufficient in relation to the identified needs of LSP teachers. Teachers lack

the knowledge and practice of conducting needs analysis among students.

3. The provision of teaching methodology in LSP teaching and learning in European higher education institutions is insufficient in relation to the identified needs of LSP teachers. The methodology provided in the few identified LSP teacher training courses is too diverse.

4. The provision of training in materials design in LSP teaching and learning in European higher education institutions is insufficient in relation to the identified needs of LSP teachers. The materials available on the market often do not correspond to the group level or subject matter. Teachers have to prepare the materials on their own. They do not always know how to this.

5. The provision of training in the use of ICT in LSP teaching and learning in European higher education institutions is insufficient in relation to the identified needs of LSP teachers. The analysis of LSP teacher training provided has shown that ICT applications are often used by LSP teachers, in particular basic applications for communication or e-learning. It is worth extending this database to include new applications that can be used in LSP didactics.

6. The provision of training in testing and assessment in LSP teaching and learning in European higher education institutions is insufficient in relation to the identified needs of LSP teachers. The training provided in testing and assessment is too varied.

7. The provision of training in research methodology in LSP teaching and learning in European higher education institutions is insufficient in relation to the identified needs of LSP teachers.

3.1.4. Bloom's taxonomy of learning objectives

Bloom suggested introducing the hierarchical learning system into educational psychology. The system aimed at structuring the expression of qualitatively different kinds of thinking, which is why it has been adapted for classroom use as a broadly adapted planning tool. It is applied to describe the degree to which students are expected to understand and use certain concepts, to demonstrate particular skills, and to have their values, attitudes, and interests affected. The main result of the Bloom study was the formulation of a division of educational objectives into three domains:

- cognitive (referring to knowing)
- affective (referring to attitudes, feelings)
- psychomotor (refereeing to physical performance)[1]

The cognitive domain contains learning skills related to mental (thinking) processes that include a hierarchy of skills involving processing information, constructing understanding, applying knowledge, solving problems, and conducting research. Within the cognitive domain there are six levels of complexity: knowledge, comprehension, application, analysis, synthesis, evaluation.

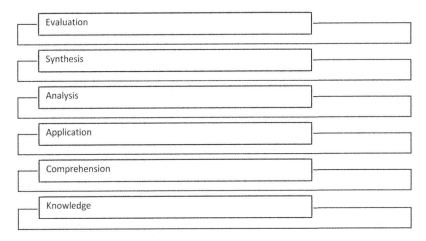

Evaluation

Synthesis

Analysis

Application

Comprehension

Knowledge

Fig. 3.1.3. Bloom's taxonomy of outcomes (on the basis of Bloom, 1956)

The higher the level, presumably, the more complex the mental operation required (higher thinking skills). However, this is not automatically related to the superiority of higher thinking skills, because the development of higher thinking skills cannot be activated without the basic level of some lower thinking skills. For example, in order to evaluate a process, it must be first analysed (Hoque, 2016, p. 46).

Tab. 3.1.1 below presents a description of certain levels of Bloom's taxonomy with "verb tables" to identify which action verbs align with each level.

---

[1] For the needs of the formulation of the outcomes described, only the cognitive level was taken into consideration.

Tab. 3.1.1. Bloom's taxonomy (based on Anderson & Krathwohl, 2001, 67–69)

Taxonomy level	Description	Verbs
Evaluation	Critical synthesis of the work, applicability to the life context	Judge, assess, compare, evaluate, conclude, measure, deduce, argue, decide, choose, rate, select, estimate, validate, consider, appraise, value, criticise, infer
Synthesis	Ability to put parts together to form a coherent or unique new whole.	Compose, produce, design, assemble, create, prepare,predict, modify, tell, plan invent, formulate, collect, set up, generalise, document, combine, relate, propose, develop, arrange, construct, organise, originate, derive, write, propose
Analysis	Analysis of the constituent parts of the material and determination how the parts relate to one another and to an overall structure or purpose.	Analyse, ascertain, attribute, connect, deconstruct, determine, differentiate, discriminate, dissect, distinguish, divide, examine, experiment, focus, infer, inspect, integrate, investigate, organise, outline, reduce, solve (a problem), test for
Application	Introducing the procedure of carry on	Apply, carry out, construct, develop, display, execute, illustrate, implement, model, solve, use
Comprehension	Construction of meaning from instructional messages, including oral, written, and graphic communication.	Categorise, clarify, classify, compare, conclude, construct, contrast, demonstrate, distinguish, explain, illustrate, interpret, match, paraphrase, predict, represent, reorganise, summarise, translate, understand
Knowledge	Retrieve relevant knowledge from long-term memory.	Choose, define, describe, find, identify, label, list, locate, match, name, recall, recite, recognise, record, relate, retrieve, say, select, show, sort, tell

The table was applied to define the outcomes based on the gaps identified in the project.

3.1.5. Outcomes formulation

Battersby (1999, p. 2) formulates the following definition of outcomes: "Learning outcomes are statements that describe the knowledge or skills students should acquire by the end of a particular assignment, class, course, or program, and help students understand why that knowledge and those skills will be useful to them." At this point it is worth mentioning the difference between learning objectives and outcomes that consists in the generality of the approach to the content being taught. Learning objectives refer to the material the instructor intends to cover. By contrast, learning outcomes refer to what the student should know and realistically be able to do by the end of an assignment, activity, class, or course (Harden, 2002, p. 152)[2].

Battersby (1999, p. 2) gives the following definition of outcomes: "Learning outcomes are statements that describe the knowledge or skills students should acquire by the end of a particular assignment, class, course, or program, and help students understand why that knowledge and those skills will be useful to them." At this point it is worth mentioning the difference between learning objectives and outcomes, a difference that relates to the generality of the approach to the content being taught. Learning objectives refer to the material the instructor intends to cover. By contrast, learning outcomes refer to what the student should know and realistically be able to do by the end of an assignment, activity, class, or course (Harden, 2002, p. 152).

The process of outcome formulation relates to "unwrapping" the expected aim through establishing cognitive requirements (with the choice of the correct verb) and refers to the content and concepts defined (using appropriate nouns). This step enables one to locate the formulated objective in the relevant level of the taxonomy and simultaneously design the procedure of its assessment. Placement is important, because different types of objectives require different approaches to the assessment. The second step includes the definition of the conditions that are necessary for the tasks to be performed. This step contains, for example,

---

[2]   The goal of the part of the project is to develop the learning outcomes.

reference to variables (with/without supervision, in small/large groups, in homogenous/heterogeneous groups, by checking a chart/looking at a photo, referring to a manual, etc.). The third step relates to defining the standard to which the task must be performed.

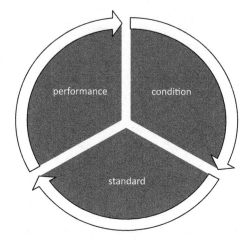

Fig. 3.1.4. Structure of the outcome

The outcomes developed were based on the seven pillars devised from the identification of gaps (see *Fig. 3.1.5. Seven pillars of LSP teacher training*).

Fig. 3.1.5. Seven pillars of LSP teacher training

The pillars formulated based on the identified gaps between LSP teacher professional development provision in Europe and LSP teachers' needs were divided among the members participating in the project.

Tab. 3.1.2. Division of pillars between participating project members

Name of partner organisation/ country	Pillar
Universidad de Cadiz (Spain)	Needs analysis
Jade Hochschule Wilhelmshaven/ Oldenburg/ Elsfleth (Germany)	Testing and assessment
Universita' degli Studi di Bergamo (Italy)	LSP materials
Univerza v Ljubljani (Slovenia)	LSP in general
Sveuciliste u Zagrebu (Croatia)	LSP teaching and learning methodology
Universite de Bordeaux (France)	Collaboration and development
Uniwersytet im. Adama Mickiewicza (Poland)	Transversal skills

The suggestions delivered formed the starting point for developing the final version of the outcomes. The performance and standard sections developed within the formulated outcomes are shown in Fig. 3.1.6.

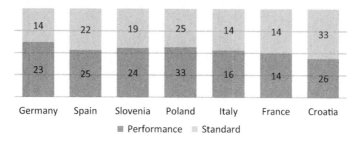

Fig. 3.1.6. Number of performance and standard sections within developed outcomes

3.1.5.1. Performance section

The performance section in the formulated outcomes refers to the lower levels of Bloom's taxonomy (application, comprehension, knowledge).

Tab. 3.1.3. Example of performance section

LSP academic discourse	
At the end of the session the trainees (PERFORMANCE) will be able to:	
Description	**Taxonomy level**
Understand the linguistic means that are typical of academic discourse	COMPREHENSION
Distinguish the differences between spoken and written academic discourse,	KNOWLEDGE
Identify the academic discourse that their learners will need in their professions or careers (e.g., presentations),	APPLICATION

3.1.5.2. Condition section

The elements included in the condition section refer to the internal and external conditions (see Tab. 3.1.3) because they both affect the learning results. Internal conditions relate to the learning-teaching process in itself, whereas external ones are dependent on the external conditions.

Tab. 3.1.4. Examples of internal and external conditions from the formulated outcomes

Internal conditions	External conditions
Characteristics of the target group and learning setting	Institutional policies
Various disciplinary genres specifics and constraints	Different theoretical aspects of needs analysis
Different stakeholders' groups	Specifics and constraints of various disciplines
Different LSP teaching/learning goals and LSP teaching/learning outcomes	
Different delivery and target languages	

3.1.5.3. Standard section

The standard section refers to the higher levels from Bloom's taxonomy (evaluation, analysis).

Tab. 3.1.5. Example of standard section

Methodology of needs analysis	
Description	Taxonomy level
choose an appropriate design/method and conduct a needs analysis	ANALYSIS
evaluate the collected data	EVALUATION
assess LSP teaching/learning goals and LSP teaching/learning outcomes based on the results of needs analysis	ANALYSIS AND EVALUATION

3.1.6. Conclusions and synopsis

The preparation of learning outcomes was an important stage of the TRAILs project, one which combines the previous stages by analysing the results of a compilation of LSP teacher training programmes in the EHEA (carried out within intellectual Output 1) and the results of interviews and surveys conducted among LSP teachers employed at universities (carried out within Intellectual Output 2). The developed outcomes give an in-depth insight into the learning-teaching process and establish realistic expectations concerning the state of knowledge and skills acquired on completing the course. The formulated outcomes will also form the starting point for the preparation of the TRAILs Winter school curriculum and the related lesson plans.

3.2

Teaching Language Skills in LSP

Snježana Kereković, Brankica Bošnjak
Terzić, Olinka Breka

3.2.1. Introduction

Does developing the skills of reading, listening, writing and speaking in a general foreign language (GFL) differ from teaching these skills in languages for specific purposes (LSP)? The participants in the LSP Teacher Training School (TRAILs) were asked this question at the beginning of a plenary session that dealt with the development of comprehension of LSP input (reading, listening and audio-visual) and the development of LSP output (writing and speaking). Twelve LSP teachers and 19 foreign language students participated in the online TRAILs School, in which an innovative curriculum for LSP teacher training was piloted. As can be seen in Fig. 3.2.1, 39% of the participants believe that there is a difference while 65% of the participants think that there is no difference between developing these skills in GFL and LSP.

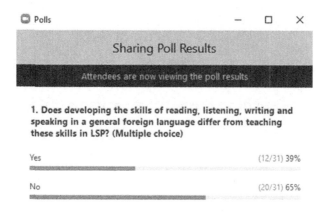

Fig. 3.2.1. Poll results – Teaching four language skills in GFL and LSP

Teaching a foreign language means teaching learners how to read, understand, write and speak in a target language, i.e. foreign language teachers develop the four basic language skills – reading, listening, writing and speaking. Obviously, teachers teaching languages for specific purposes (LSP teachers) address the same skills. In their seminal book of 1987, Tom Hutchinson and Alan Waters devote a chapter to ESP teaching methodology and explicitly state that there is nothing specific about ESP methodology and that the same principles underlie both good English for specific purposes (ESP) teaching methodology and good English language teaching (ELT) methodology (Hutchinson & Waters, 1987: 142). The fact that over a third of the TRAILs School participants believe that there is a difference between developing skills in GFL and LSP may suggest that the teaching situations in a GFL setting and an LSP setting are not identical. Thus, including this topic in the TRAILs Summer School curriculum seems very well justified.

3.2.2. TRAILs Summer school: Module 4: LSP teaching skills

The TRAILs Summer School programme included eleven different modules focusing on topics relevant to the field of teaching languages for specific purposes. The development of the comprehension of LSP input (reading, listening, audio-visual) and the development of LSP output (writing and speaking) were covered in the third and the fourth parts of Module 4. The module comprised a plenary session and three simultaneously run group sessions, held after the plenary session. Both the plenary session and each group session lasted 90 minutes. In the introduction to the part of the plenary session dealing with teaching language skills in an LSP setting, the development of the skills of reading, listening, writing and speaking in a GFL setting was compared with the development of these skills in an LSP setting. Next, each of the four language skills was briefly introduced and the reading, listening, writing and speaking activities that can be designed and used in an LSP setting were discussed. The role of the LSP teacher in the development of these language skills was also addressed.

In the group sessions, the participants discussed the criteria for selecting a text/audio-visual material for LSP teaching and developed pre-, while- and post-reading, listening, writing and speaking activities for a video material and a written text from three different domains (mechanical engineering, business and veterinary medicine). The goal of the activities carried out in the group session can be expressed in terms of the learning outcomes. As regards the topic of developing the comprehension of LSP input, the learning outcomes are as follows: At the end of the training the trainee will be able to design appropriate tasks for the development of LSP learners' reading/listening/audio-visual comprehension skills; to contrast different comprehension strategies and select those appropriate to the comprehension tasks; to prepare and present an outline of an integrated series of tasks (pre-, while- and post-tasks) for the selected LSP input; and to reflect on and evaluate other participants' outlines of text comprehension tasks. As regards the development of LSP output, the learning outcomes are the following: The trainee will be able to design appropriate tasks for the development of LSP learners' text production skills; to contrast and choose adequate text production strategies to be used in line with the production tasks; to prepare and present an outline of a series of tasks of varying cognitive difficulty (guided, semi-guided and free tasks) to enhance LSP output; and to reflect on and evaluate other participants' outlines of the tasks.

3.2.2.1. *Teaching LSP as communication*

The methodological approach to teaching LSP comprises aspects that are not of particular relevance to teaching methodology in GFL. In LSP teaching, needs analysis should be the starting point for many of the decisions an LSP teacher makes. LSP teachers need to know what their students need the language for, or what the target needs are (Hutchinson & Waters, 1987: 53). Communicative language teaching makes use of real-life situations coupled with the students' and/or professionals' communication need (Ruiz de Guerrero & Arias Rodríguez, 2011). This includes information about what skills the students will predominantly need for study and use in their future professional situations, so that they can master them during their education. Based on this information, the teacher makes decisions about what language skills may be more important for a particular group of students and then focuses on improving these particular skills.

Further, the LSP genre is to be analysed and genre-specific features are to be identified, among them the dominant text[1] type features in particular (De Chazal, 2014). This will enable the teacher to identify clearly both the content (vocabulary) and the language skills that are of primary importance to a particular group of students. For example, students who attend an LSP course for nurses would focus on the topics of medical care, including medical terminology, hospital language and patient-staff interactions. Regarding the four language skills, the teacher would realise that it is crucial to teach the skills of reading, listening and speaking and that the development of the skill of writing is of minor importance. Contrary to nurses, students who take a course in academic writing would focus heavily on developing the skills of reading and writing and the LSP teacher would select the types of texts to be read by these students, which differ considerably from the texts to be read by future nurses. Between these two extremes, there is a wide variety of professions in which the four language skills have a different significance, resulting in the LSP teacher making different choices when selecting texts and deciding which language skills to focus on. After having made these decisions, the teacher designs lesson plans that would prepare the students for communication in their profession.

---

[1] "Text" refers here to anything that conveys a set of meanings, either in written or spoken form.

3.2.2.2. *Developing reading activities in LSP teaching*

In general, there are two reasons why we read: for entertainment or to gain information. Bojovic also mentions reading for research purposes (Bojovic, 2010), but this can be categorised under reading to gain information. The primary purpose of reading in LSP is comprehension of the message conveyed by the author of the text. Therefore, the selection of an appropriate specialised text is one of the LSP teacher's greatest concerns. When selecting an appropriate text for their lessons, LSP teachers need to consider the following selection criteria: topic, language and length. The first criterion, topic, is related both to the needs analysis – what the students need the language for - and to the aim of the course – whether the content of the text meets the aim of the course with respect to the course outcomes. In addition, interesting, up-to-date content will attract students to the reading materials, with a positive attitude resulting in more effective learning. The second criterion – language – refers both to the language of a selected text and to the language proficiency level of students. The former includes questions such as: Does the text include vocabulary to be covered under the syllabus?; Does the text include structures the teacher wants to highlight and practise?; Can various communicative or writing activities be created, etc.? The latter refers to real-life teaching scenarios when teaching beginners, false beginners, advanced or mixed-ability groups. Finally, the third criterion – length – is related to the time which can be devoted to a particular topic.

Based on a particular text chosen and having established the purpose of reading, the LSP teacher will decide which of the reading strategies can be used: scanning, skimming or intensive reading. In an LSP setting, extensive reading is rarely an adequate reading strategy and is hardly employed by LSP teachers.

When reading a specialised text, students connect the new information to what they already know about the topic, and their knowledge of the topic enables them to adequately (and sometimes even intuitively) understand the text. LSP teachers facilitate this process by preparing pre-, while- and post-reading activities to accompany the selected text. The pre-reading activities activate the prior knowledge of students in particular, and it has therefore been suggested that 50–60% of the lesson should be spent on pre-reading activities (Klund, n.d.), as presented in Fig. 3.2.2.

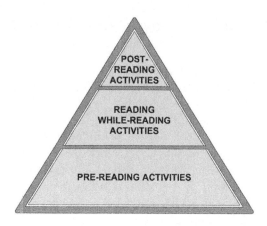

Fig. 3.2.2. Reading skill development – a traditional lesson format adapted from https://k12teacherstaffdevelopment.com/tlb/the-importance-of-pre-read ing-activities/

In our LSP teaching experience, the lesson format has changed so that the pyramid has become a shape as presented in Fig. 3.2.3. A well-selected specialised text frequently opens up the possibility of developing numerous post-reading activities, including case studies and projects, so an equal amount of activities and of time can be devoted to pre-reading and post-reading activities.

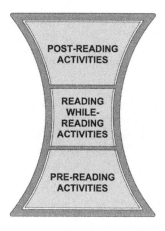

Fig. 3.2.3. Reading skill development – a lesson format in an LSP setting

There is a large body of literature dealing with developing the skill of reading, including a wide variety of reading activities. Tab. 3.2.1, shared with the participants of the TRAILs Summer School, gives a comprehensive list of pre-, while- and post-reading tasks that can be developed in an LSP setting.

Tab. 3.2.1. List of pre-, while- and post-reading tasks for an LSP setting

Pre-Reading Activities	While-Reading Activities	Post-Reading Activities
Guessing the topic from the title/key words/pictures/ sentences	Skimming the text to locate the main idea of the text	Ordering paragraphs or placing events in the right order
Commenting on quotes related to the topic	Identifying topic sentences and the main ideas of paragraphs	True or false quiz
Brainstorming – students share their background knowledge	Distinguishing between general and specific ideas	Correcting sentences that contain inaccurate information
Predicting the information presented in the text from the subtitles and pictures and captions	Checking whether predictions and guesses are confirmed	Finishing off sentences that include information from the text
Asking questions students want to find answers to in the text	Scanning the text for specific information	Answering comprehension questions
Speed chatting	Identifying the connectors – how they link ideas within the text	Matching beginnings to endings of sentences
Watching a video related to the topic	Inferring the meaning of new words using the context	Gap-fill vocabulary task
True or false quiz	Making notes	Gap-filling a summary of the text
Introducing new vocabulary	Completing a mind map	Writing key words for the text
KWL charts – students write what they KNOW, what they WANT to know and what they LEARNED after reading	Coding the text – margin marking – students place a question mark next to a statement they do not understand or an exclamation mark next to something that surprises them	Writing a summary

(Continued)

Tab. 3.2.1. Continued

Pre-Reading Activities	While-Reading Activities	Post-Reading Activities
Analysing who wrote and the audience for whom the text was written	Highlighting the key words	Discussing the topic in more detail
	Completing data charts or flow charts – extracting information from the text	Finding related information or news and reporting on them
	Identifying cause-effect relationships	Substantiating or reconsidering own ideas – critical thinking
	Student-to-student conversation after having finished a paragraph – clearing up possible confusions	Creative writing with the new vocabulary
	Writing key words for each paragraph	Watching a video related to the topic
	Writing paragraph headings	Case studies
		Team projects

3.2.2.3. Developing listening activities in LSP teaching

Listening comprehension is a complex process which is crucial in the development of second language competence. Research has shown that adults spend 40–50% of communication time listening (Gilman & Moody, 1984). Also, it has been found that when we communicate, we gain 45% of language competence from listening, 30% from speaking, 15% from reading and 10% from writing. So it can be concluded that listening has to be considered as a language forerunner (Renukadevi, 2014). Listening is also the basis for communicative competence. Without listening skills, no communication can be achieved (Croom Helm Cross, 1998). But listening is felt by learners to be a comparatively much more difficult skill as it includes interrelated subskills such as receiving, understanding, remembering, evaluating and responding (Renukadevi, 2014). At the same time, it is suggested that of the four skills listening is the one that has historically been the most neglected (White, 2006: 111) and misrepresented in second language (L2) classrooms. Hence, listening has been the skill which has been the least well taught. Nunan even calls it "the Cinderella skill in second language learning" (Nunan, 2002: 238).

In listening comprehension listeners use two listening processes: the "top-down" process and the "bottom-up" process. The former refers to the listening process whereby listeners use their prior knowledge to understand the meaning of a message, relying also on content words and contextual clues. The latter refers to the process whereby listeners use their linguistic knowledge to understand the meaning of a message (Anderson & Lynch, 1988). Vandergrift argues that listening comprehension is neither top-down nor bottom-up processing, but an interactive, interpretive process where listeners use both prior knowledge and linguistic knowledge in understanding messages, and that the degree to which listeners use the one process or the other will depend on their knowledge of the language, their familiarity with the topic or the purpose of listening (Vandergrift, 2002). In an LSP setting, learners have much more content knowledge than language knowledge and they mostly use the "top-down" process, matching what they hear with what they already know about the topic. Because of that they become active listeners capable of completing listening tasks effectively.

The LSP teacher's task of selecting an appropriate spoken text is most important. Chi discusses potential problems in listening among Vietnamese economics students and lists criteria for selecting recorded materials (Chi, 2015). Similar to the selection of a written text, the selection of an appropriate recorded material depends on the purpose of listening or on the listening situation. These may include listening for academic purposes, e.g. listening to a lecture in a foreign language, then listening to a presentation or a report on a specific topic, listening to a supervisor's instructions, etc. In addition, each of the purposes of listening will require a particular listening strategy, such as listening for gist (the main ideas only), listening for specific information, listening for details (detailed understanding), predicting, making inferences or listening for the speaker's opinion. The listening activity may also be a starting point for a discussion or can result in writing a summary. At all events, a purpose for listening must be established so that students know the specific information they need to listen for and the degree of detail required.

When selecting a spoken text, the LSP teacher needs to consider at least two criteria in addition to those discussed above in relation to selecting a written text, namely, topic, language and length. These other two are the authenticity of the spoken language and the quality of the recorded material. A spoken text that can be seen as adequate for an LSP setting is one that would enable students to cope with different real-life listening situations. Thus, the selected spoken text should include natural speech, which means that the speech may be imperfect like in real life (e.g. false starts, hesitations) and that students may also be exposed to strange pronunciation or accents. As regards the quality of the recorded material, it is vital that the background noise be reduced to a minimum and that the recording can be played even in a large lecture theatre. All the criteria need to be taken into consideration and their ranking in order of importance would depend on the purpose of listening. In addition, the selected material should be neither too easy nor too difficult. If it is at an appropriate level, it will challenge students to actively understand and form their predictions, and they will be able to clear up ambiguities; their motivation to study will be raised.

Numerous pre-, while- and post-listening activities are used by foreign language teachers to develop the listening skills of their students. Pre-listening activities seem to be very important as they help students focus their attention on the meaning while listening. Also, by using all the available information and their background knowledge of the topic, students can make predictions to anticipate what they might hear, leading to effective listening. Tab. 3.2.2 gives a list of pre-, while- and post-listening tasks that can be developed and used in an LSP setting.

Tab. 3.2.2. A list of pre-, while- and post-listening activities for an LSP setting

Pre-Listening Activities	While-Listening Activities	Post-Listening Activities
Predicting the topic from the title/key words/ sentences	Listening for gist	Answering comprehension questions
Setting the context – who is speaking, where and why	Listening for specific information	Summarising the information orally
Brainstorming – activating background/previous knowledge	Listening for main ideas	Expressing an opinion on the information (critical thinking)
If some knowledge input is required, reading a related text	Listening for the speaker's opinion	Discussing the topic in more detail
True or false quiz	Making inferences	Gap-filling a summary of the text
Introducing new vocabulary	Gap fill task (transcript)	Writing a summary of the spoken text
KWL chart (students write what they KNOW, what they WANT to know and what they LEARNED after listening)		

3.2.2.4. Developing writing activities in LSP teaching

Writing may be defined as the ability to write accurately, briefly and clearly (Kavaliauskiene & Suchanova, 2010). As mentioned before, in LSP teaching, knowledge of the genre is a key element in all communication, and it is especially significant in writing academic or professional texts (Dudley Evans & St. John, 1998). The end product of writing should be coherent and cohesive, and appropriate both to the purpose of the writing and to the intended readership. Also, there are certain conventions that have to be followed in writing. Many writing conventions will remain a mystery unless LSP teachers are able to bring these forms and patterns of language use to conscious awareness (Reppen, 2002: 321). Further, depending on the context and disciplinary domain, different levels of formality in writing are used.

Students often perceive writing as a difficult and tiring activity because good writing requires time (time for reflection and revision), patience (which young people generally lack) and a peaceful environment (which is rarely available in the classroom). Also, they struggle with the organisation of ideas, the text structure, inconsistent usage of terms, lengthy sentences, repetition of the same information and grammatical mistakes.

In every specialised area professionals write texts of different types. LSP teachers need to be familiar with the different text types that are produced in the domain whose language they teach and then need to deal with them in class, as their students would have to produce some written texts themselves both as students and later as professionals. So LSP teachers should consider the pre-service writing needs of their students as well as their in-service needs once they start their professional career. To exemplify this point, Tab. 3.2.3 gives a list of texts that are produced and/or used in the field of mechanical engineering and how these texts can be ranked in terms of frequency considering pre-service learners and in-service learners, e.g. production engineers.

Tab. 3.2.3. Text types in mechanical engineering and their ranking in terms of frequency

Texts Produced/Used in Mechanical Engineering	Ranking pre-service learners	Ranking in-service learners production engineers
Popular science articles in journals/magazines	1	5
Papers in mechanical engineering (scientific) journals	9	6
Technical reports	4	1
Textbook chapters	2	7
Case studies	5	4
Undergraduate/graduate/PhD theses	8	9
Thesis abstracts	6	8
Manuals/Instructions for use/installation	3	2
Project paperwork	7	3

It is obvious that the ranking in terms of frequency varies between different learners: a particular text type will be more frequently produced by production engineers, e.g. a technical report (ranked 1), than by students (ranked 4). For LSP teachers this means that their students need to practise writing different types of texts, ranging from those that students already have to write during their studies (an abstract of their undergraduate/graduate theses at least) to those they will be writing as engineers (e.g. instructions for use of a product or project paperwork).

The LSP teacher's task is to provide guidance throughout the writing process, as there is no spontaneity in writing in general and in technical writing in particular. This guidance can be given by highlighting the differences between different text types, potentially different conventions in the native language and the foreign language, the difficulties a topic to be covered in writing might create, the necessity to organise one's ideas, the necessity to select, generalise and reorganise information, and the necessity to analyse, criticise and summarise a text. Additionally, students who do not have the minimum language level to perform a writing task need clear and detailed guidance provided by the teacher. To this end, LSP teachers can prepare a wide variety of guided, semi-guided and free writing tasks (Tab. 3.2.4) to develop the writing skills of their students.

Tab. 3.2.4. List of guided, semi-guided and free writing tasks for an LSP setting

Guided Writing Tasks	Semi-Guided Writing Tasks	Free Writing Tasks
Providing a model paragraph	Put the questions WHO? WHAT? WHERE? HOW? WHY? to students to think about the topic and give their answers	Retelling a written or a spoken text
Comprehension questions to extract the main information	Listing ideas that are connected to the topic	Writing a draft
Language-based exercises focusing on vocabulary or sentence structure	Looking at the topic from different points of view	Writing an introductory and a concluding paragraph of the text
Tasks to practise paraphrasing	Analysing the topic (breaking it down into parts)	Writing the body of the text (topic sentence, elaboration, specific evidence, analysis)
Gap-filling a model paragraph	Rewriting a model paragraph	Writing a summary of a paper/article/ technical text
Correcting incorrect information in a model written text	Outlining a problem and presenting a solution	Writing an essay
Putting the sentences of a model paragraph in the right order	Presenting cause-effect relationships	
Putting the paragraphs of a model written text in the right order	Tasks to achieve coherence of the text by fully developing the arguments	
Tasks to practise the use of cohesive devices (e.g. contrasting, sequencing, adding, listing, concluding)	Defining concepts	
Tasks to practice hedging and paraphrasing	Listing advantages and disadvantages	
	Providing a list of key expressions for students to use	

3.2.2.5. Developing speaking activities in LSP teaching

Speaking refers to the ability to communicate in a foreign language clearly and efficiently. Davies & Pearse argue that the main aim of English language teaching is to develop in learners the ability to use English effectively and correctly in communication (Davies & Pearse, 2000). Developing the speaking skill seems to be the most important aspect of learning a foreign language and learning is successful if the learner can conduct a conversation in the language (Nunan, 1995). Speaking is one of the central elements of communication and is an aspect that needs special attention and instruction (Shumin, 2002: 210). Also, as a productive skill, it is often viewed as one of the most difficult aspects of language learning and because of that in some educational institutions it has been neglected or ignored.

A claim made by Krashen a long time ago that learners' productive abilities (writing and speaking) will arise naturally from receptive knowledge (reading and listening) (Krashen, 1982) is still discussed by many teachers. We asked the participants in the TRAILs Summer School whether they believe that learners' productive skills would arise naturally from their receptive language knowledge. Fig. 3.2.4 presents the results: 26% of the participants believe that writing and speaking skills will naturally develop in learners who have good reading and listening skills, and 74% of the participants do not believe this.

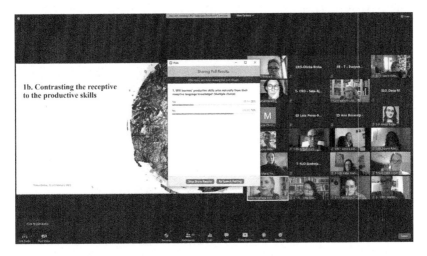

Fig. 3.2.4. Poll results – Productive vs receptive skills

Recent theories of second language acquisition no longer assume that productive skills will arise naturally from comprehension skills (Richards, 2008), so special attention needs to be devoted to developing the skill of speaking. The ability to speak fluently and efficiently in a foreign language contributes to the learner's success, both during education and in their career (Kayi, 2006). Therefore, teaching speaking skills is a very important part of LSP teaching. The main task of the LSP teacher is to create an environment in which meaningful communication can take place. The language input may be a listening or a reading activity providing the learners with the material they need to begin producing language themselves (Bahrani & Soltani, 2012). Leong and Masoumeh Ahmadi analysed factors influencing learners' English speaking skills and stressed the role of teachers in creating a friendly and cooperative environment that can help students to overcome their difficulties in oral performance and build up their self-confidence. Further, teachers are responsible for choosing the best teaching method to keep their learners involved in the speaking activity (Leong & Masoumeh Ahmadi, 2017). Obviously, all these recommendations can be implemented in an LSP setting.

As is the case with the three skills already discussed, LSP teachers should be familiar with the situations in real life in which both their students as pre-service learners and future professionals need to use their specialised language in speech. We suggest that a list of such situations should be made, including activities or tasks to be done to promote communication in class. To this end, the TRAILs Summer School participants were asked to make such a list for a particular specialised area. For illustration, Tab. 3.2.5 gives a list of situations in which mechanical engineers use technical language in speech and a list of tasks that can be carried out to develop the skill of speaking in the listed professional situations.

Tab. 3.2.5. List of professional situations in which mechanical engineers use technical language including activities for speaking skill development

Use of Specialised Language in Speech/List of Situations	Activities/Tasks to Promote Communication
Brainstorming in project teams Explaining a technical problem Presenting a solution to a technical problem Taking part in a professional discussion Dialogue with a boss/colleague/subordinate Presenting one's company Presenting a project/product/case study • to team members • to the superior • to the investor • to the public Explaining to a colleague how something is to be done Explaining to a layperson (non-professional) how something is to be done Conducting a business meeting Conducting business negotiations Taking part in a meeting	Brainstorming Presenting arguments Explaining a problem Explaining how something works Discussion after a content-based lesson Role play Simulations (e.g. meetings, negotiations) Information gap Interviews Reporting Presenting one's company Presenting a project/product/case study Describing pictures Reading graphs

Obviously, various speaking activities can help students a great deal to develop the basic interactive communicative skills necessary for study and their future career. These activities also make students more active in the learning process and, at the same time, their learning more meaningful and fun for them. The role of LSP teachers is once again crucial: they set the purpose of each activity, establishing a link to real-life professional situations; form groups of optimum size; provide clear instructions; encourage students to ask questions, paraphrase ideas and check for clarification; monitor the speaking activity so that speaking is equally divided among group members.

3.2.3. Integration of the four language skills

The four language skills need to be integrated into LSP teaching simply because in all real-life situations people use all language skills to communicate. These skills are to be supported by communicative activities to improve learners' communicative competence in their future professions so that they use accurate and fluent language. Also, it is obvious that the four skills are interconnected and that one skill reinforces another: reading and listening pave the way to speaking, speaking can stimulate writing, which in turn requires speaking, reading and listening again.

One of the tasks the participants in the TRAILs Summer School were working on in the group sessions was to develop a plan for a lesson based on a text dealing with a veterinary medical topic (Preparing for surgery[2]), and a video about a horse waking up during surgery[3] with the aim of integrating all language skills. The participants' response to the task revealed that they used the input from the plenary session to develop valuable and relevant activities aimed at practising all four language skills, thereby also showing their creativity in the process. So, in each stage of the lesson, the pre-reading stage, the reading stage and the post-reading stage, tasks to develop each of the four language skills were suggested. In the pre-reading stage, speaking activities (analysing who wrote the text and the audience for whom the text was written, brainstorming the topic, asking the questions students want to find answers to in the text, introducing the new vocabulary) and writing activities (writing a KWL chart) can be carried out. In the reading stage, writing activities (highlighting the key words, completing the flow chart, identifying the cause-effect relationship) or speaking activities (inferring the meaning of the words of Latin origin, student-to-student conversations after having finished a paragraph to clear up possible confusions) can be carried out. Then, in the post-reading stage, numerous writing activities can be done: true/false quiz, finishing off sentences, ordering events in the preparation of a horse for surgery in the right order, answering comprehension questions, finishing off sentences that include information from the text, matching beginnings to endings of sentences, gap-fill vocabulary task to practice the terminology and collocations. The speaking skill can be practised by summarising the information from the

---

[2] https://www.petplanequine.co.uk/my-petplan-equine/preparing-for-surgery.asp
[3] https://www.youtube.com/watch?v=BWCnRCcvjsg

text orally or in a discussion in which the topic would be elaborated in more detail including students' experience from the clinic. The listening skill can be also integrated as watching a video is included in the plan, so students can practise speaking by summarising the information they heard in the video, commenting on the events they saw in the video and expressing their own opinions. Finally, students can be given an additional task to further develop all language skills. For example, in groups they can prepare similar steps in the preparation of some other animal (a dog, cat…) for surgery, which would also make the whole lesson meaningful and related to real-life situations.

3.2.4. Concluding remarks

It is beyond dispute that GFL teaching methodology and LSP teaching methodology address the same language skills and that the same principles apply to both teaching settings. However, these settings are different and two aspects are to be taken into consideration in the LSP setting: needs analysis and genre-specific features. In addition, LSP teachers are required to cope with a variety of demanding and challenging tasks.

What methods will an LSP teacher use in teaching the skills of reading, listening, writing and speaking? A needs analysis would be the starting point to determine the kinds of reading, listening, writing and speaking skills students need to develop and use successfully both in their academic setting and their professional careers. Different specialised contexts (domains) result in different syllabi, not only with reference to the content (subject matter) but also to the extent to which particular language skills need to be developed. However, whatever the specialised language and the genre-specific features may be, students will need to be able to handle authentic texts for reading and/or listening comprehension, to have authentic spoken exchanges relevant to their field and to produce written texts in line with the conventions of the respective genre.

We have also shown that the LSP teacher's role is quite complex. LSP teachers need to present new, specialised language to students in rich contexts with authentic materials covering relevant terminology and language structures. This is to be followed by creating real-life professional situations in which students can practise the language they have been exposed to. To achieve the learning outcomes, LSP teachers continuously have to develop a wide variety of communicative activities and tasks, so that students can progress from the practice which is controlled in the classroom to the production required in real professional situations. In addition to this long list of demanding tasks, LSP teachers also aim at preserving language accuracy and fluency in the activities undertaken in the classroom.

Part 4

INNOVATIVE LSP TEACHER TRAINING CURRICULUM

4.1

Materials Adaptation in LSP: Processes and Techniques

Patrizia Anesa, Katharine Sherwood, Cailean Dooge

4.1.1. Introduction

This chapter investigates the adaptation of materials in LSP teaching. Starting from the acknowledgement that LSP instructors are often not involved in the selection of the book for a course, it is evident that the evaluation and potential adaptation of the materials in highly specialised courses is of fundamental importance in order for learners to be able to reach the given learning objectives.

This work presents reflections on the concept of materials adaptation and the creation of bespoke materials when adaptation leads to addition, with a particular focus on the techniques known commonly as "expansion" and "replacing". These are usually dealt with separately but are considered by us to be closely connected due to the primacy of sourcing and managing new LSP content in both techniques. A presentation of methods for selecting and managing new content is then followed by several examples of the two techniques from wide-angled fields such as Business English and from more narrow-angled specialist areas such as Automotive Engineering.

The aim of this chapter is to furnish both instructors and their trainers with a scheme for approaching materials adaptation, and the strategies that should be taken into account when planning training activities for LSP teachers, so as to provide them with the key tools to evaluate, select, prepare, integrate and review materials effectively.

4.1.2. Considerations prior to materials adaptation

Before the decision to adapt materials is made, there are several points to be taken into consideration, including whether the materials to be used are from a well-established core text, and if this core text is still up-to-date and relevant. Or if the materials are ones which have been created in the past by previous instructors on the course due to a lack of available ready-made materials. Perhaps there are political reasons for the choice of a particular set of materials to be used and the instructor needs to work within organisational constraints. Ultimately, however, the overriding consideration an instructor must bear in mind is this: Do the materials meet the needs of the learners and will they enable the learners to achieve the objectives set down for the course as established in the Needs Analysis?

4.1.2.1. Commercially-produced materials (CPMs): Advantages and disadvantages

There is little doubt that commercially-produced materials (CPMs) offer myriad and significant positives. When they provide a complete syllabus for the course, with clear learning objectives, they are motivating for learners and supply the instructor with a ready-made structure. In addition, they include content and activities which should have undergone a pre-publication trial phase with both learners and instructors, have often been written by experienced materials writers with specialist knowledge of that particular discipline, and frequently have accompanying resources such as teacher's books, companion websites, etc. Furthermore, CPMs have face validity and meet learner expectations: "… a textbook is reassurance for most students. It offers a systematic revision of what they have done and a guide to what they are going to do" (Grant, 1987: 8). Finally, coursebooks are often a requirement, whether due to a course being financed or because a percentage of the learners will not be in the classroom (online or face-to-face) during classes.

Although CPMs' advantages are apparent, their commercial necessity of a "one-size-fits-all" approach means that the contents are too generalised for a significant number of LSP courses. In addition, the instructor is married to the teaching approach and content within the CPM (syllabus, unit, lesson unit), which may steer the course in a direction less suited to the needs of the learners. Furthermore, if the materials they include are too sanitised and not necessarily authentic (Krzanowski, 2013), and if the choice of example texts is questionable, they can "over-protect" learners from the realities of language use outside the classroom (Tomlinson, 2012). CPMs can also date comparatively quickly and it may be several years before a new edition appears on the market (if a new edition does, in fact, appear). Finally, publishers tend to cater to a larger extent for more text-based disciplines such as Engineering (Krzanowski, 2013) and so the choice of materials in narrower fields may be limited. Therefore, chosen coursebooks may only be partially suitable for a particular LSP course and may need input from the instructor.

4.1.2.2. Materials evaluation

In order to be able to decide whether existing materials need adaptation or not, the instructor must be able to evaluate them first. It is beyond the scope of this chapter to discuss the initial motives for adopting a particular book for an LSP course in tertiary education or in company, or how the evaluation of said coursebook was performed.[1] For the purposes of this study on materials adaptation we are, instead, joining the process when the course has already been organised, coursebooks have already been evaluated and one selected, and the instructor is now preparing for its use in the classroom.

When evaluating materials, the key question to always keep in mind is: Do they meet the target language and course learning objectives? If not, this may be for several reasons and other questions include: Are the scenarios in the book realistic and memorable? Do they include real language found in the discourse community? Are the tasks challenging, topical, relevant, and thought-provoking (Krzanowski, 2013)? Do the materials provide opportunities for learner autonomy (McDonough & Shaw, 2003)? Charles and Pecorari (2016) state that ultimately, "the main impetus for adaptation is the necessity to align the materials more closely with the teaching circumstances and characteristics of your students", while Graves (2000) summarises the reasons for adaptation as: teacher beliefs and understanding, students' needs and interests, institutional context, and time factor.

---

[1] For this we could turn to, among others, McDonough & Shaw's Two-Stage Predictive Evaluation Criteria (2003).

At this juncture, an LSP instructor may find themselves in one of several different situations: Is the coursebook wholly suitable to meet the course objectives and also respond to the needs of the students? If not, is the coursebook partially suitable? Perhaps it has potential, and some useful and relevant materials, but cannot be used as the sole source of classroom work. This is more likely the case and, in this respect, Tomlinson (2006: 1) aptly states: "[m]ost materials, whether they be written for a global market, for an institution or even for a class, aim to satisfy the needs and wants of an idealized group of target learners who share similar needs and levels of proficiency … No matter how good the materials are, they will not by themselves manage to cater to the different needs, wants, learning styles, attitudes, cultural norms and experiences of individual learners".

Thus, if the coursebook is only somewhat satisfactory, why is this? Is it because some units or activities are appropriate and others are not? Is that due to the choice of subject matter (maybe it is not relevant, outdated, too complex for the level, etc.) or the design of the materials (maybe they lack scaffolding, focus on the wrong skills, there is an absence of variety of activity type, etc.)? Perhaps, in the worst-case scenario, the coursebook is truly unsuitable for the needs of the learners and there is very little usable content in it.

4.1.2.3. Identifying gaps in materials

At this point, task/activity/exercise (hereafter referred to as "activity") evaluation is paramount in order for the instructor to start identifying where the materials need to be reformulated in some way.

When looking at the book units, lesson units and individual activities (hereafter referred to as "sets of activities"), the instructor must always first look at the purpose of, and the reasoning behind, any activity and so must always ask themselves what the aim is and what the rationale behind it is[2].

To give an example, the aims of a "warmer" activity at the start of a lesson could be:

---

[2]   By "aim" we mean "Why is the activity here? What is its motive? What is the objective to be reached?" and by "rationale" we mean "What is the logical explanation and fundamental reasons for its inclusion?"

1. To generate interest in the topic and activate learners' schematic knowledge.
2. To have learners retrieve vocabulary from their existing knowledge bank.
3. To prepare learners for the following listening task.

The rationales behind the same activity could be:

1. Instructors must allow learners to take advantage of their existing subject-matter knowledge to facilitate their learning of the topic in the L2.
2. Context setting, and activating schemata, before a listening activity aids with its top-down processing.

Having identified the aim and rationale of sets of activities, the instructor should also be able to reflect on the following areas of importance:

1. Will the learners understand the purpose of the activity? Will it meet their expectations? Is the activity engaging, useful, and challenging?
2. What is the natural language outcome? Is it the one claimed or intended? How generative is the activity? How efficient is it in terms of language used/gained?
3. Are the content and the activity "real-world"? Are there any authenticity issues?
4. What enablement language is needed to start/manage/complete the activity? Are the instructions clear? And in appropriate language for the learners' level?
5. Is the subject appropriate? Is it the right target language/skill, etc. for the learners?
6. Do learners have enough subject knowledge and language training to do it?
7. What interaction does it encourage? What roles are the instructor and learners to take on?
8. How can the instructor check/monitor performance and give feedback?
9. What is the activity's complexity, i.e. what is the number of steps the learners need to perform in order to complete the activity?

10. Is there a gradual increase in the cognitive demands? Is it scaffolded?

11. Can the activity be used in a mixed-ability group?

12. What types of learners will it appeal to? Do the materials include a variety of activity types so as to avoid being repetitive?

13. Does the activity lend itself to follow-up/extension work for learner autonomy?

14. How are skills covered? Are they covered discretely or integrated? How much time is spent on them? Are they the appropriate skills for the specialisation with authentic and real-world content and activity types?

15. Reading passages – what is the quality and appropriateness? Are discourse skills included?

16. Listening passages – are there authentic recordings or specially written?

17. Speaking activities – is there real interaction or artificial dialogue?

18. Writing activities – do they include model answers?[3]

Upon completion of the evaluation, the instructor is in a position to decide whether sets of activities can be used in their complete form or whether there is a need for adaptation. McDonough, Shaw, and Masuhara (2013) give various reasons for materials to be "wanting", including: inappropriate/irrelevant subject matter for the specific needs/ objectives of the learners; grammar coverage is not suitable (not enough, not enough practice at the right level, grammar presented unsystematically); reading passages contain too much unknown vocabulary or comprehension questions are not appropriate, i.e. answers can be lifted directly from the text with little understanding of content; listening passages are not authentic, or not at the right level for the learners, or audio activities are difficult to include due to classroom issues; dialogues are not natural and reflective of everyday usage; and other considerations such as cultural appropriacy, outdated materials, lack of variety of activities, too little/too much material, group work or role-plays difficult to manage, etc.

Hence, any "gaps" in the materials should be seen as an opportunity and not as a threat, as they allow instructors to achieve greater

---

[3] Adapted from Anthony (2018).

appropriacy from materials, through: individualising (catering to different learning styles); personalising (encouraging learners to use their own experiences); localising (being perceived as relevant to learners); and modernising (being up to date) (see, inter alia, Islam & Mares 2003: 89). The instructor has evaluated the activities (the "what") and identified the weaknesses (the "why"). They have decided that they need to alter the materials in some way and so now, let us focus on the "how".

4.1.3. Materials adaptation

Materials adaptation applies to every type of language teaching, and not just to the field of LSP. There will inevitably be activities or units which are less preferable and which instructors regularly adapt or omit. As Maley aptly writes, "[m]aterials will always be constraining in one way or another, so that teachers will always need to exercise their professional judgement (or 'sense of plausibility') about when and how a particular piece of material is implemented in any particular case" (Maley, 2003: 392).

Adaptation is "[p]art of the creative dialogue between teachers and published materials" (Islam & Mares, 2003: 86) and there are several lists of adaptation techniques which have been published, including Islam and Mares (2003), Maley (2003) and Masuhara (2004). As we will be referencing Islam and Mares' list, we include a useful visualisation from Bocanegra-Valle (2010) below:

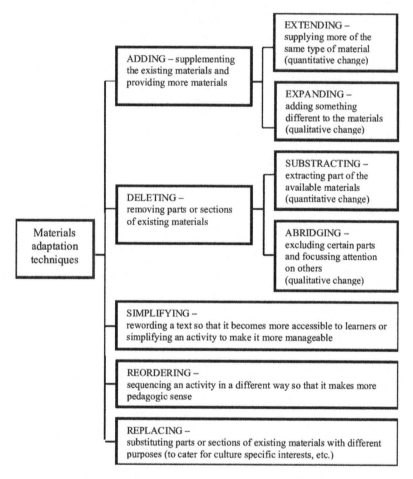

Fig. 4.1.1. Techniques for adapting materials (based on Islam and Mares 2003: 91–92). Reproduced with permission from Bocanegra-Valle (2010: 153).

Masuhara (2004) refers to Adding as the "Plus" category, Deleting as the "Minus" category and other modifications (Simplifying, Reordering, etc.) as the "Zero" category. Masuhara also subdivides the categories and adds "Reorganisation" to mean a change in the position of texts or illustrations, and "Conversion" to mean when an instructor changes the genre of a text, for example from a poem to a piece of narrative text.[4]

At this point, however, as our aim in this chapter is to concentrate on issues of materials adaptation which we feel are the most common in the specific field of LSP, we would like to introduce a new perspective. From our experience and observations in LSP instruction we posit that the most common types of materials adaptation used are the ones Islam and Mares refer to as Expansion (part of Adding, or Masuhara's "Plus"), when the instructor chooses to add content/activities to existing ones in the coursebook, and Replacing (part of modification, or Masuhara's "Zero"), when the instructor chooses to swap content/activities deemed unsuitable with alternative materials.[5]

We are not suggesting that the other techniques are not used. In fact, deduction is also a common mode of materials management in LSP whereby the purpose of the activity or its content do not align with the learners' needs and the activity is jettisoned. However, for the purposes of this chapter, and with the field of LSP consistently in mind, we are directing our attention to the melding of new materials onto existing ones.

4.1.4. Materials fusion

Rather than separate the two techniques of expansion and replacing, we would like to bring them together under the new umbrella term "Fusion". We believe Masuhara's classification of replacing in the "Zero" category is misleading as it involves the same sourcing and management of new content as expansion does. The instructor is 'fusing' new content with the original material, whether through augmentation or through substitution (see *Fig. 4.1.2: Materials adaptation: Fusion*):

---

[4] Altering genre would be something rarely done in LSP instruction as, as we will see, genre is fundamental to effective LSP materials.

[5] In fact, research conducted at the Gazi University Research and Implementation Centre for the Teaching of Foreign Languages in Turkey found that, for both inexperienced and experienced instructors, addition/supplementation was by some way the most used technique when planning lessons (Çoban, 2001).

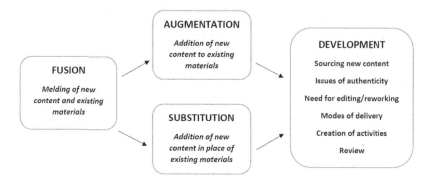

Fig. 4.1.2. Materials adaptation: Fusion

The next section will focus on the process of managing this type of adaptation and the strategies involved.

4.1.5. Materials development

The same considerations to material design can be made here, as if an instructor were creating their own materials from scratch, and this process will include a profound reflection on some key elements such as: sourcing new content; issues of authenticity; need for editing/reworking; modes of delivery; creation of activities; and review. There will be an additional need to marry the new materials with the existing ones and so this must be considered as well.

4.1.5.1. Sourcing new content

Sourcing the new subject-specific content is a priority. As the instructor is teaching in LSP, there must also be a balance of, and emphasis on, various field-specific skills and subject-specific vocabulary, and a need to look at the genres and registers for that particular discipline, and what approaches and methods are best suited to it (Day & Krzanowski, 2011).

Then, depending on the aims of the lesson, where should the content come from? Where does it "sit" in the existing sequence of materials? What is its purpose? Is it for general practice of issues/topics in the field? Is it to consolidate lexis or a language point? Is it to develop a skill? What is the level of subject-matter knowledge the students are bringing with them to the course?

In LSP instruction two terms are used with frequency when considering content – carrier content and real content. Carrier content is also known as subject-matter content, informative content, specific content, and specialist knowledge. "Real content" refers to the linguistic content, i.e. the language or skills content of an exercise, and is also known as language content (Bocanegra-Valle, 2010). If the carrier content is right, the lesson will work, even if not every activity functions exactly as intended on the day. If the choice of carrier content is wrong, then the lesson will always be weak and no amount of editing, restructuring, or rewriting will transform the lesson into a successful one.

The difference between carrier content and real content may be clarified as follows: "The notions of 'carrier content' and 'real content' are essential to the understanding of ESP work and to an understanding of motivation in ESP" (Dudley-Evans & St John, 1998: 11). Moreover, it can be argued that the development of LSP materials is ultimately "a trade-off between learning needs, language content, and subject-matter content" (Bocanegra-Valle, 2010: 143). In this respect, Ouarinki (2018) provides an instructive example: in a lesson with architecture students on the stages involved in building a solar-powered house, the specific vocabulary associated with building such energy-efficient homes would function as the carrier content, while the language of sequencing of the different stages would be the real content. Therefore, the real content is presented through the carrier content. Another example would be learners on a Marketing course looking at a market report (carrier content) and identifying collocations with the word 'market' such as "market research", "market segment", "market growth", "overseas market", "domestic market", etc. (real content).

Selecting the right carrier content is the key to the success of a lesson. If the carrier content is relevant, interesting, exemplifies the genre traits and lexis from a particular specialism, is able to be mined, and stimulates discussion, then, with the right scaffolding and sequencing, it will lend itself to memorable and useful activities.

It can be assumed that the majority of instructors would choose not to write their own carrier content as this would be entering a potential minefield. As a non-specialist in the subject, how can the instructor understand the content at the right level, even if they are *au fait* with the genre conventions of that specialism? Thus, using authentic language samples produced by members of the target discourse community, even if modified (and therefore "pseudo-authentic"), is by far the most beneficial option.

There are considerations, however, which need to be made when searching for suitable carrier content. Questions to ask include: Is it at the right level for the learners?[6] Is it challenging, relevant and usable? Does it need to be simplified/modified in any way or can it/should it be used in an unedited form? Is it suitable content for language work or is the objective for it to provide new vocabulary or as a springboard for discussion? Texts need to be appropriate for learning aims and learners, and suitable and exploitable, as well as relevant, accessible, and engaging in content (Charles & Pecorari, 2016).

The issue for the instructor working in LSP is where to find the new material and how to decide on its suitability or unsuitability. Nowadays, finding material is not difficult on the internet, where a wealth of information and examples of every genre are available. In fact, the issue is that there is an overwhelming amount of content disseminated, including from newspaper and magazine articles, specialist-interest websites and blogs, professional organisations and associations, company websites and government webpages, YouTube videos, films and documentaries, and even materials that already come with lesson plans (TedEd, specialist web pages for educationalists). Accessing all these different channels and distinguishing quality content with classroom potential from inappropriate content can be a difficult path to negotiate.

4.1.5.2. Sourcing multimodal content

Traditional LSP classrooms (whether face-to-face or online) can be dominated by Teacher Talking Time. They can also be heavily text-based with a lot of reading activities built around long passages (whether authentic, semi-authentic, or written especially for the purpose). In this regard, multimodality can play a decisive role in the classroom and may involve the incorporation of different media into a lesson in the form of video, podcasts, websites, interactive activities like quizzes, etc. In the

---

[6] In line with Krashen's input hypothesis of "*i* + *1*", where "i" is the learner's current level of language and "1" is the next stage of acquisition (Krashen, 1985).

digital age, as Dressman (2020: 39) affirms, "multimodality has become even more central to communication, and this is especially true for language learners, who depend on the multiplicity of channels available on a screen to help them 'pick up' meaning in a target language".

As LSP CPMs have little extra content available (i.e. e-books or blended learning), except for subjects with a wider focus such as Business English, how can the LSP instructor bring multimodality into the classroom to vary the pace and keep the learners engaged? And how can the instructor select appropriate content and maintain control of the learning steps? According to Krzanowksi (Atlanta TESOL Convention, 2019), suitable video content should be short and complete (i.e. have no need of editing), have memorable content and striking imagery, have a natural narration at a reasonable speed, include good spoken grammar with restricted colloquial language, have the appropriate academic register and have no overload of language.

Once suitable content has been found there is the decision to be made on how to incorporate it into a lesson. What type of activities will be built around the subject matter? What skills will be practised and how? As well as traditional text-based tasks, LSP instructors can also now take advantage of myriad applications and websites which are changing all the time, such as *Socrative*, *Kahoot*, *Wooclap*, and *Quizlet* for quizzes and surveys, *EdPuzzle* for scaffolding existing video content, and video creation/editing websites such as *Panopto*.

4.1.5.3. Issues of authenticity

In the process of adaptation, issues of authenticity have to be considered very judiciously. We will use the definition of authentic texts as those which were written for a non-language-learning audience but which are then used/mined/adapted for the language-learning classroom. When looking at authentic carrier content, authenticity does not guarantee suitability and judicious selection is fundamental to a successful lesson. A wisely-chosen authentic text can be motivating, present a wealth of usable real-world language, and help learners develop learning strategies for use outside the classroom. In contrast, an unwisely-chosen authentic text can be demotivating and dull, and can disrupt the aims of the lesson.

Suitable authentic texts are vital to help learners in the world of LSP to prepare themselves for life outside the classroom, as "[i]t is argued that without a basis in authentic texts, there is a high risk the materials will fail to meet the real-world communicative needs of the learners." (Charles & Pecorari, 2016: 75). In this regard, as Widdowson (1996: 67) states, "[t]he authenticity idea gives primacy to the goal of learning: if real communicative behaviour is what learners have eventually to learn, then that is what they have to be taught".

The obvious advantages of authentic materials include: they are content-specific with more complexity of subject matter and a high exposure to relevant language; a wide variety of content is easy to source due to the accessibility of the internet; they include natural language for the genre at hand; and a small amount of material can include a lot of useful information. Ultimately, they are motivating for learners as they provide a link between the classroom and real-world situations which learners face (or will face in the future), enabling learners to acquire coping strategies which will be important to them.

However, the palpable issues with using authentic content include: too much information compared to learnable/useful language and a high density of unknown (and non-inferable) words; overly complex structures which can make the language impenetrable and may be demotivating and dull for learners; learners may not have knowledge of the subject in their L1 yet and so cannot bring content knowledge with them to aid comprehension; and, finally, it can be very time-consuming for instructors to find the right materials.

4.1.5.4. Need for editing/reworking

The decision to edit or rework the content can serve different purposes, e.g. to improve coherency, reduce the number of unknown words, include visuals, remove colloquialisms, or target a reduced number of words (i.e. by repeating the same lexical item in different contexts to aid memorisation). Simplifying or abridging texts, in order to make them more appropriate to the level and needs of the learners, is a valid action if done judiciously. However, an instructor must be attentive to the genre conventions of the field they are teaching in and to the message contained in the text. Too much interference may distort the message and create a confusing piece of content and, in this respect, "it is often

suggested that the aim should be to vary the task rather than the text"
(Charles & Pecorari, 2016: 76).

4.1.5.5. Modes of delivery

More and more often a professional-looking mode of content delivery
is expected from instructors. In the past, teacher-made materials were in
danger of looking amateurish – glued-on pieces of texts or images on
unbound photocopied handouts. Nowadays, however, there is both a
demand and an expectation from learners that materials are presented in
a more coherent and visually attractive way.

With these demands, when creating materials the instructor must be
conscious of the appearance. Whether placing pieces of text or images
into a one- or two-page document, or preparing a lesson to be delivered
entirely through MS PowerPoint – a platform for displaying effective and
appropriate written materials and/or visuals (Muhlise Cosgun, 2017) –
the instructor must have an awareness of what does and does not work
on screen. Useful instructions for creating a MS PowerPoint presentation include: keeping text on the page to a minimum; utilising bullet
points or numbered points; making visuals arresting and purposeful and
inserting them sparingly; reducing extraneous features such as unnecessary icons; and, finally, a judicious use of bold text, colours, titles/sub-
titles, and the right font. If these rules are applied, they will go a long
way towards making the presentation clean, easier to navigate for both
instructor and learner and, ultimately, more memorable. In addition,
applying these rules to other instructor-created materials, e.g. a pdf file
or a MS Word document, will often guarantee better-designed and more
usable materials for the learner.[7]

A brief note is appropriate at this point to offer advice for when an
instructor is delivering content online which was originally designed
for face-to-face teaching. Materials which were designed for one type
of teaching situation do not necessarily transpose well to another mode
without alterations and must therefore be re-evaluated at both the macro
and the micro levels. At the macro level this may mean a change in
approach; for example, rather than presenting language in the lesson,

---

[7] https://www.makeuseof.com/tag/design-rules-word-documents/, accessed 24/03/
2021.

should the online lessons be used to clear up doubts and manage activities after materials have been shared beforehand? This flipped classroom approach may be beneficial. Another consideration would be: Do the course objectives themselves need reworking? What was possible in the physical classroom may be more difficult to achieve online. Reducing the amount of lesson content online, in order to avoid overloading learners, is a serious consideration. At the micro level it can mean the inclusion of a greater variety of material types to avoid a 'uni-directional' lesson and to maintain learner engagement, as well as the practicalities of moving activities to chat boxes or breakout rooms when class discussion activities are no longer feasible.

4.1.5.6. Creation of activities

Having found suitable content, the instructor then needs to analyse it and identify how it can be transformed into a coherent teaching resource in the classroom. What predicted difficulties may the students have with the content? What non-inferable words, if any, are included? What is the expected knowledge of the carrier content among learners? Does the activity assist learners in perceiving what and how the specialist lexis learned in class can be used in the real world?

Nation and Macalister (2010) identify four strands which need balancing: meaning-focused input, meaning-focused output, target language and fluency development. The variety of activities included would then be the same as in the arsenal of any language-learning instructor. Jigsaw readings, dictations, reformulating/retelling, comparing and contrasting, role-plays, rewriting activities, summarising, gap-fills, matching, etc. are all activity types with which to construct engaging learning segments. Instructors should also consider the increasing complexity of activities (i.e. those to engage higher cognitive skills such as decision making, reflective thinking, problem solving or critical thinking would come at the end of the session), grading, instructions, roles, sequencing and scaffolding, format and delivery, along with a decision on approaches such as a top-down processing structure (carrier content) or a bottom-up processing structure (real content). An extra element with LSP instruction, however, is that there will likely be more activities with the aim of genre work, specific skills practice or specific vocabulary acquisition and use.

4.1.5.7. Review

After their use in the classroom, the success, or not, of the fusion of the new content with existing materials needs to be considered and the question to ask is whether the materials have reached the intended objectives. Materials can be evaluated at a variety of different times – during the lesson, immediately after the lesson, or at the end of the course. They can be evaluated informally through instructor impressions based on the learners' interest in class or through their ability to perform the task well. In fact, it needs to be decided how the instructor can judge the success of an activity as, if the task is a "closed" task (i.e. a gap-fill), it is easy to evaluate how the learners performed, but if the task is an "open" one then how can the accuracy/performance be rated?

Ellis (1996) writes that questions to be asked at the micro level (i.e. sets of activities) can include:

- How did the learners react (observed or in evaluation)?
- Did the learners find the materials engaging and useful?
- How did the learners do in the performance of the task?
- Did anything unexpected happen?
- Did it take shorter/longer than predicted? Why?
- How could the instructor modify it?
- Were there any missing stages?
- Did the instructor need to make any extra language available?

When receiving task feedback from learners, an instructor should always bear in mind that the learners may have found the task enjoyable but may not have performed well in it. Maybe they were not able to use the target language either during the activity or later. Alternatively, the learners may find the task less interesting to complete but, in terms of task achievement, they may perform it more successfully and retain the target language more effectively.

We would suggest that it is rare for an instructor to be unaware of the success, or not, of classroom materials during an actual lesson. Also, as the class is progressing, the instructor probably needs to assess why the materials are being problematic: Were the instructions rushed or unclear or not logical? Was the choice of text not the right one? Was the time management of the lesson not well organised? Would the activity have been done better as a pair and not a small group? Was the content of interest to the instructor, but less so to the recipients? All these reasons as to why a lesson may not have reached its intended objectives are relevant to any language lesson and not specifically to LSP instruction. However, we would suggest that there will be a larger number of issues with the choice of carrier content in LSP and so the lesson's success or failure will rest more frequently on this selection.

4.1.6. Materials fusion case studies

To illustrate approaches which could be useful for the LSP instructor who is equipped with existing materials but who needs to adapt them for use in the classroom, we have included some examples of both augmentation and substitution, considering different motives for change, a diversity of specialisms and teaching situations and a variety of content.

4.1.6.1. Augmentation example: Carrier content and learning outcomes ambiguity

Market Leader Intermediate by Pearson was the core textbook on a B2-level Business English course in an Economics and Business Department at a university, assessed by way of an end-course speaking exam.

The unit on "Leadership" focused on the qualities of good business leadership and language to describe its characteristics. It included several reading activities using an article on the career of the current Chairman of L'Oréal, Sir Lindsey Owen-Jones. The primary issue with the activity was the lack of clarity regarding the purpose of the article. It was difficult to find how the information in the text exemplified good leadership. There was a lot of extraneous information about Owen-Jones's personal life but little about his leadership style and specifically how/why this had contributed to the successful expansion of L'Oréal. The exercises based around the article did little to aid learners' understanding, with unclear aims.

Thus, it was felt that there needed to be more information included on Owen-Jones in order to make this section of the lesson more relevant, pertinent, and beneficial. An article was sourced from a business website which contained just this information.[8] It was a more in-depth

---

[8] https://www.referenceforbusiness.com/biography/M-R/Owen-Jones-Lindsay-1946.html, accessed 23/03/2021.

description of Owen-Jones' leadership at L'Oréal, the company's subsequent achievements, and how Owen-Jones' decision-making contributed to those successes. The article was lengthy and so was adapted with key information being extracted and placed in a new document, along with the use of bullet points, visuals, etc. in order to aid the learners.

During the lesson, as an introduction to Owen-Jones, the learners completed selected exercises from the existing reading in *Market Leader Intermediate* first (including a warmer to activate schemata, a skim reading, and then a scan reading). However, at this point, the new material was inserted. First, the learners had to skim read the new information and match the paragraphs to their correct headings. Then they had to do two detailed activities: the first, regarding real content, was to identify vocabulary connected to describing business strategy and sales growth, and the second, regarding carrier content, was to answer specific multiple-choice questions about subject information found in each paragraph. Finally, the learners had to work with a partner to identify five key points about Owen-Jones' contribution to L'Oréal's success, make notes together, and present them to another pair for comparison.

The key point here is that not all reading passages in textbooks are apt in terms of activity aim or carrier content. The instructor must ask what the learners will take away from the existing activity. The judicious selection of alternative materials is imperative in terms of both language input and learner motivation. However, it is still decisive to identify what the objective of the new activity is as well and what the learners will take away from it.

4.1.6.2. Augmentation example: Real content/real world

A unit from *English for International Tourism Pre-Intermediate* by Longman deals with language for Tour Guides to describe the particular attractions of a city. The (inauthentic) listening activity of a tour guide describing an attraction and the activities built around it were deemed useful, but it was felt that further exposure to more authentic input and practice for the "real world" was needed, as well as a widening of the scope of the topic to make it truly "international". A section on "Attractions of Botswana" from an online safari brochure was therefore selected.[9]

---

[9]　https://www.senseofafrica.com/destinations/botswana/, accessed 24/03/2021.

The reasons for its choice were multitudinous: it was sufficiently exotic as to be memorable and cognitively engaging; there was no need to re-write it and it could be used for a mixed-ability class; it was in sections and so easily manageable; and it was suitable for mining real content, such as work on lexical sets (including flora and fauna, geographical features, terminology around safaris, etc.), and further noticing activities, such as identifying descriptive language. The website included a map of Botswana which was a useful, visual warmer activity to introduce the topic and then the vocabulary work centred on categorising activities, matching words with visuals or definitions, describing images, etc. This was then added to the functional language the learners had already covered for presenting information. Therefore, the scaffolded set of activities could build up to a final collaborative task divided into two parts: firstly, the learners had to work in pairs, outside class time, to research one of the tourist attractions mentioned in the brochure (of their choosing) and create a welcome speech/introduction as through addressing a group of tourist clients and, secondly, the learners performed their work in class to the other members as an authentic activity.

This was a real-world example of how this type of language is used, and it was mined to have learners use the knowledge gained in class for an authentic communicative purpose, thereby making it motivating as well as preparing the learners to function in the target community.

4.1.6.3. Augmentation example: Personalising content

While doing the unit on Accounting Policies and Standards in *Professional English in Use: Finance* (Cambridge University Press, 2006), during the "Over to You" activity at the end of the materials, the subject of financial fraud came up. After completing the lesson unit, the learners (accountants in the Finance Department of an international printing company) asked to do some work in a subsequent lesson on financial fraud as they found the topic of great interest. As this presented an opportunity to introduce more finance-related vocabulary with real-world examples, use a variety of media, and provide the course with a motivating and bespoke element, it was decided to respond positively to the request and, to this end, the following materials were sourced. Firstly, a clear and concise presentation on financial fraud from the Bank of Mauritius[10] was used as an activation activity to provide a generalised introduction to the topic. Secondly, a podcast about Ponzi schemes from the Australian Securities and Investment Commission[11] was chosen. The podcast, which gave a brief and clear explanation, history, examples, indication of penalties and advice on how to avoid this type of fraud, was then "chunked" and used for more in-depth analysis and a variety of sets of activities, in order to also give listening-skills practice. Finally, a simplified and abridged article from the Corporate Finance Institute entitled "Bernie Madoff's Greatest Scam Ever" was chosen as an engaging and memorable example, giving reading-skills practice and the opportunity to develop writing skills through writing a summary or speaking skills through describing the case in learners' own words.

The three sources augmented the topic in the coursebook, providing a variety of authentic (podcast from a financial services regulator) and semi-authentic (the article was abridged to make it more accessible) material. This gave learners exposure to challenging input and the opportunity to consolidate a variety of skills mining the material, while using both top-down and bottom-up scaffolded activities. The instructor was able to tailor the course to learner needs and there was pertinent field-focused vocabulary input. By sourcing relevant, authentic, interesting and diverse materials an instructor can build engaging and memorable content in direct response to the learners' interests.

4.1.6.4. Substitution example: Localising materials

Cambridge English for Engineering (Cambridge University Press, 2008) was the core textbook for a B1+/B2-level English for Engineering course at a company that manufactured brakes for cars. The learners were brake engineers who worked for the racing department and were sent around the world to work with other engineers on racing tracks. Therefore, there was a need to improve their communication skills by practising scenarios based on everyday engineering situations and to give them the specialist language knowledge they required in order to enable them to work effectively and confidently in their sector. Part of the book

---

[10] https://www.bom.mu/sites/default/files/types-of-financial-frauds_4.pdf, accessed 10/03/2021.

[11] https://asic.gov.au/about-asic/news-centre/videos-and-podcasts/the-asic-podcast/episode-47-the-power-of-a-ponzi-scheme/, accessed 10/03/2021.

unit called "Breaking point", focusing firstly on technical problems with racing and endurance cars, had a section on assessing and interpreting faults. This contained a listening activity – a phone conversation in a mining plant regarding a technical problem with a diesel engine. After evaluating the unit, the instructor opted for the substitution of the inauthentic listening (obviously specially recorded for the book) with a video of a car mechanic assessing a specific fault related to brakes – a shaking steering-wheel. The video was sourced from *YouTube*[12] and chosen because of its suitable length and its completeness (with no need for editing); the speed of delivery was deemed appropriate for the target audience; and the technical vocabulary was strictly related to the learner needs. A lesson was built around the video with pre-listening activities: activating schemata and learners' subject knowledge, prediction and pre-teaching of some vocabulary, and post-listening activities including a gap-fill, matching activity, language work on modals of deduction and a pair-work discussion. Consolidation was in the form of homework, where the students accessed an *EdPuzzle* version of the video (edited with true/false and multiple-choice questions inserted) and tested what they had retained from the lesson.

Through this substitution, there was an opportunity to build on the previous topic and focus on a more specific problem related to brakes, to personalise and localise the course by choosing a topic more pertinent to the learners' actual jobs, increasing their engagement and motivation, to widen their lexis around their own field and give them practice in analysing and discussing a more real-world scenario, to vary the lesson by introducing a multimodal element and, most importantly, to expose the learners to more authentic input.

4.1.6.5. Substitution example: Outdated content

Included in the Oxford Express Series tile, *English for the Automobile Industry* is a magazine article on the subject of Smart Cars. The book was published in 2007 (there has been no new edition since), when Smart Cars were a relatively new and increasingly popular city car. When assessing the article now, however, it was felt that it did not reflect the modern automobile industry and more up-to-date content may be of more interest to learners working or studying in this field in the present day.

---

[12] https://www.youtube.com/watch?v=jEdDY2SKoWA, accessed 06/03/2021.

In addition, the activity lacked scaffolding and purpose, with only a brief instruction to read the article and consider the advantages and disadvantages of these types of cars and in which countries they might be most successful. Therefore, it was felt that visiting the Fiat company's website (aimed at the general public), and its section on city cars,[13] gave a lot of relevant and useful content to enable a discussion on the pros and cons of city cars in 2021. This could then be extended by looking at an article on the new 2021 Fiat Mobi city car, available in South America, from a car review website[14] which gives a concrete and very up-to-date example with field-specific vocabulary suitable for a more detailed look at the type of car under discussion. Finally, if appropriate for the learners on a particular course, a full technical performance review is available[15] which could be used as a source of work for a higher-level automobile engineering focus.

In this way, a short, dated, general article on city cars could be substituted with three levels (general, new model of car description and technical performance review) of new content on an ultra-modern car, thereby demonstrating to the learners how recent the materials are.

4.1.6.6. *Substitution example: Inauthentic dialogue*

On an English for the Tourism Industry programme, designed for B1 learners who, at the end of the course, would be working in hotels and restaurants, a decision was made to swap a hotel check-in listening activity from the coursebook, *English for International Tourism* by Longman, for a video of a check-in. The substitution was done for two reasons: firstly, the coursebook dialogue was very simplistic – dealing with the very basics of a hotel check-in such as spelling someone's name – and had obviously been written and recorded for inclusion in the book. Secondly, it felt outdated with no mention of wifi or other more current issues. Consequently, in order to be more "real-world", and to cover more varied scenarios during a check-in, a video from Lingua TV[16] was

---

[13] https://www.fiat.com/city-car, accessed 06/03/2021.

[14] https://moparinsiders.com/meet-the-2021-fiat-mobi-city-car-for-south-america/, accessed 06/03/2021.

[15] https://www.automobile-catalog.com/performance/2021/2988935/fiat_mobi_t rekking_1_0_flex_etanol.html, accessed 06/03/2021.

[16] https://www.youtube.com/watch?v=wyqfYJX23lg accessed 06/03/2021.

sourced. Although not completely authentic (as recorded especially for learners on an English for Hospitality course), it included a lot of natural language, a variety of situations which could arise during a check-in, clear dialogue spoken at a natural pace and a large amount of useful lexis. The video was used for both top-down and bottom-up language work (real content was identified as modal verbs for requests and offers) and role-plays.

As genuine, unscripted hotel check-in videos are difficult to find (for data privacy reasons), the video worked as an alternative to the limited original listening. It fitted neatly into the start of the lesson unit from the book and the following coursebook material on giving health and safety advice was kept to deepen the topic and lexis and to provide further practice of the linguistic content from the video.

4.1.7. Conclusion

This study argues for the need to ensure that all the phases of the learning process are adequately supported with appropriate materials to yield meaningful learning experiences for learners; this objective can be achieved through a profound knowledge of the strategies and techniques which may be employed in the adaptation of materials within course-books. There has been a particular focus on the "creation" of materials through augmentation and substitution and the considerations which are needed, from selecting appropriate content to its management through design and delivery to its post-use evaluation.

As this chapter focuses mainly on adding materials which are part of an existing plan, Block's (1990) three reasons for producing DIY materials prove to be particularly relevant: better contextualisation than in CPMs (real-world examples, relevant to the learners), timeliness (up to date), and the personal touch (learners appreciate that "bespoke" materials have been created to match their needs exactly). Evidently, instructors, by not following a lesson designed by a writer in a faraway publishing house, can focus purely on the needs of their learners, and adding content to materials which are "lacking" for a particular LSP course signifies that the needs of the learners are being specifically catered for.

We can reason with Krzanowski (2013) that the most important skills needed when creating materials are a willingness to experiment through trial and error, as well as a reasonably good knowledge of the particular LSP specialism in order to be able to address the wants/needs of the learners; otherwise, the specialist subject instructor may lack confidence in their ability to select and deliver the relevant content.

From the instructor's perspective, sourcing content and creating materials to add to a lesson can be professionally rewarding, enabling teachers to develop new skills and insights into the discipline. These processes can also help instructors become more adept at evaluating materials produced by themselves and by others, and, ultimately, to enhance their professional development, while aiding learners to reach their LSP objectives.

4.2

Teaching Vocabulary in LSP

Brankica Bošnjak Terzić, Olinka Breka,
Snježana Kereković

4.2.1. Introduction

Vocabulary learning is an indispensable component of language acquisition. It is an essential building block of language (Schmitt, Schmitt, & Clapham, 2001: 55) for both general foreign language and LSP learners. While without grammar very little can be conveyed, without vocabulary nothing can be conveyed (Wilkins, 1972). Since vocabulary knowledge enables language use, language use enables the increase of vocabulary knowledge, and knowledge of the world enables the increase of vocabulary knowledge and language use (Nation, 1993).

LSP vocabulary refers to the vocabulary of a particular area of study or professional use (Coxhead, 2018). LSP vocabulary is important because learners need to express concepts in their fields (Basturkmen, 2006: 69) and because it is linked to learners' language learning needs, specialised knowledge, and goals (Coxhead, 2018). Therefore, identifying LSP vocabulary or what vocabulary should be taught at the tertiary level in the LSP context is of great importance. Many factors influence the process of LSP vocabulary learning, the main part of which is the ability to identify technical vocabulary and implement a wide range of vocabulary learning strategies (VLS) through various productive and receptive activities in an LSP classroom.

4.2.2. Identifying technical vocabulary

Vocabulary is an integral part of LSP, and LSP learners need to acquire a wide range of terms that are specific to and common in their field of study. LSP vocabulary includes vocabulary that is specific to a particular field of study and it is tied to learners' needs. Research suggests that up to one in three words in a specialised text is technical (Coxhead, 2018), indicating the importance for LSP learners to identify technical vocabulary in spoken or written texts and acquiring it. Teachers involved in teaching LSP vocabulary are usually faced with the difficulty of deciding which words to teach and how to implement technical terminology in their classes. Moreover, if technical vocabulary can be identified in authentic texts, it would be easier for LSP teachers to decide what to focus on in vocabulary teaching.

Technical vocabulary can be referred to by various terms in the literature. These terms include special purpose, specific content, subject-specific, semi-technical and sub-technical vocabulary (Coxhead, 2013).

Approaches to determining which words are technical terms and what vocabulary LSP teachers should teach have generated a lot of interest among researchers. To our knowledge, there are several approaches to identifying subject vocabulary in the literature.

Chung and Nation (2004: 251) state that there are no well-established approaches to deciding which words are technical terms and which are not, and that there are virtually no studies that compare the effectiveness of the approaches. However, they state that this can be done in four ways: using a rating scale as the most valid, using a technical dictionary, using clues where learners find contextual clues in the text to help them understand new terminology, and using a computer-based approach.

Consulting an expert for vocabulary guidance can be a helpful approach when identifying technical vocabulary. However, Schmitt (2010) lists several difficulties with this method, including referring to different vocabulary lists from several experts on the same topic, as the selection depends on their expertise in a specific field.

Selecting words according to their frequency of occurrence in a particular subject area and comparing their frequency of occurrence or non-occurrence in another area or range of areas (Chung & Nation, 2004) is also one of the approaches. Accordingly, words that occur more frequently in a particular domain would be technical.

The use of digital vocabulary profiling tools such as the General Service List (GSL) (West, 1953), the New General Service List (NGSL) (Brown, Culligan, & Phillips, 2013), Academic Word List (AWL) (Coxhead, 2000) and subject-specific vocabulary lists, particularly important for LSP teachers and available online or through journal publications, are important tools for identifying technical vocabulary.

The General Service List, developed by West in 1953, contains approximately 2,000 high-frequency headwords that are important to L2 learners and is still the best general-purpose list for covering the most frequent words in English. The New General Service List (NGSL) is an updated and expanded version of the GSL, and contains 2,800 high-frequency words that are useful for L2 learners of English.

The Academic Word List is a great tool for teachers and learners to identify and learn new terms and to compare words in a specific corpus with words in a general corpus. It was created using a corpus of texts from four disciplines (science, law, commerce, and art). It consists of 570 items and is divided into 10 sub-lists according to their frequencies.

There are several subject-specific lists on the Internet. They usually contain a list of words used in a specific professional field and can help to determine whether the word chosen is technical or academic.

Beck, McKeown, and Kucan (2013) use a three-tier system of vocabulary. Tier One words are referred to as everyday words. Tier Two words are referred to as general academic words, which consist of high-frequency words that are essential to understanding a text and occur frequently in various academic texts. General academic words usually have one or more general language meanings and take on extended meanings in technical contexts. For example, the meaning of the noun article in general language refers to a specific subject or object, whereas in the context of ESP it may refer to a single clause of paragraph of a legal document or agreement, typically a single rule or regulation. Tier Three words are technical or content-specific words with low frequency. These words are closely related to the subject area of the text and are specific to a particular subject area. For learners studying LSP, the second and third-level words are considered to be high-frequency vocabulary and therefore need to be carefully selected and taught.

In addition, reading field-related articles and watching many field-related video clips can offer an important insight into relevant terminology, as can the use of technical dictionaries. The LSP teacher should provide learners with general skills on how to use a dictionary and how to select relevant technical dictionaries.

The choice of approach depends on the knowledge level and the needs of the learners, the materials used in class, the teacher's preferences, and collaboration with subject teachers.

To help learners learn and use new terminology effectively, LSP teachers should introduce and teach learners a wide range of vocabulary learning strategies.

4.2.3. Vocabulary language learning strategies

Learning foreign language vocabulary is a long-lasting and challenging task, not only because of the complex nature of lexical competence, but also because of the myriad factors that influence the learning process, such as the nature of lexical items, individual learner differences, and external, learner-independent factors (Bošnjak Terzić & Pavičić Takač, 2020). The importance of strategic vocabulary learning, which implies deliberate and proactive action towards more effective learning, has been recognised as an important and useful approach in the acquisition of new terminology and has been acknowledged as an important predictor of learners' academic achievement. Nation (2001) defines VLS as a part of language learning strategies, which in turn are a part of general learning strategies. Vocabulary learning strategies are specific strategies utilised in the isolated task of learning vocabulary in the target language (Pavičić Takač, 2008: 52). By employing learning strategies, learners take more control over their learning and more responsibility for their studies (Nation, 2001: 222).

Several VLS taxonomies have been proposed (Gu & Johnson, 1996; O'Malley & Chamot, 1990; Schmitt, 1997). Gu and Johnson's list describes metacognitive strategies (planning, monitoring, evaluating strategies) and cognitive strategies (attention, rehearsal, and production strategies). O'Malley and Chamot's taxonomy (1990) includes metacognitive, cognitive, and social/affective strategies. The most comprehensive and precise taxonomy is Schmitt's classification (1997), which is based on Oxford's classification (1990). Schmitt categorises strategies into direct strategies (memory, cognitive, compensation) and indirect strategies (metacognitive, social, affective).

Memory strategies are classified under direct strategies because they directly and explicitly involve the target language and help learners to store and retrieve information. Memory strategies consist of creating new words through imagery, key words, grouping, associating, creating mental images, reviewing (Oxford, 1990). They assist long-term retention. Cognitive strategies directly affect the incoming language information and are the most preferred strategies among language learners (Rafik-Galea, & Wong, 2006). Cognitive strategies involve deliberate manipulations of language to improve learning. They include repetition, organising new language, summarising meanings, guessing meanings from the context, using imagery to memorise, and using mechanical means to learn vocabulary, including keeping vocabulary notebooks (Schmitt, 2000). Compensation strategies help learners to compensate for limitations in a language and are needed to overcome any gaps in knowledge of the language (Oxford, 1990: 71). Guessing intelligently and overcoming limitations in speaking and writing are the two compensation strategies described in Oxford's taxonomy.

Indirect strategies help the learner regulate the learning process and support or control language learning without directly involving the language. Metacognitive strategies belong to the category of indirect strategies and include consciously monitoring the learning process and making decisions, monitoring or evaluating the best learning methods (O'Malley & Chamot, 1990; Schmitt, 1997, 2000). Social strategies involve interacting with other people to improve vocabulary learning (Oxford, 1990; Schmitt, 2000), while affective strategies refer to emotions, attitudes, motivation, and values (Oxford, 1990). These are the effective factors that significantly influence learning.

Several studies confirm a positive relationship between the effective use of strategies and academic achievement in FLL (Andrade &Evans, 2013; Gu, 2005; Oxford, 2011a; Schmitt, 1997; Seker, 2015). Although there is a growing interest among researchers in investigating the effective use of VLS, there is still a dearth of VLS research in the field of LSP.

Jurkovič (2010) found a statistically significant effect of metacognitive strategies on ESP achievement test scores. The results of a study by Bošnjak Terzić (2018) showed a statistically significant correlation between strategy use and academic achievement on vocabulary test scores. Although there is a lack of VLS research in the LSP field, based on the findings of FLL and a few studies in the LSP field, it seems safe to presume that successful learners employ a wide range of strategies while less successful learners employ a limited range of strategies.

Effective strategies are needed to stimulate and help learners retrieve their receptive vocabulary and use it in productive skills. Receptive vocabulary knowledge is the ability to understand a word when the learner hears or sees it, while productive vocabulary knowledge is the knowledge needed to produce a word when the learner can use it in his/her writing or speaking. Productive or active learning activities are associated with learning language through its use in speech and writing, while receptive or passive learning activities are associated with learning language through reading and listening.

4.2.4. TRAILS Summer School

The TRAILs Summer School was organised to promote high-quality and innovative instruction in LSP because most teachers have not received pre-service LSP training/education. The TRAILs Summer School programme was presented in the form of 11 teaching/learning modules covering different topics relevant to LSP teacher education. Of the 11 modules offered and presented in the TRAILs Summer School, Module 4, entitled LSP Teaching Skills, took place in the afternoon session of the TRAILs Summer School on Tuesday 23 February, 2021. There were 30 participants (from all partner countries) who actively participated in all sessions, including 12 LSP practitioners and 18 future LSP practitioners (foreign language students and PhD students).

The plenary session was divided into five parts: LSP vocabulary teaching/learning; Selective grammar (form-based) teaching/learning in LSP settings; Development of the comprehension of LSP input: reading, listening, audio-visual; Development of LSP output: writing, speaking; and Teacher Talk.

For the purposes of this article, we will describe the part that dealt with the teaching and learning of LSP vocabulary. The topic was presented in the first part of the interactive plenary session, followed by three simultaneously run group sessions. The main aim of the plenary session was to increase the awareness and knowledge level of trainee teachers on teaching LSP vocabulary.

The learning outcomes of Module 4 for the part dealing with teaching/learning LSP vocabulary were defined as follows: Participants will be able to design and perform various activities for receptive and productive learning/learning of LSP vocabulary; help their learners to expand their LSP vocabulary; enhance their learners' proficiency in understanding and using the vocabulary of professional and academic texts; and prepare and present a design of various tasks for receptive and productive learning/teaching of LSP vocabulary.

In particular, the aim of the plenary session was to help participants define and understand the basic concepts, principles and theories used in LSP vocabulary teaching and to raise awareness and provide a wide range of ways to distinguish between technical and academic vocabulary, among which digital tools for vocabulary profiling were presented. In addition, the importance of using different activities for receptive and productive LSP vocabulary learning, as well as the importance of implementing VLSs in LSP classrooms and understanding which VLSs can be applied to learning/teaching LSP vocabulary, were addressed in the session.

Following the interactive session, the participants were divided into three groups, each group comprising in-service and pre-service teachers. In the group sessions, the participants implemented the topics covered in the plenary session through numerous activities. They were given a text from The Engineer magazine on the topic of the future of electric vehicles in the world.

In the first task, the participants had to carefully decide what vocabulary to choose for the lesson and divide it into academic and technical vocabulary groups. They also had to outline how they selected the words and what they based the classification on. The LSP practitioners indicated that they usually made their selections based on their teaching experience, prior knowledge, and research, comparing words in a specific corpus with words in a general corpus. Many of the LSP practitioners noted that the frequency of occurrence is very important when dealing with and identifying new vocabulary. They usually lack collaboration with subject teachers and mostly rely on collaboration with other foreign language teachers. On the other hand, the language students lack teaching experience and prior knowledge. They found that the suggested online vocabulary lists can be very useful in tandem with the experience they share with their more experienced colleagues. In addition, the use of specialised dictionaries proved to be a source of information that both groups of participants trusted.

For the next task, the participants had to prepare and present an outline of the receptive and productive activities they would use to teach the selected LSP vocabulary and suggest the strategies they would employ when learning new terminology from the selected text.

As all participants reported, the focus when preparing activities, whether receptive or productive, is on language in context. The aim is to develop vocabulary knowledge through real-life situations and topics that are of the greatest interest to learners and, accordingly, to develop a wide range of activities that could help learners to acquire productive and receptive vocabulary knowledge. Participants also indicated that learners are more motivated to participate in all activities when exposed to new vocabulary and specific content in real-life situations. In addition, when teaching learners at tertiary level, LSP teachers need to take into account different levels of learners' knowledge, so the range of activities should be broad and suitable for a certain level.

Several activities were designed and proposed among the participants:

1. highlighting the key words
2. finding collocations
3. describing how the electric vehicle works using the key words
4. a matching exercise (matching the definitions of the words to the words in the text)
5. word formation
6. word family gap-fill activity
7. discussion of the advantages of electric vehicles
8. retelling the text
9. discussion of advantages and disadvantages of electric vehicles
10. cloze text without multiple choice or word bank
11. cloze text with multiple choice or word bank
12. discussion of advantages and disadvantages of investing in new technologies and vehicle architecture
13. discussion of hybrid vehicle features (design)
14. retelling the article
15. predicting the information presented in the text
16. summarising the main idea

In terms of strategies, the basic concept is to make learners permanently familiar with the specialised vocabulary and encourage them to develop an awareness of their strategic approach to learning. The role of an LSP teacher is to employ and teach language learning strategies through various productive and receptive activities which should be related to the professional context and be based on authentic materials and real-life situations. By providing multiple examples of VLS when introducing a new concept, learners expand their learning strategy repertoire. The LSP practitioners stated that they do not rely only on incidental acquisition of strategies, but that explicit strategy learning should also be implemented. It should also be kept in mind that a strategy does not work the same way for every learner. Therefore, implicit or explicit strategy learning and knowledge of each learner's strategic approach in the LSP context as well as setting learning objectives, are valuable assets when teaching LSP vocabulary.

Associating new terminology with existing concepts or images that have meaning for learners, i.e., applying expertise to new terminology, is considered to be an effective VLS. In addition, organisational strategies such as creating mental maps, grouping information into meaningful categories, and highlighting, were also suggested by LSP practitioners.

Other strategies presented by the participants included: skimming for the main idea, finding key words in the text, paraphrasing and summarising strategies, and translating strategies. Other suggested strategic approaches to vocabulary learning were using synonyms and collocations to learn new terms, i.e., using the new word in a sentence to help learners memorise new terms. Guessing from the context, i.e., using the content of the text to guess the meaning of the new word and then confirming the meaning in a dictionary, i.e., using dictionary strategies, were described as strategies frequently used by LSP teachers.

4.2.5. Conclusion

Teachers and learners need to find out what vocabulary is used in different contexts, what company it keeps, and what might be the most efficient way of teaching and learning it (Coxhead, 2018). The role of LSP teachers is to prepare LSP learners to autonomously use language in their professional settings. LSP teachers often have difficulty when providing up-to-date context-related vocabulary because they themselves often do not have a technical background. In addition, most LSP teachers have not received training in LSP teaching and usually find themselves in situations where they are self-taught or rely only on the help of their more experienced colleagues. One of the main problems in teaching LSP is to identify technical vocabulary and meet the needs of learners. Accordingly, LSP teachers need to design numerous activities and an appropriate methodology to implement a wide range of LSP strategies, thus enabling learners to retain vocabulary in their long-term memory. It should be kept in mind that the strategies and activities employed in the LSP setting are no different from those used in any foreign language teaching and learning. However, LSP teachers need to expand the repertoire of their learners' strategies to use it in a different academic context and to relate it to the professional context, as well as develop an awareness of the importance of highly specialised terminology and its frequency. Using a wide range of strategies should help learners to develop vocabulary knowledge that they would use receptively and productively in their future careers. In addition, LSP teachers should carefully plan their lessons, methodology, activities, and strategies to motivate learners to participate in the lessons so that they can independently apply LSP in their professional settings after completing their higher education.

4.3

Task/Problem/Project-Based Learning and Teaching in LSP: How Do They Correspond to 21st Century Learning?

Olinka Breka, Snježana Kereković, Brankica Bošnjak Terzić

4.3.1. Introduction

What and how we teach in LSP settings should depend on the learner's reason for learning (Hutchinson & Waters, 1987). LSP teaching has constantly changed with the ever-growing needs and demands defined by new professional contexts (Jendrych, 2013). Therefore, in LSP, what specific refers to is not only specialised terminology and grammatical structures typical of a target discourse community, but also and primarily the specific purpose for which learners learn (Gatehouse, 2001).

Besides linguistic accuracy and knowledge of specialised terminology, what else do modern professionals need to master today? What competences and skills are they expected to acquire and develop to navigate the challenges of the present and future world?

Learners should develop abilities to 'connect knowledge and skills, learning and competence, inert and active learning, codified and tacit knowledge, and creative and adaptive learning and transform them into valuable skills' (Carneiro, 2007: 156). These skills should enable them not only to plan and manage, but to actively shape the complex challenges they are facing and will be facing in the future.

4.3.1.1. Critical thinking

Critical thinking is fundamental to 21st-century learning. In higher education, learners should be taught how to access, analyse and synthesise information, while at the same time developing their interpretative abilities. Ennis (1985) proposes that learners should also be capable of reasonable reflective thinking in order to decide what to believe or do, while Davies (2015) argues that by practising critical thinking learners can be prompted to take action, thus becoming critical thinkers. There is another aspect of critical thinking that is essential to learning in higher education settings: an ability to not only access information but assess its relevance, i.e. to decide what resources as well as data are relevant to them in relation to the purpose they have in mind. Since a huge amount of information is available at any moment to everyone, the relevance of this skill is absolutely essential.

4.3.1.2. Communication and collaboration

The ability to express yourself and communicate your ideas clearly and effectively, in writing and in speech, is crucial in both professional and educational contexts.

Collaborative working, as Johnson et al. (1991) understand it, is more than just working in groups. It includes positive interdependence between team members who are well aware that they are reliant on one another, so that each member of the team is held accountable for doing their share of work. Furthermore, group work entails interaction between all members, who, by cooperating closely on a task, at the same time learn from each other, give feedback to each other, and challenge and encourage each other. The underpinning idea is that by working together the members of the group form a learning community (Kilpatrick et al., 2003) based on mutual trust, which enhances members' motivation and willingness to improve their work in order to upgrade their performance. Collaboration also offers group members an opportunity to hone a wide array of relevant skills such as critical thinking, leadership, decision-making and interpersonal skills, to mention but some.

4.3.1.3. *Creativity and productivity*

Creative learners pursue new ideas and concepts. They seek solutions to ambiguities and deal with uncertainties or multiple solutions to problems. Creativity also enables learners to innovate and create new products to present their ideas. Divergent thinking and innovative capacity are required for professional and personal success, while the ability to create a product that will meet a need is also a source of personal satisfaction and self-esteem. The task of LSP teachers is to identify and encourage creativity in LSP learners. They should also provide or direct learners to multi-faceted forms of visual, verbal, and auditory communication, using multiple media types to achieve relevance, immediacy, and clarity (McLauglin & Lee, 2008).

4.3.1.4. *Personalisation and participation*

Learning should be driven by personal needs and choices. Hence, learners should engage in personally relevant and meaningful learning. They should set their goals and decide how best to reach them. Mayer et al. (2008) suggest that learners' ownership of learning, taking responsibility for their own learning, has a great impact on their attitudes and level of independence in relation to learning. This ownership of learning, personal engagement in the process of learning, largely affects both the process itself and its results. It boosts learners' motivation and their performance. Wenger argues that participation in a community of practice involves both action and connection. It is a social experience that assumes mutual engagement, joint enterprise and shared repertoire (Wenger, 2007: 83).

4.3.1.5. *Metacognition*

Active learners are able to plan and organise their own learning; they self-monitor and self-evaluate the learning process and tend to know what, why and how they progress through it. Put simply, to be active participants in a learning process, they need to develop and practise metacognition, which is, in fact, thinking about thinking and learning. In other words, they should develop and adopt a set of procedures that will enable them to reflect on what they are doing and how, and raise their awareness of what is involved in the process. This is not only an intrinsic talent. It can and should be explicitly taught and practised. By embedding metacognitive strategies in the learning process which deals with content areas, teachers can create and promote a metacognitive culture in learning environments. Metacognition is considered to be a critical element of successful learning. Dewey argued that we learn more from reflecting on our experiences than from the actual experiences themselves (Stanford Encyclopedia of Philosophy, 2018).

4.3.2. Task/problem/project-based learning and teaching

Having listed and discussed some of the 21st-century skills, we naturally should ask ourselves how to purposefully and explicitly teach these skills in LSP contexts. In the subsequent sections we will discuss task-based language learning, problem-based learning and project-based learning in an attempt to address the question of whether these teaching and learning methods can cater to the needs of 21st-century learners in LSP settings, and to what extent.

4.3.2.1. Task-based language teaching

Based on the constructivist theory of learning and communicative language teaching methodology, task-based language learning and teaching (TBLT) can be defined as a learner-centred approach that focuses on learner needs (Ellis, 2003). It enhances language acquisition and facilitates effective instruction by providing learners with both opportunities for comprehensible input (Long, 1985) and negotiation of meaning, as well as opportunities for interaction and comprehensible output (Swain, 1995) by encouraging authentic communication in which learners use target language to discuss their personal experiences, express their own ideas and feelings (Nunan, 2004; Willis, 1996). Since there is a strong inclination towards bringing the real world into the classroom, authentic texts are exploited and classroom language learning is connected to language use outside the classroom. Learners do not only focus on the language, but also on the learning process itself. Richards and Rodgers (2004) noted that engaging learners in task work provides a better context for the activation of learning processes.

Various definitions of tasks have been provided, depending on the perspective of the person making the definition and the purpose for which the definition is made (Samuda & Bygate, 2008: 64). Willis (1996: 23) defines a task as an activity where the target language is used for a certain communicative purpose or goal with the aim of achieving an outcome. For Nunan (2004: 4) a task is a piece of classroom work which involves learners in comprehending, producing or interacting in the target language while their attention is principally focused on meaning rather than form. Samuda and Bygate (2008) claim that key language processes take place in holistic language work, which makes tasks invaluable in achieving this purpose. Therefore, they define a task as a holistic activity which engages language use in order to achieve a non-linguistic outcome while meeting a linguistic challenge, with the overall aim of promoting language learning, through process or product or both.

Regardless of certain differences, various definitions of tasks share the same essential ideas and point to some common features:

(1) meaning is primary, while focus on form is secondary to meaning,

(2) tasks are goal-oriented and completion of the non-linguistic outcome is the priority,

(3) tasks are related to the real world in terms of their communicative purposes, and the discourse that emerges is comparable to that emerging in the real world,

(4) learners' needs are central to the selection of content,

(5) completion of the outcome in tasks is the priority and the performance itself is evaluated by the outcome achieved,

(6) learners are personally involved in tasks (Prabhu, 1987 as cited in Littlewood, 2004: 323 referred to personal involvement as "mind-engagement"), and

(7) tasks should have a sense of completeness, being able to stand on their own as communication acts.

One of the most valuable aims and possible effects of TBLT, as Willis and Willis argue, is that this approach gives learners opportunities to "have a go" regardless of their language competence (Willis & Willis, 2007: 2).

There have been many models for implementing TBLT (Ellis, 2003; Nunan, 2004; Willis, 1996). Here we will present the framework for

TBLT outlined by Willis (1996), which results from the author's experience as a teacher educator.

This framework is based on a three-stage task cycle: pre-task, task cycle and language focus.

(1) During the pre-task stage the teacher introduces the topic and brings up the language that might be useful to learners when performing the task. Very often this stage starts with learners being informed or familiarised with the topic by reading a text, listening to a text/dialogue or watching a video clip, etc. The teacher then sets the task and gives clear guidelines.

(2) During the second stage, learners do the task. They get involved in purposeful communication, preferably in pairs or small groups, with the goal to be achieved. The teacher monitors the process, encourages learners and provides scaffolding. After having completed the task, learners plan how to present the outcome of their activity. This might be in the form of a presentation, poster, video, podcast, written report, or any other appropriate medium. The teacher can still be asked for advice in this phase. Finally, learners report on their outcome while the teacher listens and then comments.

(3) In the final phase, learners focus on language. They first reflect on the process and the language, how well they did the task, what problems they encountered and how they dealt with them. This is the analysis part of the language focus stage, in which self-reflection and peer-reflection are involved; at the end, the teacher conducts an exercise of language expressions or, if necessary, language form. Obviously, throughout the framework cycles the learner's focus is primarily on meaning and language, although when required the teacher provides a focus on form outside the context of communicative activity, providing what learners need (Willis & Willis, 2007).

4.3.2.2. Problem-based learning

Problem-based learning (PBL) is another learner-centred method that fosters meaningful and experiential learning (Hmelo-Silver, 2004). Learners work collaboratively to investigate, explain and solve meaningful problems (Hmelo-Silver, ibid.). They play an active role in this process, aiming at transferable learning supported by the learner's personal engagement and intrinsic motivation. Basically, learners learn by solving complex, meaningful, real-world problems and reflecting on their learning process and the experiences gained (Barrows, 2000; Duch et al., 2001; Hmelo-Silver, 2004). It is argued that PBL empowers learners to conduct research, integrate theory and practice, and apply knowledge and skills to develop a viable solution to a defined problem.

Schmidt et al. (2011) state that PBL can be approached from three different perspectives, namely, (1) as a process of inquiry: learners investigate problems, ask questions and search for solutions, (2) as "learning to learn": learners get involved in self-directed learning and learn skills and strategies that can be transferred to other areas of their personal or professional lives, and, finally, (3) as a cognitive approach: learners acquire knowledge about the relevant content. Learners are presented with a problem which triggers questions which, in turn, activate the learners' prior knowledge. They do not only activate their prior knowledge related to the problem, they also elaborate on it through self-explanation, discussion with peers and practising or responding to questions. By engaging in these activities, learners better comprehend and retain important new information.

What distinguishes PBL from other experiential learning techniques is that (a) the process starts with the problem, (b) learners need to be engaged constantly in self-directed learning (SDL), (c) they also need to self-reflect throughout the process on the process itself and learning, (d) learners work in small groups, and (e) they require facilitation and guidance to navigate through the process (Hmelo-Silver, 2004; Hmelo-Silver & Eberbach, 2012; Schmidt et al., 2011; Scott, 2017). For this process to be effective, the starting point, the problem, needs to meet the essential requirements. What are the features of a good problem?

A good problem, one that will help the learner engage in the learning process and will result in flexible thinking and effective learning, should be authentic, complex, ill-structured and open-ended, fostering free enquiry. It should be realistic and relevant to learners, allowing for constant feedback and evaluation of learners' knowledge and practices. The problem should be complex enough to present a challenge, though adapted to learners' prior knowledge, and will encourage discussion, research (gathering knowledge from many different sources) and SDL, and boost learners' need to know and learn. Collaboration is essential and the activities learners engage in should be valued in the real world (Hmelo-Silver, 2004; Hmelo-Silver & Eberbach, 2012; Savery, 2006).

When solving problems, learners go through a learning cycle (Hmelo-Silver, 2004), or the PBL tutorial process, which consists of several stages. Learners are presented with a problem scenario. The problem is complex while the information that learners get is minimal. First, learners need to identify what they already know about the problem. Once they have identified the facts, analysed them and formulated the problem, learners engage in questioning and research, trying to obtain additional information pertaining to the problem and possible solution(s). Based on the new knowledge acquired, learners make hypotheses about the problem. Throughout the process learners take time to reflect on what they have done, how they did it and whether it was productive and fruitful. They conduct self- and peer-reflection, which helps them clarify different aspects of the problem and its challenges, and become aware of knowledge deficiencies. These deficiencies become learning issues that learners then research and investigate, during their self-directed learning process. This is the process learners go through individually, investigating the issues defined and collecting relevant data. Then learners re-group, share and discuss the information gathered so that they can evaluate their hypotheses and, if required, reformulate them or generate new ones. Upon completion of each problem, learners reflect on the abstract knowledge gained and evaluate their understanding of the problem and practices that lead to the resolution of the problem.

Self-directed learning is an essential component of problem-based learning. It should be understood as a process in which learners conceptualise and design their learning, i.e. they set their goals, decide what resources to use and how to use them and, finally, they evaluate the learning process they have conducted (Brookfield, 1994; Hiemstra, 1994; Knowles, 1975; Loyens, Magda, & Rikers, 2008; Voskamp, Kuiper, & Volman, 2020). Although in doing so learners are independent to a large extent, that does not necessarily mean that learning takes place in isolation. On the contrary, teachers can and often do play a role in SDL, participating in dialogues with learners and helping them decide which resources to access. In particular, teachers play a significant role in enhancing critical thinking in self-directed learners (Hiemstra, 1994). Another important task of the teacher is to help learners develop the skills for self-direction (Voskamp et al., 2020), which requires a change in teaching strategy. Williamson Hawkins (2018) notes that since SDL is characterised by autonomy and self-regulation, it is critical to teach language learning strategies (Oxford, 2011b) along with self-directed learning skills. To help students who are struggling to build SDL habits and develop SDL skills, teachers should also adopt the same behaviours and try to self-manage, self-monitor and self-modify themselves in their teaching (Costa & Kallick, 2004).

4.3.2.3. Project-based learning

Like the two instructional methods discussed above, task-based teaching and learning and problem-based learning, project-based learning (PjBL) is a learner-centred, inquiry-based teaching method based on the constructivist theory that claims that learners learn better and their understanding of what they are learning goes deeper if they participate in authentic activities performed in authentic, real-life contexts. Project-based learning is thus a form of situated learning in which learning is centred on the whole person and results from the interaction between three areas of influence: agent, activity and world (Lave & Wenger, 1991). Since learners learn by doing, knowing is not separated from doing. On the contrary, learners build their knowledge and construct meaning by solving problems, making decisions, creating, sharing and explaining their ideas and experiences and reflecting on what they are doing. In a word, they do what is relevant to them in a meaningful way, in collaboration with other learners and as part of a community of learners, with the aim of developing real-world products and interacting with the world (Krajcik & Shin, 2014).

For Thomas (2000), projects are central to the curriculum, which means that through projects learners learn relevant concepts of the discipline. Their conceptual knowledge is built through inquiry-based activities initiated by setting a driving question. Activities are to a large extent learner-driven and are authentic in the way that they resemble real-life activities performed by professionals in the discipline. Thomas summarises these features as: centrality, driving question, constructive investigation, autonomy and realism. In addition, all the actors and participants, learners as well as teachers or members of the community, collaborate on finding a solution or solutions to a problem, and learners are scaffolded with learning technologies that enable them to go beyond their ability (Krajcik & Blumenfeld, 2006; Krajcik & Shin, 2014). Another important feature is continuous reflection on what they are learning, how they are doing it, and why. This can be done by introducing learning journals, formative assessment or discussions about the project, the learning process itself and the resulting gains, challenges and future goals or modified actions. Also, learners are encouraged and trained to give and take constructive feedback, using appropriate rubrics, protocols and similar guiding tools. To really benefit from these practices, it is important to create the classroom culture that fosters collaboration and metacognition.

All the aforementioned features are relevant, but the two most essential components are: (1) a driving question and (2) a final outcome of a project. The function of a driving question is to initiate and guide instruction, to provide a context for exploratory learning and to motivate and inspire learners to engage in a relevant problem-solving process. To fulfil these requirements, a good driving question should be: (a) feasible, (b) worthwhile, (c) contextualised, (d) meaningful, and (e) ethical (Krajcik & Blumenfeld, 2006). Learners get involved in the activities in order to create a tangible product, artefact (report, presentation, videotape, brochure, etc) or event that addresses the driving question. Creating a tangible product is definitely a critical feature of any project, which makes project-based learning different from problem-based learning. In summary, when applying project-based learning our primary goals should be: (1) to support deep disciplinary content learning, (2) to engage students in authentic work, (3) to support student collaboration, (4) to build an iterative culture (Grossman et al., 2019), and (5) to create an end product to be presented to and shared with the wider public.

4.3.3. TRAILs Summer School: Module 7 – Task/project/ problem-based learning in LSP

In the second phase of the TRAILs project (see Bocanegra-Valle and Perea-Barberá, this edition), an online questionnaire was designed to obtain relevant data on LSP teacher needs. The data from 621 respondents was collected and synthesised. According to the results, 61 % of the LSP practitioners either strongly agreed or agreed that teacher training programmes were a prerequisite for qualifying as an LSP teacher. When asked to specify the knowledge and training issues needed, from a total list of 43 items, the respondents selected as the first five most important LSP teacher needs the following: (1) analysis of target and learner needs, (2) materials design and development, (3) course design and development, (4) general principles of LSP, and (5) task-based language teaching. When asked to add further relevant competences and training issues, the respondents emphasised the importance of project-based and problem-based learning. As a result, one of the modules (Module 7) of the TRAILs Summer School focused on task-based language learning and teaching, problem-based learning and project-based learning. Module 7 comprised an interactive plenary session followed by three group sessions, running concurrently. Thirty participants, twelve LSP teachers and nineteen future LSP teachers coming from all partner countries took part in both the plenary and group sessions.

The plenary session was divided into three parts. In the first part we dealt with TBLT/PBL/PjBL. The second part was about SDL, while the last section focused on multimodal learning in LSP.

The aim of the plenary session was twofold. First, we discussed the fundamental theoretical principles these methods are based upon. Another aim of the plenary session was to let the participants explore and discover for themselves what kind of learning these methods promote or reconsider, whether they confirm or revise their previous ideas and beliefs about them. To this end, the plenary session was made interactive, so that the participants were engaged in a number of appropriate activities.

Clearly stated objectives help us to focus our attention and efforts and indicate what we want to achieve (Anderson et al., 2001). The learning outcomes of the plenary session and group sessions, encompassing task/problem/project-based teaching/learning, self-directed learning, multimodal learning as well as time management and teamwork as relevant components of the methods discussed, were defined. However, since in this chapter we are concerned with TBLT/PBL/PjBL, we will present only the learning outcomes that point to the most pertinent information in relation to the methods in focus and the desired behaviours of the participants. They are as follows: At the end of the training the trainee will be able to define and understand the main theoretical assumptions of, and differences between, task/problem/project-based teaching/learning in LSP settings; and will be able to understand, explain and analyse the process and structure frameworks of the TBLT/PBL/PjBL cycle as well as understand and analyse the basic features of a well-designed task/problem/driving question. One of the learning outcomes was also understanding and using online tools for collaborative learning. Due to the limited time, however, this was considered to be unattainable for less experienced or inexperienced participants. Next, the participants were required to take part in activities that would enable them to achieve the following learning outcomes: At the end of the training, the trainee will be able to contrast TBLT/PBL/PjBL; to develop the skills of higher order thinking, effective communication, cooperation and teamwork; to prepare and present a sample of task/problem/project-based syllabus outline for a specific group of LSP learners and to evaluate other participants' task/problem/project-based syllabus outlines. Obviously, our goal was to take the participants through an exploratory and active learning process, starting with lower-order thinking skills such as understanding and applying through analysing to evaluating and creating new meaning (Anderson & Krathwall, 2001).

In both the plenary and group sessions, the participants worked in small mixed groups (in-service and pre-service LSP teachers). The plenary session was divided into six sections and the participants were provided with six handouts.

Handout 1 – In the first set of tasks the definitions of TBLT/PBL/PjBL were analysed and the very central concepts/points in each method identified. Also, similar or shared ideas and principles were pinpointed.

Handout 2 – The fundamental features of a task, a problem and a driving question were identified based on the texts presenting them. Those features were analysed and ranked in terms of their capacity to empower learners to develop the 21st-century skills. In addition, two examples of driving questions were provided in order to be refined. This activity was aimed at demonstrating participants' ability to transfer the acquired new or improved prior knowledge about the central points of PjBL.

Handout 3 – In the third set of tasks, three incomplete frameworks for the TBLT/PBL/PjBL cycle were offered and the individual stages of each process were discussed. Possible solutions were then negotiated and finally group decisions on how to complete the frameworks were reached.

Handout 4 – Seven principles of TBLT, namely scaffolding, task dependency, recycling (of language), active learning, integration (of language meaning, function and form), reproduction to recreation, and reflection were in focus here. The definitions were matched to the principles after being discussed and analysed. The rationale for including these principles and encouraging the participants to discuss them is that the principles can be universally applied to language learning activities.

At the end, the participants' creativity skills were tested: the participants were challenged to formulate one more principle along with an explanation of why it should be added to the list.

Handout 5 – All the tasks in the handout were related to self-directed learning. They ranged from completing the unfinished statements about SDL, doing a SWOT analysis of SDL, brainstorming and ranking SDL strategies, to sharing and discussing personal experiences in relation to using SDL in LSP teaching.

Handout 6 – Multimodal learning was addressed in this set of tasks. The handout had originally been used by students of aeronautical engineering in LSP classes at the Faculty of Mechanical Engineering and Naval Architecture, University of Zagreb. It consisted of an article accompanied by two activities. In the first activity, the article was read and the relevant information to be used later to write a summary was highlighted and annotated. In the second activity, a version of the summary was provided for the participants to edit and write an improved version. To facilitate the comprehension of a very demanding text, in terms of both the ideas dealt with and the language, especially its highly specialised terminology, different modes of the same content (article information) were provided: (a) a set of photographs illustrating the helicopter components and techniques discussed in the article, (b) an animation without any text, (c) an animation with text, and (d) a video clip. They were compared and contrasted and, finally, evaluated in terms of: (1) gaining and keeping learners' attention, (2) information conveying, (3) language-noticing, (4) meaning-making, (5) contextualisation of the target language (terminology), (6) enhancing vocabulary range, (7) affecting learner motivation, engagement and awareness, (8) fostering critical thinking, and (9) catering to the development of language skills.

In group sessions, the fundamental features of TBLT/PBL/PjBL were revisited and discussed in terms of the position they occupy in the language-content continuum (Anthony, 2018). Then, the participants were further divided into three smaller groups. Each group was provided with an authentic course syllabus to analyse and identify the method it was based upon. Next, each group negotiated and conceptualised a syllabus following the instructions (type of the course, teaching hours, language level), formulated the learning objectives and learning outcomes of the course, and designed outlines (samples) of tasks based upon the allotted method. Finally, after completing their tasks, all three groups reunited to conduct self- and peer-evaluation of the created syllabus concepts, learning objectives, learning outcomes and the task outlines in terms of whether (a) the syllabi were based on the given method, (b) the goals were achieved within the given time, (c) the syllabi contained activities requiring teamwork, (d) the syllabi contained activities requiring autonomous and self-directed learning, and (e) the syllabi contained multimodal activities.

As stated above, there were two goals we wanted to accomplish: First, to focus on the essential concepts, theories and issues of TBLT/PBL/PjBL; Second, to foster the participants' active involvement.

On the one hand, in the plenary and group sessions, the participants were offered a comprehensive overview of the relevant aspects of the major topics, while on the other, they were given an opportunity to pose questions, seek answers, check their hypotheses and reflect on their ideas and practices. What was especially valuable from the participants' point of view was that they worked collaboratively and were involved in the activities applicable to their particular situations and practices, while at the same time studying the relevant theories. Additionally, they had an opportunity to apply the ideas discussed. Both in-service LSP teachers and their less experienced or inexperienced pre-service colleagues showed great enthusiasm and either shared the insights they had gained through years of teaching LSP or made their contribution by adding fresh new perspectives to the issues discussed. This interactivity and active involvement helped the pre-service LSP teachers to better process the newly acquired knowledge, while the in-service teachers got the opportunity to integrate their knowledge in a different context in which they were required to explain, justify and exemplify their ideas. Since we had an opportunity to closely observe and monitor the participants as well as to communicate with them, we were able to observe that they formed real communities of practice that included routines, words, tools, ways of doing things, stories, gestures, symbols, genres, actions, or concepts that the community has produced or adopted in the course of its existence, and which have become part of its practice (Wenger, 2007: 83). This aspect of the sessions organised in the TRAILs Summer School was probably one of its most valuable experiences and visible results. But most importantly, the participants understood the relevant implications of the activities conducted for their teaching and future professional development. To sum up, if teachers are to come together to learn about and improve their instruction, it is critical for them to have a shared language with which to analyse and reflect on their work in the classroom (Grossman et al., 2019). That is exactly what we strove to offer the participants – an insight into most prominent learner-centred methods of teaching LSP along with peer- and self-reflection.

4.3.4. Concluding remarks

Higher education has to change dramatically in order to educate young people so that they function effectively in the 21st century. The development of specific skills such as critical thinking, communication and collaboration skills, creativity skills, problem solving skills, metacognitive skills, in a word, life and career skills, are to be fostered. Likewise, LSP should be aimed at developing the 21st-century skills. To achieve this aim, pedagogies and methods that support deeper learning are to be adopted. Deeper learning occurs when learners engage in real-life situations or those that imitate them, working in collaboration with other learners (Barron & Darling-Hammond, 2008). At the beginning of this chapter a question was posed as to whether task-based language learning and teaching, problem-based learning and project based-learning are methods that can respond to the new demands placed on teaching LSP in higher education contexts. To this end, the fundamental theoretical concepts and principles of these three methods were discussed and the possibilities of their implementation in a number of activities presented. Common features of these three methods were identified, namely, task-based language learning and teaching, problem-based learning and project-based learning, which are learner-centred methods which situate learners in authentic learning environments. Learners are encouraged to communicate meaningfully and purposefully, in collaboration with other learners using all their language resources. Learners are encouraged to apply multidisciplinary skills from other subjects which make the methods more relevant and authentic. These methods foster higher-order thinking as well as reflective thinking and learning. Learners take responsibility for their own learning and create opportunities for themselves to further explore and challenge ideas and issues present in the real world. With the features of task-based language teaching and learning, problem-based learning and project-based learning listed above, we believe that these methods could be an answer to the pressing need to equip our learners in LSP learning contexts with the required 21st-century skills. However, this calls for new roles for both LSP learners and LSP teachers. Learners, as stated above, need to take an active role in their own learning. LSP teachers, who already have to take on a multitude of roles such as course designers, materials providers, collaborators, researchers and evaluators (Dudley-Evans & St John, 1998), should, in addition, adopt some new roles, such as those of motivators, facilitators and organisers, or those of intercultural mediators and mentors for lifelong learning (Basturkmen, 2014). Since we live in exciting and fast-changing times, some new roles will probably be created in the future for LSP teachers. To conclude, each new method to be applied in LSP teaching contexts means that LSP teachers need to learn how to play new roles. It is crucial, therefore, to respond to LSP teachers' needs with appropriate and effective education and professional development.

References

Aguirre Beltrán, B. (2012). *Aprendizaje y enseñanza de español con fines específicos. Comunicación en ámbitos académicos y profesionales.* Madrid: SGEL.

Ahmed, M. K. (2014). The ESP Teacher: Issues, Tasks and Challenges. *English for Specific Purposes World*, 42, 1–33.

Airey, J. (2016). EAP, EMI or CLIL? In K. Hyland & P. Shaw (Eds.), *The Routledge Handbook of English for Academic Purposes.* New York: Routledge, 71–83.

Alebaid, M. Y. (2020). Training Needs of ESP Practitioners in Vocational Education. *Multi-Knowledge Electronic Comprehensive Journal for Education and Science Publications*, 32, 1–20.

Alexander, O. (2007). Groping in the dark or turning on the light: Routes into teaching English for Academic purposes. Paper presented at the IALS Teacher Education Symposia 2006. University of Edinburgh. Available at http://www.uefap.com/baleap/teap/oa_ials_symposium.pdf (13 February 2021).

Algan, Y. (dir.) (2021). *Quels professeurs au XXIème siècle ?* Paris: Conseil Scientifique de l'Éducation Nationale.

Alshenqeeti, H. (2014). Interviewing as a Data Collection Method: A Critical Review. *English Linguistics Research*, 3(1), 39–45.

Anderson, L. W., & Krathwohl, D. R. (2001). *A taxonomy for learning, teaching, and assessing: A revision of Bloom's taxonomy of educational objectives.* New York: Longman.

Anderson, A., & Lynch, T. (1988). *Listening.* Oxford: Oxford University Press.

Andrade, M. S., & Evans, W. N. (2013). Principles and Practices for Response in Second Language Writing: Developing Self-regulated Learners. *Applied Linguistics*, 35(2), 234–237.

Anthony, L. (2018). *Introducing English for Specific Purposes.* Abingdon: Routledge.

Bahrani, T., & Soltani, R. (2012). How to Teach Speaking Skill? *Journal of Education and Practice*, 3(2), 25–29.

Bárcena, E., Read, T., & Arús, J. (2014). On LSPs in the Digital Era. In E. Bárcena, T. Read, & J. Arús (Eds.), *Languages for Specific Purposes in the Digital Era*, v-ix. New York: Springer.

Barron, B., & Darling-Hammond, L. (2008). *Teaching for Meaningful Learning. A Review of Research on Inquiry-Based and Cooperative Learning*. Retrieved from https://files.eric.ed.gov/fulltext/ED539399.

Barros García, P., & Barros García, M. J. (2008). El profesor de ELE: factores que influyen en su formación. *Actas del XIX Congreso Internacional de la Asociación para la Enseñanza del Español como Lengua Extranjera (ASELE)*, 267–276.

Barrows, H. S. (2000). *Problem-Based Learning Applied to Medical Education*. Springfield IL: Southern Illinois University Press.

Basturkmen, H. (2006). *Ideas and Options in English for Specific Purposes*. Mahwah, NJ: Lawrence Erlbaum.

Basturkmen, H. (2010). *Developing Courses in English for Specific Purposes*. New York: Palgrave Macmillan.

Basturkmen, H. (2014). LSP Teacher Education: Review of Literature and Suggestions for the Research Agenda. *Ibérica*, 28, 17–34.

Basturkmen, H. (2017). ESP Teacher Education Needs. *Language Teaching*, 1–13.

Basturkmen, H. (2019). ESP Teacher Education Needs. *Language Teaching*, 52(3), 318–330.

Battersby, M. (1999). *So, What's a Learning Outcome Anyway?* Vancouver: Centre for Curriculum, Transfer and Technology, British Columbia Ministry of Advanced Education.

Beauchamp, C., & Thomas, L. (2009). Understanding Teacher Identity: An Overview of Issues in the Literature and Implications for Teacher Education. *Cambridge Journal of Education*, 39(2), 175–189.

Beck, I., McKeown, M., & Kucan, L. (2013). *Bringing Words to Life: Robust Vocabulary Instruction by Beck, McKeown & Kucan* (2nd ed.). New York: Guilford Press.

Beijaard, D., Meijer, P. C., & Verloop, N. (2004). Reconsidering Research on Teachers' Professional Identity. *Teaching and Teacher Education*, 20(2), 107–128.

Belcher, D. (2006). English for Specific Purposes: Teaching to Perceived Needs and Imagined Futures in Worlds of Work, Study, and Everyday Life. *TESOL Quarterly*, 40, 133–156.

Belcher, D., & Lukkarila, L. (2011). Identity in the ESP Context: Putting the Learner Front and Center in Needs Analysis. In D. Belcher, A. Johns, & B. Paltridge (Eds.), *New Directions for English for Specific Purposes Research*. Ann Arbor: University of Michigan Press, 73–93.

Belcher, D. (2013). The Future of ESP Research: Resources for Access and Choice. In B. Paltridge & S. Starfield (Eds.), *The Handbook of English for Specific Purposes*. Oxford: Blackwell, 536–551.

Bell, S. (2010). Project-Based Learning for the 21st Century: Skills for the Future. *The Clearing House: A Journal of Educational Strategies, Issues and Ideas*, 83(2), 39–43.

Blaxter, L., Hughes, C., & Tight, M. (2006). *How to Research*. New York: McGraw-Hill Education.

Block, D. (1990). Some Thoughts on DIY Materials Design. *ELT Journal*, 45/3, 211–217.

Bloom, B. S. & Krathwohl, D. R. (1956). *Taxonomy of Educational Objectives: The Classification of Educational Goals, by a Committee of College and University Examiners. Handbook I: Cognitive Domain.* NY: Longmans, Green.

Bocanegra-Valle, A. (2010). Evaluating and Designing Materials for the ESP Classroom. In M. F. Ruiz-Garrido, J. C. Palmer-Silveira, & I. Fortanet-Goméz (Eds.), *English for Professional and Academic Purposes*. New York: Rodopi, 143–168.

Bocanegra-Valle, A. (2016). Needs Analysis for Curriculum Design. In K. Hyland & P. Shaw (Eds.), *The Routledge Handbook of English for Academic Purposes*. Abingdon: Routledge, 560–576.

Bocanegra-Valle, A. & Basturkmen, H. (2019). Investigating the Teacher Education Needs of Experienced ESP Teachers in Spanish Universities. *Ibérica*, 38, 127–149.

Bojovic, M. (2010). *Reading Skills and Reading Comprehension in English for Specific Purposes*. The International Conference on the Importance of Learning Professional Foreign Languages for Communication between Cultures 2010. Retrieved from https://www.researchgate.net/publication/261213403_Reading_Skills_and_Reading_Comprehension_in_English_for_Specific_Purposes

Bošnjak Terzić, B. (2018). *Samoregulirano učenje vokabulara u engleskom jeziku struke* [Self-regulated vocabulary learning in English for specific purposes]. Doctoral dissertation, University of Zagreb.

Bošnjak Terzić, B. & Pavičić Takač, V. (2020). Cognitive and Metacognitive Vocabulary Learning Strategies: Insights from Learning Diaries. In M. Dodigovic & M. Agustin-Llach (Eds.), *Vocabulary in Curriculum Planning.* Grad Cham: Palgrave Macmillan, 121–142.

Brookfield, S. D. (1994). Self-Directed Learning. In YMCA George Williams College, *ICE301 Lifelong Learning, Unit 1 Approaching Lifelong Learning.* London: YMCA George Williams College. Retrieved from: https://infed.org/mobi/self-directed-learning/.

Brown, J. D. (2001). *Using Surveys in Language Programs.* Cambridge: Cambridge University Press.

Brown, J. D. (2016). *Introducing Needs Analysis and English for Specific Purposes.* Abingdon: Routledge.

Browne, C., Culligan, B., & Phillips, J. (2013). *The New General Service List.* Retrieved from http://www.newgeneralservicelist.org

Brudermann, C., Mattioli, M. A., Roussel, A. M., & Sarré, C. (2016). Le secteur des langues pour spécialistes d'autres disciplines dans les universités françaises: résultats d'une enquête nationale menée par la SAES. *Recherche et pratiques pédagogiques en langues de spécialité. Cahiers de l'Apliut*, 35(spécial 1),48p.

Bukor, E. (2015). Exploring Teacher Identity from a Holistic Perspective: Reconstructing and Reconnecting Personal and Professional Selves. *Teachers and Teaching: Theory and Practice*, 21(3), 305–327.

Campion, G. C. (2016). 'The Learning Never Ends': Exploring Teachers' Views on the Transition from General English to EAP. *Journal of English for Academic Purposes*, 23, 59–70.

Carneiro, R. (2007). The Big Picture: Understanding Learning and Meta-Learning Challenges. *European Journal of Education. Research, Development and Policy*, 42(2), 151–172.

Catapult Project. http://catapult-project.eu/wp-content/uploads/2019/05/O1_Full_Report_Final_CATAPULT.pdf

Causa, M., Derivy-Plard M., Lutrand-Pezant M. et Narcy-Combes J.P.(dir.), Les Langues dans l'enseignement supérieur. Quels contenus pour les filières non linguistiques ? , *Recherche et pratiques pédagogiques en langues de spécialité*, Vol. XXXII N° 2 | 2013, 158-163.

Cedefop (2014). *Terminology of European Education and Training Policy: A Selection of 130 Key Terms* (second edition). Luxembourg: Publications Office. Retrieved from http://www.cedefop.europa.eu/en/publications-and-resources/publications/4117

Cedefop (2017). *Defining, Writing and Applying Learning Outcomes. A European Handbook.* Luxembourg: Publications Office of the European Union.

Cervero, R. (1999). Strategic Choices for the Academy: How Demand for Lifelong Learning Will Re-Create Higher Education. *The Journal of Higher Education*, 70(6), 735–737. https://doi.org/10.2307/2649175

Cestero Mancera, A. M. (2011). La formación del profesor de ELE desde la universidad, grado y máster. *Actas de los II Encuentros de ELE*. Comillas: Fundación Comillas y Ministerio de Educación de España, 43–50.

Chapelle, C. A. & Hegelheimer, V. (2004). The Language Teacher in the 21st Century. In S. Fotos & C. Browne (Eds.), *New Perspectives on CALL for Second Language Classrooms*. Mahwah, NJ; London: Lawrence Erlbaum Associates, 299–316.

Charles, M. & Pecorari, D. (2016). *Introducing English for Academic Purposes*. London: Routledge.

Chostelidou, D., Griva, E., & Tsakiridou, E. (2009). A Record of the Training Needs of ESP Practitioners in Vocational Education. *Selected Papers from the 18th ISTAL*, 131–143.

Chi, T. M. (2015). *Learners' Potential Problems in Listening and Criteria of Selecting Recorded Materials*. Retrieved from http://nnkt.ueh.edu.vn/wp-content/uploads/2015/12/16-2015.pdf

Chung, T. M. & Nation, P. (2004). Identifying Technical Vocabulary. *System*, 32, 251–263.

Çoban, Z. (2001). *Experienced and Novice English Language Teachers' Use of Textbook Adaptation Strategies at Gazi University*. Master's Thesis, Bilkent University, Ankara, Turkey.

Codó, E. (2008). Interviews and Questionnaires. In L. Wei & M. G. Moyer (Eds.), *The Blackwell Guide to Research Methods in Bilingualism and Multilingualism*. Oxford: Blackwell, 158–176.

Commission Européenne. (2015). *La profession enseignante en Europe : Pratiques, perceptions et politiques*. Luxembourg: Office des Publications de l'Union Européenne.

Consejo de Europa. (2002). *Marco común europeo de referencia para las lenguas: Aprendizaje, enseñanza, evaluación.* Madrid: Secretaría General Técnica del MEC – Grupo Anaya – Instituto Cervantes.

Consejo Europeo. (2007). *Conclusiones del Consejo y de los representantes de los gobiernos de los Estados miembros sobre la mejora de la calidad de la educación del profesorado.* Diario Oficial de la Unión Europea 207/C 300/07, de 12.12.2007.

Council of the European Union) (2002). Council Resolution of 14 February 2002 on the promotion of linguistic diversity and language learning in the framework of the implementation of the objectives of the European Year of Languages 2001. Official Journal C050 , 23/02/2002, pp. 0001 – 0002. Retrieved 10 January 2021 from https://eur-lex.europa.eu/legal-content/HU/TXT/?uri=CELEX:32002G0223(01)

CoE (Council of the European Union) (2008). "Council Resolution of 21 November 2008 on a European strategy for multilingualism", Official Journal of the European Union, C 320 (16.12.2008), pp. 1-3.

Coolahan, J. (2002). La formation et la carrière des enseignants à l'ère de l'apprentissage à vie. *Documents de travail de l'OCDE sur l'éducation*, n°2, Éditions OCDE, Paris, https://doi.org/10.1787/226408628504.

Costa, A. L. & Kallick, B. (2004). *Assessment Strategies for Self-Directed Learning.* Thousand Oak, California: Corwin Press.

Coxhead, A. (2000). *Academic Word List.* Retrieved from https://www.wgtn.ac.nz/lals/resources/academicwordlist

Coxhead, A. (2013). Vocabulary and ESP. In B. Paltridge & S. Starfi (Eds.), *The Handbook of English for Specific Purposes* (1st ed.). John Wiley & Sons, Inc.

Coxhead, A. (2018). *Vocabulary and English for Specific Purposes Research: Quantitative and Qualitative Perspectives.* London, England: Routledge.

Croom Helm Cross, D. (1998). *Teach English.* Oxford: Oxford University Press.

Darling-Hammond, L. (2017). Teacher Education Around the World: What Can we Learn from International Practice? *European Journal of Teacher Education*, 40(3), 291–309.

Davies, P. & Pearse, E. (2000). *Success in English Teaching.* Oxford: Oxford University Press.

Davies, M. (2015). A Model of Critical Thinking in Higher Education. In M. B. Paulsen (Ed.), *Higher Education: Handbook of Theory and Research*. Dordrecht, Netherlands: Springer, 41–92.

Day, J. & Krzanowski, M. (2011). *Teaching English for Specific Purposes: An Introduction*. Cambridge: Cambridge University Press.

De Chazal, E. (2014). *English for Academic Purposes*. Oxford: Oxford University Press.

De Santiago Guervós, J. (2008). Qué enseñar a los que van a enseñar. *Actas del XIX Congreso Internacional de la Asociación para la Enseñanza del Español como Lengua Extranjera* (ASELE), 101–106.

Deyrich, M.-C. (2019). Professionnalisation et formation des enseignants du secteur LANSAD: spécificités, enjeux et défis. In C. Chaplier & A.-M. Connell (Eds.), *Épistémologie à usage didactique Langue de spécialité (secteur LANSAD)*, 199–222.

Deyrich, M.-C., Bian, B., & Begin-Caouette, O. (2016). Internationalisation de la formation des enseignants du supérieur: contextes et impacts. *Éducation comparée*, 15, 7–17.

Deyrich, M.-C. & Leroy, N. (2017). *Teacher Training for LSP: Strategies, Issues and Challenges, 1st International Conference of the Slovene Association of LSP Teachers, Languages for Specific Purposes: Opportunities and Challenges of Teaching and Research*. Rimske Terme Thermal Resort, Slovenia, 18–20 May 2017.

Deyrich, M.-Ch. & Stunnel, K. (2014). Language Teacher Education Models: New Issues and Challenges. In J. de Dios Martinez Agudo (Ed.), *English as a Foreign Language Teacher Education. Current Perspectives and Challenges*. Amsterdam, New York: Rodopi, 84–102.

Ding, A. & Bruce, I. (2017). *The English for Academic Purposes Practitioner. Operating on the Edge of Academia*. Cham: Palgrave Macmillan.

Ding, A. & Campion, G. C. (2016). EAP Teacher Development. In K. Hyland & P. Shaw (Eds.), *The Routledge Handbook of English for Academic Purposes*. Abingdon: Routledge, 547–559.

Dirckx, J. (1983). *The Language of Medicine, Its Evolution, Structure and Dynamics*. New York: Praeger.

Dörnyei, Z. (2003). *Questionnaires in Second Language Research. Construction, Administration, and Processing*. Mahwah, NJ: Lawrence Erlbaum.

Dörnyei, Z. (2016) [2007]. *Research Methods in Applied Linguistics*. Oxford: Oxford University Press.

Dudley-Evans, T. & St John, M. J. (1998). *Developments in English for Specific Purposes. A Multi-disciplinary Approach*. Cambridge: Cambridge University Press.

Du Toit-Brits, C. (2018). Towards a Transformative and Holistic Continuing Self-directed Learning Theory. *South African Journal of Higher Education*, 32(4), 51–65.

Duch, B. J., Groh, S. E., & Allen, D. E. (2001). Why Problem-Based Learning? A Case Study of Institutional Change in Undergraduate Education. In B. Duch, S. Groh, & D. Allen (Eds.), *The Power of Problem-Based Learning*. Sterling, AV: Stylus, 3–11.

Dumbrăvescu, D. & Merino Mañueco, S. (2013). La formación del profesorado en ELE en el marco de las competencias clave del profesorado de lenguas segundas y extranjeras del Instituto Cervantes. *Actas del III Congreso Internacional del Español en Castilla y León*, 367–374.

Dressman, M. (2020). Multimodality and Language Learning. In M. Dressman & W. S. Sadler (Eds.), *The Handbook of Informal Language Learning*. New Jersey: John Wiley & Sons Ltd, 39–55.

Egger M, Zellweger-Zähner T, Schneider M, Junker C, Lengeler C, Antes G. (1997) Language bias in randomised controlled trials published in English and German. *Lancet*. 2;350(9074):326-9. doi: 10.1016/S0140-6736(97)02419-7. PMID: 9251637.

Ellis, R. (1996). Does It 'Work'? Evaluating Tasks in Language Teaching. *The Language Teacher*, Issue 20.9. Accessed at https://jalt-publications.org/old_tlt/files/96/sept/eval.html.

Ellis, R. (2003). *Task-Based Language Learning and Teaching*. Oxford: Oxford University Press.

Ellis, R. (2009). Task-Based Language Teaching: Sorting Out the Misunderstandings. *International Journal of Applied Linguistics*, 19, 221–246.

Ennis, R. H. (1985). Critical Thinking and the Curriculum. *National Forum: Phi Kappa Phi Journal*, 65(1), 28–31.

Esteve, O. (2004). Nuevas perspectivas en la formación de profesorado de lenguas: Hacia el aprendizaje reflexivo o aprender a través de la práctica. *Actas de las Jornadas Didácticas de Español como Lengua Extranjera del Instituto Cervantes en Bremen*, 8–21.

EC (European Commission) (2012). Language competences for employability, mobility and growth, Accompanying the document. Communication
from the Commission. "Rethinking Education: Investing in skills for better socio-economic outcomes". SWD(2012) 372 final. Brussels: European
Commission

European Commission. (2013). *High Level Group on the Modernisation of
Higher Education: Report to the European Commission on Improving the
Quality of Teaching and Learning in Europe's Higher Education Institutions.*
Publications Office of the European Union. Available at: https://publicati
ons.europa.eu/en/publication-detail/-/publication/fbd4c2aa-aeb7-41ac-
ab4c-a94feea9eb1f.

European Commission. (2017). *Communication from the Commission to
the European Parliament, the Council, the European Economic and Social
Committee and the Committee of the Regions. A Renewed EU Agenda for
Higher Education.* Available at: https://www.cmepius.si/wp-content/uplo
ads/2014/02/Renewed-EU-agenda-for-higher-education_Accompany
ing-document.pdf (31 January 2019).

Faure, P. (2010), Des discours de la médecine multiples et variés à la langue
médicale unique et universelle , *ASp*, 58 , 73–86.

Faure, P. (2014). Enjeux d'une professionnalisation de la formation des
enseignants de langue(s) de spécialité: exemples de l'anglais et du français
de la médecine. *Recherche et pratiques pédagogiques en langues de spécialité,*
Vol. XXXIII N°1 |, 50–65.

Faure, P. (2018). From Accouchement to Agony: A Lexicological Analysis of
Words of French Origin in the Modern English Language of Medicine.
Lexis [en ligne], 11, <http://journals.openedition.org/lexis/1171>.

Flowerdew, L. (2013). Needs Analysis and Curriculum Development. In
B. Paltridge & S. Starfield (Eds.), *The Handbook of English for Specific
Purposes.* Oxford: Blackwell, 325–346.

Fortanet-Gómez, I. & Räisänen, C. (2008). *ESP in European
Higher Education: Integrating Language and Content.* Amsterdam/
Philadelphia: John Benjamins.

Gao, X. (2008). Teachers' Professional Vulnerability and Cultural
Tradition: A Chinese Paradox. *Teaching and Teacher Education*, 24(1),
154–165.

García-Romeu, J. y Jiménez, M. (2005). *Análisis de necesidades (II), una
propuesta para negociar los objetivos del curso.* Madrid: Didactired, Centro

Virtual Cervantes. http://cvc.cervantes.es/aula/didactired/anteriores/enero_05/17012005.htm

Garcia Romeu, J. (2006). *Análisis de necesidades para la programación de cursos de fines específicos. Actas del Tercer congreso internacional es Espanol para fines específicos (Ciefe) Utrecht.* II. Aplicaciones y experiencias didácticas Centro Virtual Cervantes, 145–161. https://cvc.cervantes.es/ensenanza/biblioteca_ele/ciefe/pdf/03/cvc_ciefe_03_0014.pdf

Gatehouse, K. (2001). Key Issues in English for Specific Purposes (ESP) Curriculum Development. *The Internet TESL Journal,* VII(10).

Gaussel, M. (2021). Croyances et connaissances pour enseigner. *Édubref: L'essentiel pour comprendre les questions éducatives.* Lyon: ENS.

Ghafournia, N. & Sabet, S. A. (2014). The Most Prominent Roles of an ESP Teacher. *International Education Studies,* 7(11), 1–9.

Gilman, R. A. & Moody, L. M. (1984). What Practitioners Say About Listening: Research Implications for the Classroom. *Foreign Language Annals,* 17, 331–34.

Goigoux, R., Riou, J. & Serres, G. (2015). La régulation de l'action des enseignants. *Travail et Apprentissages,* 15, 66-83. https://doi.org/10.3917/ta.015.0066

Gómez de Enterría, J. (2015). El español lengua de especialidad con fines profesionales. *Les cahiers du GÉRES,* revista del Groupe d'Étude et de Recherche en Espagnol de Spécialité, 7, 49–60.

Gold Standard PBL: Essential Project Design Elements Buck Institute for Education 2015. Retrieved from https://www.pblworks.org/blog/gold-standard-pbl-essential-project-design-elements

Goldman, B. (2014). *The Secret Language of Doctors.* Chicago: Triumph Books.

Gollin-Kies, S. (2014). Methods Reported in ESP Research Articles: A Comparative Survey of Two Leading Journals. *English for Specific Purposes,* 36, 27–34.

González, M. V. & Atienza, E. (2010). El docente reflexivo: ventajas e inconvenientes del portafolio docente. *Revista Lenguaje,* 38(1), 35–64.

Górska-Poręcka, B. (2013). The Role of Teacher Knowledge in ESP Course Design. *Studies in Logic, Grammar and Rhetoric,* 34(47), 27–42.

Grant, N. (1987). *Making the Most of Your Textbook.* Boston: Addison-Wesley.

Graves, K. (2000). *Designing Language Courses: A Guide for Teachers.* Boston: Heinle & Heinle.

Grosse, C. U., & Voght, G. M. (2012). The Continuing Evolution of Languages for Specific Purposes. *The Modern Language Journal*, 96, 190–202.

Grossman, P., Pupik Dean, C. G., Kavanagh, S. S., & Herrmann, Z. (2019). Preparing Teachers for Project-Based Teaching. *Phi Delta Kappan*, 100(7), 43–48.

Gu, P.Y. (2005). *Vocabulary Learning Strategies in the Chinese EFL Context*. Singapore: Marshall Cavendish Academic.

Gu, P. Y. & Johnson, R. K. (1996). Vocabulary Learning Strategies and Language Learning Outcomes. *Language Learning*, 46, 643–679.

Gutiérrez Araus, M. L. (2008). Nuevos tiempos y nuevos retos en la formación del profesor de español como segunda lengua. *Actas del XIX Congreso Internacional de la Asociación para la Enseñanza del Español como Lengua Extranjera* (ASELE), 77–87.

Hálasz, G., Looney, J., Michel, A., & Sliwka, A. (2018). *Des enseignants mieux préparés et plus efficaces : pistes d'action pour la qualité*. Luxembourg: Office des Publications de l'Union Européenne.

Hall, D. R. (2013). Teacher Education for LSP. In C. A. Chapelle (Ed.), *The Encyclopedia of Applied Linguistics*. Oxford: Wiley-Blackwell, 5537–5542.

Harden, R. (2002). Learning Outcomes and Instructional Objectives: Is There a Difference? *Medical Teacher*, 24(2), 151–155.

Heck, D., Grimmett, H., & Willis, L. (2019). Teacher Educators Using Cogenerative Dialogue to Reclaim Professionalism. In A. Gutierrez, J. Fox, & C. Alexander (Eds.), *Professionalism and Teacher Education: Voices from Policy and Practice*. Singapore: Springer, 137–156.

Hiemstra, R. (1994). Self-Directed Learning. In T. Husen & T. N. Postlethwaite (Eds.), *The International Encyclopedia of Education* (2nd ed.). Oxford: Pergamon Press.

Hismanoglu, M. & Hismanoglu, S. (2011). Task-Based Language Teaching: What Every EFL Teacher Should Do. *Procedia Social and Behavioral Sciences*, 15, 46–52.

Hmelo-Silver, C. E. (2004). Problem-Based Learning: What and How Do Students Learn? *Educational Psychology Review*, 16(3)235–266.

Hmelo-Silver, C. E. & Eberbach, C. (2012). Learning Theories and Problem-Based Learning. In S. Bridges, C. McGrath, & T. Whitehill

(Eds.), *Researching Problem-Based Learning in Clinical Education: The Next Generation*. New York: Springer, 3–17.

Hoque, M. E. (2016). Three Domains of Learning: Cognitive, Affective and Psychomotor. *The Journal of EFL Education and Research* (JEFLER), 2(2). Retrieved from file:///C:/Users/www/Downloads/ThreeDomainsofLearning-CognitiveAffectiveandPsychomotor.pdf.

Huang, L.-S. (2018). A Call for Critical Dialogue: EAP Assessment from the Practitioner's Perspective in Canada. *Journal of English for Academic Purposes*, 35, 70–84.

Huhta, M., Vogt, K., Johnson, E., & Tulkki, H. (2013). *Needs Analysis for Language Course Design. A Holistic Approach to ESP*. Cambridge: Cambridge University Press.

Humbley, J. (2001). La terminologie dans les langues de spécialité. In M. Mémet & M. Petit (Eds.), *L'anglais de spécialité en France. Mélanges en l'honneur de Michel Perrin*. Collection ASP – GERAS Editeur, 47–53.

Hutchinson, T. & Waters, A. (1987). *English for Specific Purposes. A Learning-centred Approach*. Cambridge: Cambridge University Press.

Hüttner, J., Smit, U. & Mehlmauer-Larcher, B. (2009). ESP teacher education at the interface of theory and practice: introducing a model of mediated corpus-based genre analysis. *System*, 37(1), 99–109.

Hyland, K. (2006). *English for Academic Purposes*. London: Routledge.

Hyland, K. (2008). The Author Replies. *TESOL Quarterly*, 42, 113–114.

INCLUDE (2016d). *Roadmap for Integration of Language Learning in Inclusion Policies in Europe. Education, Audiovisual and Culture Executive Agency of the European Union (EACEA)*. Project Number 530938-LLP-1-2012-1-IT-KA2-KA2NW. Brussels: European Commission. Retrieved 10 July 2017 from http://www.ardaa.fr/wp-content/uploads/2017/07/D9-ROADMAP.pdf.

Instituto Cervantes. (2012). *Las competencias clave del profesorado de lenguas segundas y extranjeras*. Alcalá de Henares: Dirección académica del IC.

Islam, C. & Mares, C. (2003). A Framework for Materials Writing. In B. Tomlinson (Ed.), *Developing Materials for Language Teaching: Chapters from the First Edition*. London: Bloomsbury, 86–100.

John, P., Greenwood, R., Jurković, V., Kereković, S., & Kic-Drgas, J. (2019). *Identification and Analysis of LSP Teacher Training Programmes in*

Europe. Proceedings of the 3rd ESP conference. Liverpool: Liverpool Hope University.

Johns, A. M. & Price-Machado, D. (2001). English for Specific Purposes (ESP): Tailoring Courses to Students' Needs – And to the Outside World. In M. Celce-Murcia (Ed.), *Teaching English as a Second or Foreign Language* (3rd ed.). Boston: Heinle and Heinle, 43–54.

Jendrych, E. (2013). Developments in ESP Teaching. *Studies in Logic, Grammar and Rhetoric,* 34(1), 43–58.

Johnson, D. W., Johnson, R. T., & Smith, K. A. (1991). Cooperative Learning: Increasing College Faculty Instructional Productivity. *ASHE-ERIC Higher Education Report,* No. 4, George Washington University.

Jurkovič, V. (2005). *Ed. Guide to Problem-Based Learning.* Ljubljana: Slovene Association of LSP Teachers

Jurkovič, V. (2010). Language Learner Strategies and Linguistic Competence as Factors Affecting Achievement Test Scores in English for Specific Purposes. *TESOL Journal,* 1(4), 449–469.

Kanno, Y. & Stuart, C. (2011). Learning to Become a Second Language Teacher: Identities-in-practice. *The Modern Language Journal,* 95(2), 236–252.

Kakoulli Constantinou, E., Papadima-Sophocleous, S., & Souleles, N. (2019). Finding the Way Through the ESP Maze: Designing an ESP Teacher Education Programme. In S. Papadima-Sophocleous, E. Kakoulli Constantinou & C. N. Giannikas (Eds.), *ESP Teaching and Teacher Education: Current Theories and Practices,* 27–46. Research-publishing.net. Available at https://research-publishing.net/book?10.14705/rpnet.2019.33.9782490057450.

Kavaliauskiene, G. & Suchanova, J. (2010). "Read-to-write-tasks" in English for Specific Purposes Classes. *Santalka. Filologija. Edukologija,* 18(4), 57–64.

Kayi, H. (2006). Teaching Speaking: Activities to Promote Speaking in a Second Language. *The Internet TESL Journal,* 12(11). Retrieved from http://iteslj.org/; http://iteslj.org/Techniques/Kayi-TeachingSpeaking.html.

Keeley, B. (2007). *Le capital humain – Comment le savoir détermine notre vie.* Paris: Éditions de l'Organisation de Coopération et de Développement Économique. (Les Essentiels de l'OCDE).

Kelchtermans, G. (2009). Who I Am in How I Teach is the Message: Self-understanding, Vulnerability and Reflection. *Teachers and Teaching*, 15(2), 257–272.

Kelly, M., Grenfell, M., Allan, R., Kriza, C., & McEvoy, W. (2004). *European Profile for Language Teacher Education – A Frame of Reference*. Southampton: University of Southampton.

Kennedy, C. (1983). An ESP Approach to EFL/ESL Teacher Training. *The ESP Journal*, 2, 73–85.

Kilpatrick, S., Barrett, M., & Jones, T. (2003). Defining Learning Communities. *International Education Research Conference AARE – NZARE*. Retrieved from: www.aare.edu.au/03pap/jon03441.

Kırkgöz, Y. (2018). Recent Developments in ESP/EAP/EMI Context. In Y. Kırkgöz & K. Dikilitaş (Eds.), *Key Issues in English for Specific Purposes in Higher Education*. Cham: Springer, 1–10.

Kırkgöz, Y. (2019). ESP in Teacher Education: A Case Study. In S. Papadima-Sophocleous, E. Kakoulli Constantinou, & C. N. Giannikas (Eds.), *ESP Teaching and Teacher Education: Current Theories and Practices*, 13–26. Research-publishing.net. Available at https://doi.org/10.14705/rpnet.2019.33.923 (13 February 2021).

Klund, S. (n.d.). Reading Across the Curriculum. In *Professional Learning Board's Online Continuing Education Course for Teachers*. Retrieved from https://k12teacherstaffdevelopment.com/tlb/the-importance-of-pre-reading-activities/

Knezović, A. (2016). Rethinking the Languages for Specific Purposes Syllabus in the 21st Century: Topic-Centered or Skills-Centered. *International Journal of Information and Communication Engineering*, 10(1), 1–16.

Knowles, M. S. (1975). *Self-directed Learning*. New York: Association Press.

Kokotsaki, D., Menzies, V., & Wiggins, A. (2016). Project-Based Learning: A Review of the Literature. *Improving Schools*, 19(3), 267–277.

Krajcik, J. & Blumenfeld, P. (2006). Project-Based Learning. In R. K. Sawyer (Ed.), *The Cambridge Handbook of the Learning Sciences*. New York, NY: Cambridge University Press, 317–333.

Krajcik, J. S. & Shin, N. (2014). Project-Based Learning. In R. K. Sawyer (Ed.), *The Cambridge Handbook of the Learning Sciences* (2nd ed.). New York, NY: Cambridge University Press, 275–297.

Krashen, S. D. (1982). *Principles and Practice in Second Language Acquisition.* Oxford: Pergamon Press Inc.

Krashen, S. (1985). *The Input Hypothesis: Issues and Implications.* New York: Longman.

Krzanowski, M. (2013). Self-Designed Teaching Materials for the Enhanced Harmony in the ESP Classroom: A Practitioner's Perspective. A presentation delivered at the *TESOL 2013 EPIS-CALLIS-VDMIS Conference,* Dallas, 23/03/2013.

Krzanowski, M. (2019). Creative Ways of Adapting and Using Authentic Materials in the ESP Classroom. *Atlanta TESOL Convention,* 12–15 March 2019.

Kubanyiova, M. & Crookes, G. (2016). Re-visioning the Roles, Tasks, and Contribution of Language Teachers in the Multilingual Era of Language Education Research and Practice. *The Modern Language Journal,* 100(supplement), 117–118.

Lagarde, C. (2013), Un hispanisme en chantier, in , Transversalité et visibilité disciplinaires : les nouveaux défis de l'hispanisme, Christian LAGARDE et Philippe RABATÉ (eds.), HispanismeS, n°2 (juin 2013)

Lagarde, C. & Rabaté P. (2013) (eds), Transversalité et visibilité disciplinaires : les nouveaux défis de l'hispanisme, *HispanismeS,* n°2.

Lave, J. & Wenger, E. (2012). *Situated Learning: Legitimate Peripheral Participation.* Cambridge: Cambridge University Press.

Leong, L. M. & Masoumeh Ahmadi, S. (2017). An Analysis of Factors Influencing Learners' English Speaking Skill. *International Journal of Research in English Education,* 2;134–41. Retrieved from http://ijreeonline.com/files/site1/user_files_68bcd6/sma1357-A-10-26-1-fefa0eb.pdf

Lison, C. (2018). COMPTE-RENDU – Journée d'étude – Fabrique Pédagogique – 18/10/2018 http://www.cue-aquitaine.fr/docs/fabrique-pedagogique/CR_journee_etude_FP_18.10.2018.pdf

Littlewood, W. (2004). The Task-Based Approach: Some Questions and Suggestions. *ELT Journal* 58/4, October, 319–326.

Long, M. H. (1985). Input and Second Language Acquisition Theory. In S. Gass & C. Madden (Eds.), Input in Second Language Acquisition (pp. 377-393). Rowley, Mass.: Newbury House.

Long, M. H. (2005). Methodological Issues in Learner Needs Analysis. In M. H. Long (Ed.), *Second Language Needs Analysis*. New York, NY: Cambridge University Press, 19–76.

Loyens, S. M. M., Magda, J., & Rikers, R. M. J. P. (2008). Self-Directed Learning in Problem-Based Learning and Its Relationships with Self-Regulated Learning. *Educational Psychology Review*, 20, 411–427.

Mackiewicz, W. (2002, May). Lifelong Foreign Language Learning. In *European Seminar on Foreign Language Learning Needs in Education Systems*, 5–7. http://userpage.fu-berlin.de/elc/docs/Mackiewicz-Valen cia.pdf

Majhanovich, S. & Deyrich, M. (2017). Language Learning to Support Active Social Inclusion: Issues and Challenges for Lifelong Learning. *International Review of Education*, 63, 435–452 (2017). https://doi.org/10.1007/s11159-017-9656-z

Maley, A. (2003). Squaring the Circle – Reconciling Materials as Constraint with Materials as Empowerment. In B. Tomlinson (Ed.), *Developing Materials for Language Teaching: Chapters from the First Edition*. London: Bloomsbury, 379–402.

Marra, M. (2013). English in the Workplace. In B. Paltridge & S. Starfield (Eds.), *The Handbook of English for Specific Purposes*, 175–192. Hoboken: Wiley-Blackwell.

Marrero, J. E. (2010). Escenarios, saberes y teorías implícitas del profesorado. *El pensamiento reencontrado*. Barcelona: Octaedro Universidad, 9–47.

Martín Peris, E. (2009). El perfil del profesor de español como lengua extranjera: necesidades y tendencias. *Monográficos MarcoELE*, 8, 167–180.

Masuhara, H. (2004). Materials Adaptation. In B. Tomlinson & H. Masuhara (Eds.), *Developing Language Course Material*. RELC Portfolio Series, 11, 1–7. Singapore: RELC.

Mateva, G., North, B., Rossner, R., Tashevska, S., &Vitanova, A. (2013). *La grille de compétences EPG. Guide d'utilisation*. Bruxelles: Union Européenne (Programme de formation et d'éducation tout au long de la vie).

McDonough, J. & Shaw, C. (2003). *Materials and Methods in ELT* (2nd ed.). Maine: Blackwell Publishing.

McDonough, J., Shaw, C., & Masuhara, H. (2013). *Materials Evaluation in EFL: A Teacher's Guide* (3rd ed.). Hoboken, New Jersey: Wiley-Blackwell.

McLoughlin, C. & Lee, M. J. W. (2008). The 3 P's of Pedagogy for the Networked Society: Personalization, Participation, and Productivity. *International Journal of Teaching and Learning in Higher Education*, 20(1), 10–27.

Meyer, B., Haywood, N., Sachdev, D., & Faraday, S. (2008). Independent Learning: Literature Review (Research Rep. No. DCSF-RR051). London: Learning and Skills Network.

Moreno Fernández, F. (2011). *¿Qué es ser un buen profesor o una buena profesora de ELE?* Alcalá de Henares: IC (Departamento de Formación de Profesores del Instituto Cervantes).

Muhlise Cosgun, O. (2017). The Effectiveness of PowerPoint Presentations and Conventional Lectures on Pedagogical Content Knowledge Attainment. *Education and Teaching International*, 54/5, 503–510.

Munby, J. (1978). *Communicative Syllabus Design*. Cambridge: Cambridge University Press.

Nation, I. S. P. (1993). Vocabulary Size, Growth and Use. In R. Schreuder & B. Weltens (Eds.), *The Bilingual Lexicon*. Amsterdam/Philadelphia: John Benjamins, 115–134.

Nation, I. S. P. (2001). *Learning Vocabulary in Another Language*. Cambridge: Cambridge University Press.

Nation, I. S. P. & Macalister, J. (2010). *Language Curriculum Design*. New York & London: Routledge.

Nickerson, C. (2013). English for Specific Purposes and English as a Lingua Franca. In B. Paltridge & S. Starfield (Eds.), *The Handbook of English for Specific Purposes*. Oxford: Blackwell, 445–460.

North, B., Mateva, G., & Rossner, R. (2011). *Grille de compétences EPG* (European Profiling Grid). Bruxelles: Union Européenne (Programme de formation et d'éducation tout au long de la vie).

Nunan, D. (1988). *The Learner-Centred Curriculum: A Study in Second Language Teaching*. Cambridge: Cambridge University Press.

Nunan, D. (1995). *Language Teaching Methodology: A Textbook for Teachers*. New York: Phoenix, Ltd.

Nunan, D. (2002). Listening in Language Learning. In J. C. Richards & W. A. Renandya (Eds.), *Methodology in Language Learning: An Anthology of Current Practice*. Cambridge: Cambridge University Press, 238–241.

Nunan, D. (2004). *Task-Based Language Teaching*. Cambridge: Cambridge University Press.

O'Connell, A. M. & Chaplier, C. (2015). ESP/ASP in the Domains of Science and Law in a French Higher Education Context: Preliminary Reflections. *The European English Messenger*, 24(2), 61–76.

O'Malley, J. M. & Chamot, A. V. (1990). *Learning Strategy in Second Language Acquisition*. Cambridge: Cambridge University Press.

Ouarniki, O. (2018). Evaluation and Analysis of the Current ESP Courses. *TRANS*, 23. Available at https://www.inst.at/trans/23/evaluation-and-analysis-of-the-current-esp-courses/. Accessed 03/03/2021.

Oxford, R. L. (1990). *Language Learning Strategies: What Every Teacher Should Know*. Boston, MA: Heinle and Heinle.

Oxford, R. L. (2011a). *Teaching and Researching Language Learning Strategies*. London: Longman.

Oxford, R. L. (2011b). Strategies for Learning a Second or Foreign Language. *Language Teaching*, 44(2), 167–180.

Paltridge, B. (2013). Genre and English for Specific Purposes. In B. Paltridge & S. Starfield (Eds.), *The Handbook of English for Specific Purposes*. Hoboken: Wiley-Blackwell, 347–366.

Papadima-Sophocleous, S., Kakoulli Constantinou, E., &Giannikas, C. N. (2019). Introduction. In S. Papadima-Sophocleous, E. Kakoulli Constantinou, & C. N. Giannikas (Eds.), *ESP Teaching and Teacher Education: Current Theories and Practices*, 1–12. Research-publishing. net. Available at https://doi.org/10.14705/rpnet.2019.33.923 (13 February 2021).

Pavičić Takač, V. (2008). *Vocabulary Learning Strategies and Foreign Language Acquisition*. Clevedon, UK: Multilingual Matters Ltd.

Pellegrino, J. W. & Hilton, M. L. (2012). *Developing Transferable Knowledge and Skills in the 21st Century*. Washington, DC: National Research Council.

Pizarro, M. (2013). Nuevas tareas para el profesor de español como lengua extranjera: la reflexión sobre su concepción de la enseñanza. *Porta Linguarum*, 19, 165–178.

Porcher, L. (2004). *L'Enseignement des langues étrangères*. Paris: Hachette. 21

Moskowitz, G. (1978). *Caring and sharing in the foreign language class*. Rowley, MA: Newbury House.

Nishino, T. & M. Watanabe (2008). Classroom-oriented policies versus classroom realities in Japan. *TESOL Quarterly 42* (1), 133-138.

Norris, J. M. (2009). Task-based teaching and testing. In M.J. Long & C.J. Doughty (Eds.), *The Handbook of Language Teaching* (pp. 578-594). Chichester: Wiley Blackwell.

Nunan, D. (2003). The impact of English as a global language on educational policies and practices in the Asia-Pacific region. *TESOL Quarterly, 37* (4), 589-613.

Nunan, D. (2004). *Task-based language teaching*. Cambridge: Cambridge University Press.

Orafi, S. & S. Borg (2009). Intentions and realities in implementing communicative curriculum reform. *System, 37* (2), 243-253.

Park, S.W. & Manning, S.J. (2012). L1 vs. L2 use and classroom interaction in team-taught elementary school classes in Korea. *English Teaching, 67* (2), 105-134.

Pennycook, A. (1994). *The cultural politics of English as an International Language*. London: Longman.

Prabhu, N. S. (1987). *Second language pedagogy*. Oxford: Oxford University Press.

Pujol Berché, M. (2003). Le professeur, élément clé dans la qualité de l'enseignement. *Recherche et pratiques pédagogiques en langues de spécialité*, XXII(1), 40–53.

Rafik-Galea, S. & Wong, B. E. (2006). Vocabulary Learning Strategies Among Adult Foreign Language Learners. In W. M. Chan, K. W. Chin, & J. T. Suthiwan (Eds.), *Foreign Language Teaching in Asia and Beyond: Current Perspectives and Future Directions*. Singapore: Centre for Language Studies, 145–188.

Räsänen, A. (2008). Tuning ESP/EAP for Mobility, Employability and Expertise. In I. Fortanet-Gomez et C. A. Räisänen (Eds.), *ESP in European Higher Education. Integrating Language and Content*. AILA Applied Linguistics series 4, John Benjamins, 247–266.

Renukadevi, D. (2014). The Role of Listening in Language Acquisition; the Challenges & Strategies in Teaching Listening. *International Journal of Education and Information Studies*, 4(1), 59–63.

Reppen, R. (2002). A Genre-Based Approach to Content Writing Instruction. In J. C. Richards & W. A. Renandya (Eds.), *Methodology in Language*

Learning: An Anthology of Current Practice. Cambridge: Cambridge University Press, 321–327.

Richards, J. C. (2008). *Moving Beyond the Plateau: From Intermediate to Advanced Levels in Language Learning*. Retrieved from https://www.professorjackrichards.com/wp-content/uploads/moving-beyond-the-plateau.pdf.

Richards, J. & Lockhart, C. (1998). *Estrategias de reflexión sobre la enseñanza de idiomas*. Cambridge: Cambridge University Press.

Richards, J. & Rodgers, T. (2004). *Approaches and Methods in Language Teaching*. Cambridge: Cambridge University Press.

Richardson, P. W. & Watt, H. M. G. (2018). Teacher Professional Identity and Career Motivation: A Lifespan Perspective. In P. A. Schutz, J. Hong & D. Cross Francis (Eds.), *Research on Teacher Identity Mapping Challenges and Innovations*. Cham: Springer, 37–48.

Richer, J.-J. (2011). De l'enseignant de langue(s) au professionnel des langues. *ELA: Études de Linguistique Appliquée*, 161(1), 63–77.

Rodríguez-Piñeiro Alcalá, A. I. & García Antuña, M. (2009). Lenguas de especialidad y lenguas para fines específicos: precisiones terminológicas y conceptuales e implicaciones didácticas. *El español en contextos específicos: enseñanza e investigación*. Comillas: Fundación Comillas/ASELE, 907–932.

Ruiz de Guerrero, N. Y. & Arias Rodríguez, G. L. (2011). Reading under the ESP Approach. *Hallazgos*, 8(15), 199–211.

Ruohotie-Lyhty, M. (2016). Dependent or Independent: The Construction of the Beliefs of Newly Qualified Foreign Language Teachers. In P. Kalaja, A. M. F. Barcelos, M. Aro, & M. Ruohotie-Lyhty (Eds.), *Beliefs, Agency and Identity in Foreign Language Learning and Teaching*. London: Palgrave, 149–171.

Sabater, M. L. (2000). Aspectos de la formación del profesorado de español para fines específicos. *Actas del I Congreso Internacional de Español para Fines Específicos* (CIEFE), 184–193.

Sachs, J. (2005). Teacher Education and the Development of Professional Identity: Learning to Be a Teacher. In D. M. Pam & M. Kompf (Eds.), *Connecting Policy and Practice: Challenges for Teaching and Learning in Schools and Universities*. New York, London: Routledge, 5–21.

Samuda, V. & Bygate, M. (2008). *Tasks in Second Language Learning*. New York: Palgrave. Macmillan.

Savery, J. R. (2006). Overview of Problem-Based Learning Definitions and Distinctions. *Interdisciplinary Journal of Problem-Based Learning*, 1, 9-20

Sawyer, K. R. (2006). *The Cambridge Handbook of the Learning Sciences*. Cambridge: Cambridge University Press.

Schmidt, H. G., Rotgans, J. I., & Yew, E. H. J. (2011). The Process of Problem-Based Learning: What Works and Why. *Medical Education*, 45, 792–806.

Schmitt, N. (1997). Vocabulary Learning Strategies. In D. N. Schmitt & M. McCarthy (Eds.), *Vocabulary Description, Acquisition and Pedagogy*. Cambridge: Cambridge University Press, 199–227.

Schmitt, N. (2000). *Vocabulary in Language Teaching*. Cambridge: Cambridge University Press.

Schmitt, N. (2010). *Researching Vocabulary: A Vocabulary Research Manual*. New York: Palgrave Macmillan.

Schmitt, N., Schmitt, D., & Clapham, C. (2001). Developing and Exploring the Behavior of Two New Versions of the Vocabulary Levels Test. *Language Testing*, 18(1), 55–88.

Schutz, P. A., Nichols, S. L., & Schwenke, S. (2018). Critical Events, Emotional Episodes, and Teacher Attributions in the Development of Teacher Identities. In P. A. Schutz, J. Hong, & D. Cross Francis (Eds.), *Research on Teacher Identity Mapping Challenges and Innovations*. Cham: Springer, 49–60.

Schön, D. A. (1994). *Le praticien réflexif. A la recherche du savoir caché dans l'agir profession nel*.Traduit et adapté par J. Heynemand & D. Gagnon. Québec : Les éditions Logiques.

Scott, K. S. (2017). An Integrative Framework for Problem-Based Learning and Action Learning: Promoting Evidence-Based. Design and Evaluation in Leadership Development. *Human Resource Development Review*, 16(1), 3, 34.

Seker, M. (2015). The Use of Self-regulation Strategies by Foreign Language Learners and Its Role in Language Achievement. *Language Teaching Research*, 20(5), 600–618.

Shumin, K. (2002). Factors to Consider: Developing Adult EFL Students' Speaking Abilities. In J. C. Richards & W. A. Renandya (Eds.), *Methodology in Language Learning: An Anthology of Current Practice*. Cambridge: Cambridge University Press, 204–211.

Silverman, J., Kurtz, S., & Draper, J. (2013). *Skills for Communicating with Patients* (3rd ed.). London: Radcliff Publishing.

Stanford Encyclopedia of Philosophy (2018). John Dewey. Retrieved from: https://plato.stanford.edu/entries/dewey/.

Stes, A. &Van Petegem, P. (2013). La formation pédagogique des professeurs dans l'enseignement supérieur. *Recherche et formation* [En ligne], 67 | 2011, mis en ligne le 01 juillet 2013, consulté le 23 avril 2020. URL: http://journals.openedition.org/rechercheformation/1360; https://doi.org/10.4000/rechercheformation.1360.

Swain, M. (1995). Three Functions of Output in Second Language Learning. In G. Cook & B. Seidlhofer (Eds.), *Principles and Practice in Applied Linguistics*. Oxford: Oxford University Press, 125–144.

Swales, J. (1990):Genre Analysis: English in Academic and research settings, Cambridge, England: University Press, 260 pp.

Taillefer, G. (2008). Transformations, évolution : un regard sur la dynamique de notre métier , *Cahiers de l'APLIUT*, Vol. XXVII N° 2 | 2008, 49–65.

Taillefer, G. (2013). CLIL in Higher Education: The (Perfect?) Crossroads of ESP and Didactic Reflection. *ASp*, 63, 31–53.

Talbot, L. & Arrieu-Mutel, A. (2012). Décrire, comprendre et expliquer les pratiques d'enseignement d'un professeur de lycée. *Éducation et didactique*, 6(3) | 2012, 65–95.

Talmy, S. (2010). Qualitative Interviews in Applied Linguistics: From Research Instrument to Social Practice. *Annual Review of Applied Linguistics*, 30, 128–148.

Tano.M. (2013) L'émergence en France d'un réseau d'enseignants et enseignants-chercheurs dans le domaine de l'Espagnol sur Objectifs Spécifiques , *Actes du 41ème congrès de l'UPLEGESS*, IÉSEG École de Management, Lille, France. pp. 122–133.

Tano, M. (2016). Enseigner l'espagnol à un public ingénieur : compétences pour la professionnalisation des enseignants. *Les cahiers du GÉRES* (revue du Groupe d'Étude et de Recherche en Espagnol de Spécialité), 8, 95–121.

Tano, M. (2017a). *L'analyse des besoins langagiers en espagnol sur objectifs spécifiques : le cas des formations françaises d'ingénieurs*. Thèse de doctorat en langues, littératures et civilisations romanes, Université Paris Nanterre.

Tano, M. (2017b). État des lieux sur l'enseignement et la recherche dans le champ de l'espagnol de spécialité en France. *Les Langues Modernes,* Dossier : «Les langues de spécialité», 3, 9–20.

Tano, M. (2018). Orientaciones metodológicas y programáticas de un curso de español para fines específicos. *Crisol* (revista del Centre de Recherches Ibériques et Ibéro-américaines de l'Université Paris Nanterre), 1, 1–36.

Tano, M. (2020). *El perfil de profesores e investigadores universitarios implicados en el campo del español de especialidad.* Informe de investigación, Groupe d'Étude et de Recherche en Espagnol de Spécialité.

Tano, M. (2021a). Hacia una identificación profesional de profesores e investigadores universitarios implicados en el campo del español de especialidad. *MarcoELE: Revista de Didáctica Español Lengua Extranjera*, 32, 1–19.

Tano, M. (2021b). Balisage terminologique dans le domaine de la langue espagnole spécialisée. *HispanismeS* – Revue de la Société des Hispanistes Français, 15 (sous presse), 1–22.

Tao, J. & Gao, X. (2017). Teacher Agency and Identity Commitment in Curricular Reform. *Teaching and Teacher Education*, 63, 346–355.

Tao, J. (Tracy) & Gao, X. (Andy) (2018). Identity Constructions of ESP Teachers in a Chinese University. *English for Specific Purposes*, 49, 1–13.

Tashakkori, A. & Creswell, J. W. (2007). Editorial: The New era of Mixed Methods. *Journal of Mixed Methods Research*, 1, 3–7.

Thomas, J. W. (2000). *A Review of Research on Project-Based Learning.* San Rafael, CA: Autodesk Foundation.

Tomlinson, B. (2012). Materials Development for Language and Teaching. *Language Teaching*, 45/2, 143–179.

Tomlinson, B. (Ed.) (2006). *English Language Learning Materials: A Critical Review.* London: Continuum.

Trowler, P. & Bamber, R. (2005). Compulsory Higher Education Teacher Training: Joined-up Policies, Institutional Architectures and Enhancement Cultures. *International Journal for Academic Development*, 10(2), 79–93. https://doi.org/10.1080/13601440500281708.

Upton, T. A. (2012). LSP at 50: Looking Back, Looking Forward. *Ibérica*, 23, 9–28.

Van Der Yeught, M. (2016). A Proposal to Establish Epistemological Foundations for the Study of Specialised Languages. *Asp*, 69, 41–63.

Vandergrift, L. (2002). *Listening: Theory and Practice in Modern Foreign Language Competence.* Retrieved from https://www.llas.ac.uk/resources/gpg/67.

Vandermeeren, S. (2005). Foreign Language Need of Business Firms. In M. H. Long (Ed.), *Second Language Needs Analysis.* New York, NY: Cambridge University Press, 159–82.

Vangehuchten, L. & Moreno Bruna, A. (2015). *La enseñanza del español para fines económicos y comerciales hoy día: hacia un nuevo diseño del curso ELEFEC.* Actos del V congreso del CIEFE.

Verdía Lleó, E. (2011). De la adquisición del conocimiento al desarrollo de la competencia docente: profesionalización de los profesores de ELE. *Actas de los II Encuentros de ELE.* Comillas: Fundación Comillas y Ministerio de Educación de España, 59–70.

Vez, J. M. (1998). Enseñanza y aprendizaje de las lenguas. *Conceptos clave en Didáctica de la Lengua y la Literatura.* Barcelona: SEDLL, 75–86.

Voskamp, A., Kuiper, E., & Volman, M. (2020). Teaching Practices for Self-directed and Self-regulated Learning: Case Studies in Dutch Innovative Secondary Schools. *Educational Studies.* Retrieved from https://doi.org/10.1080/03055698.2020.1814699.

Wenger, E. (2007). *Communities of Practice: Learning, Meaning, and Identity.* Cambridge: Cambridge University Press.

West, M. (1953). *A General Service list of English Words.* London: Longman, Green & Co.

Widdowson, H. (1996). Authenticity and Autonomy in ELT. *English Language Teaching Journal,* 50/1, 67–68.

Wilkins, D. (1972). *Linguistics in Language Teaching.* London: Arnold.

White, G. (2006). Teaching Listening: Time for a Change in Methodology. In E. Usó-Juan & A. Martínez-Flor (Eds.), *Current Trends in the Development and Teaching of the Four Language Skills.* Berlin: De Gruyter Mouton, 111–135.

Whyte, S. (2016). Who Are the Specialists? Teaching and Learning Specialised Language in French Educational Contexts. *Recherche et pratiques pédagogiques en langues de spécialité. Cahiers de l'Apliut,* 35(spécial 1), 283p.

Williamson Hawkins, M. (2018). Self-directed Learning as Related to Learning Strategies, Self-regulation, and Autonomy in an English

Language Program: A Local Application with Global Implications. *Studies in Second Language Learning and Teaching*, 8(2): Special Issue: Language Learning Strategies: Linking with the Past, Shaping the Future (R. Oxford & M. Pawlak, eds.), 445–469.

Willis, J. (1996). *A Framework for Task-Based Learning*. London: Longman.

Willis, D. & Willis, J. (2007). *Doing Task-Based Teaching*. Oxford: Oxford University Press.

Woodrow, L. (2018). *Introducing Course Design in English for Specific Purposes*. Abingdon: Routledge.

Wright, T. (1987). *Roles of Teachers and Learners*. Oxford: Oxford University Press.

Yang, J., Schneller, C., & Roche, S. (Eds.). (2015). *The Role of Higher Education in Promoting Lifelong Learning*. Hamburg: UNESCO Institute for Lifelong Learning. http://www.sel-gipes.com/uploads/1/2/3/3/12332 890/unesco_-_2015-_the_role_of_higher_education_in_promoting_li felong_learning.pdf

Zavasnik, M. (2007). ESP Teacher Training Needs: The Case of Slovenia. In *XVI Symposium on Language for Special Purposes (LSP). Specialised Language in Global Communication*, 97–98. Hamburg: University of Hamburg.

Zohrabi, M. (2013). Mixed Method Research: Instruments, Validity, Reliability and Reporting Findings. *Theory and Practice in Language Studies*, 3(2), 254–262.

List of Authors

Dr. Patrizia Anesa is an Associate Professor in English Language and Translation at the University of Bergamo, Italy. She holds a Ph.D. in English Studies, with a specialisation in professional communication. She is a member of the Research Centre on Specialised Languages (CERLIS) and is also an Associate Editor of the IDEA project (International Dialects of English Archive). Her research interests lie mostly in the area of specialised discourse. In particular, she is currently interested in the applications of Conversation Analysis in LSP and the investigation of knowledge asymmetries in expert-lay communication.

Dr. Ana Bocanegra-Valle is a Senior Lecturer at the University of Cadiz (Spain). Her main research interests include Maritime English, ESP/ EAP methodology, English for research publication, and ESP/EAP discourse. She is at present Book Review editor for *ESP Today* and *RESLA*. She has published articles and book chapters in prestigious journals and publishing houses and has served as peer reviewer for a wide number of journals both in Spain and abroad. Her latest books are *Applied Linguistics and Knowledge Transfer. Employability, Internationalisation and Social Challenges* (Peter Lang, 2020) and *Ethnographies of Academic Writing Research. Theory, Methods and Interpretation* (John Benjamins, co-edited, 2021).

Dr. Brankica Bošnjak Terzić is a technical English teacher at the Faculty of Mechanical Engineering and Naval Architecture of the University of Zagreb, Croatia. She has 19 years of experience in teaching ESP. She obtained her Ph.D. degree in 2018 with a dissertation titled Self-regulated vocabulary learning in ESP. She has authored and co-authored several case reports, review and research papers. She has also authored ESP textbooks for secondary schools. The fields of her scientific and professional interests are: language strategies, vocabulary learning strategies, ESP, self-regulated learning and motivation in ESP and e-learning.

Dr. Olinka Breka is a technical and business English teacher at the Faculty of Mechanical Engineering and Naval Architecture, University of Zagreb, with more than 25 years of experience in teaching ESP. Her main fields of interest are language teaching methodology, materials development, and professional teacher development. She has authored and co-authored several review and research papers, a number of series for teaching general and business English, and two technical English textbooks for students of mechanical engineering. In her doctoral dissertation, she focuses on the role of textbooks and teachers in the development of intercultural competence in foreign language teaching and learning.

Dr. Marie-Anne Châteaureynaud is a senior lecturer at the University of Bordeaux where she teaches Spanish, Occitan, language teaching and courses on the education system, in the teacher training school INSPE. She holds a Ph.D. and a habilitation to direct researches. Its areas of investigation concern Occitan sociolinguistics, inclusive plurilingualism, language teaching, LSP teaching, applied linguistics and minority languages. Also learning processes, higher education issues, research training, and lifelong learning are an important part of her research.

Dr. Marie-Christine Deyrich is Professor Emerita of applied linguistics at the University of Bordeaux and member of the LACES laboratory. She has been involved in several European projects funded by the Council of Europe among which LILAMA (language learning for the labour market), INCLUDE (Language learning for active social inclusion) and TRAILs (LSP teacher training). Her writings deal with ethical language teaching in intercultural issues, linguistic policy, LSP learning and teaching in higher education.

Cailean Dooge works as an English teacher and LSP trainer at the University of Bergamo and is also currently the Director of Studies of a language school, where her role includes management of courses and teacher training. She has over 20 years' experience teaching English in Italy, Ireland, and Taiwan, and has organised and taught LSP courses in the medical, tourism, and automotive fields. She is originally from Zimbabwe and has a BA in English Literature and Drama from Rhodes University in South Africa. Her research interests lie in LSP materials design.

Dr. Pascaline Faure is a Senior Lecturer at Sorbonne Université School of Medicine. Her research interests are the linguistic and didactic aspects of medical languages. Her research focusses on medical terminology in a comparative approach between English and French as well as on the teaching of English for medical purposes in Higher Education. She is the author of Les langues de la médecine: analyse comparative interlingue (Peter Lang, 2021) and of L'anglais médical et le français médical: analyse linguistico-culturelle et modélisations didactiques (EAC, 2012), and one of the editors of Apprendre les langues à l'université au 21e siècle (Riveneuve, 2013).

Russell Henry Greenwood is a lecturer of Nautical and Logistical English and a researcher at the Jade University of Applied Sciences, Germany. He has provided ESP to various businesses, faculties, private clients and universities since 2011. His research into Languages for Specific Purposes includes content creation for the MariLANG project, which created testing, teaching and learning facilities for Maritime English pursuant to IMO Model Course 3.17, and Output 1 of the TRAILs project, which sought to create an ambitious curriculum for LSP teacher training in the EHEA.

Dr. Peter John is a Professor for Digital Technologies and Technical Language at Flensburg University of Applied Sciences where he teaches translation and natural language processing. He is also a senior researcher at the Fraunhofer Institute for Digital Media Technology (IDMT). His research interests lie in the automatic assessment of natural language and, generally, in technical communication. He has been involved in a series of projects on Languages for Specific Purposes both in written and in spoken form.

Dr. Violeta Jurkovič is a teacher of ESP and ESAP at the Faculty of Maritime Studies and Transport of the University of Ljubljana, Slovenia. Currently, she teaches Maritime English for students of navigation and marine engineering, and English for Academic Purposes for students of transport technology and logistics at the undergraduate level. She holds a Ph.D. in language teaching methodology. Her research interests lie in maritime communication, Maritime English, online informal learning of languages, and professional development of teachers of languages for specific purposes.

Dr. Snježana Kereković is a technical and business English teacher at the Faculty of Mechanical Engineering and Naval Architecture, University of Zagreb, with more than 25 years of experience in teaching ESP. Her main fields of interest are language teaching methodology, applied linguistics, terminology and translation. She authored and co-authored several research and review papers, case reports as well as two technical English course books for students of mechanical engineering. She completed her Ph.D. studies with a dissertation on multi-word lexical units in technical English and their equivalents in Croatian.

Dr. Joanna Kic-Drgas graduated from linguistics and economics and is employed as an Assistant Professor in Teaching Languages for Specific Purposes in the Institute of Applied Linguistics at the Faculty of Modern Languages and Literature of the Adam Mickiewicz University in Poznań. Joanna Kic-Drgas has ten years of experience in teaching languages for specific purposes and has authored and co-authored academic and professional papers focused on teaching methodology, intercultural communication, multilingualism and international cooperation.

Dr. Paloma López-Zurita is a Senior Lecturer at the Faculty of Social Sciences and Communication, University of Cadiz, Spain. She holds a Ph.D. in English Philology and has wide experience of teaching English for Specific Purposes both to undergraduates and Master's students. Her main research areas are terminology, lexicology and cross-cultural interference, particularly as applied to specific discourse. She has published in a range of journals including Iberica, Onomázein, Estudios Filológicos, etc. and is at present the Director of the Language for Specific Purposes Panel at the Spanish Society for Applied Linguistics (AESLA).

Dr. M. Dolores Perea-Barberá is a Senior Lecturer in the Faculty of Maritime Studies and in the School of Engineering at the University of Cádiz, Spain, where she teaches Maritime English, English for Engineering, and English for the Shipping Business both at graduate and post-graduate levels. She holds a Ph.D. in Applied Linguistics. Her research interests are specialised vocabulary, vocabulary learning strategies, language education technology, and Integrating Content and Language in Higher Education (ICLHE). She has been the Coordinator of the Bilingual (English/Spanish) Education Program at the School of Engineering since 2017.

Katharine Sherwood works as an English teacher and LSP teacher trainer at the University of Bergamo, alongside her role as an external speaking examiner. Katharine has 20 years' experience of teaching English in Italy, Spain, the UK and China, including several years focusing on LSP in-company (textile engineering, automotive engineering, financial, medical) and at tertiary education level (legal, business). She has also been responsible for teacher training, and the management of language courses, in language schools in both Italy and the UK. Katharine holds a first-class BA in American History and Literature and an MPhil in Publishing Studies. She also worked for several years as a Marketing Manager in the reference and education publishing sector. Her LSP research interests lie in materials evaluation and adaptation.

Dr. Marcelo Tano after studying French Philology and Communication Sciences in Argentina, began his training and work experience in France. He holds a Master's degree in Information-Communication at the University of Nancy, and a doctorate in Spanish from the University of Paris Nanterre. For more than two decades, he has been teaching Spanish (LSP) at the University of Lorraine, where he is also in charge of cooperation relations with Spanish-speaking countries at the Ecole Nationale d'Ingénieurs de Metz. He is an associate researcher at the Laboratoire Inter-universitaire de Recherche en Didactique Lansad and an elected member of the Board of Directors of the Groupe d'Étude et de Recherche en Espagnol de Spécialité. He was elected president of this group from 2011 to 2019 and editorial director of Les Cahiers du GÉRES. He is currently coordinator for France of the research project "Spanish in Europe", conducted by the Universities of Heidelberg and Zurich in collaboration with the Cervantes Institute.

Dr. María Vázquez-Amador is an Assistant Lecturer in the Faculty of Social Sciences and Communication at the University of Cadiz, Spain, where she teaches English for Tourism. In the last twenty years she has taught other ESP subjects such as Business English, English for Marketing, Commercial English and English for Nursing, both at graduate and post-graduate levels. She holds a Ph.D. in Applied Linguistics. She has published on a range of topics in English for Specific Purposes. Her research focuses on the influence of English in the Spanish press, terminology, lexicology, ESP methodology and specialised vocabulary.

Dr. Joanna Woźniak is an Assistant Professor at the Institute of Applied Linguistics, at the Adam Mickiewicz University, Poznań. She holds a Ph.D. in Applied Linguistics. Her research interests lie mostly in the area of discourse linguistics, contrastive German-Polish phraseology, languages for specific purposes, and foreign language learning and teaching. She is a member of the European Society of Phraseology (EUROPHRAS) and the editorial team of the scientific journal Glottodidactica. An International Journal of Applied Linguistics.

Champs didactiques plurilingues :
données pour des politiques stratégiques

The Book Series «Champs didactiques plurilingues» aims to promote practice and research about foreign language teaching and learning from a triple bond between subjects, objects and contexts, each with their individual and interacting dynamics. It involves the disciplinary fields involved in the production of practical and theoretical ideas, and of the concrete, educational and professional contexts of teaching and learning, together with school and university language policies which influence the learning of a particular language, the choice of languages and their status. The series is divided into three strands: one strand, "Research in action" is intended for researchers, student-researchers, and practitioner-researchers, which can include many teachers; a second strand "Knowledge for know-how" is intended especially for students, practitioners and decision-makers; the other strand "Research exchanges"specially designed for papers written from conferences and congress papers.

«Champs didactiques plurilingues» publish books in English, French, Portuguese or Spanish and a partnership with the journal Matices en Lenguas Extranjeras of the Universidad Nacional de Colombia (https://revistas.unal.edu.co) allows authors to publish a podcast presenting their book.

Series editor: Patrick Chardenet

Ouvrage parus

Savoirs pour savoir faire

Vol. 1 – Laurent Puren et Bruno Maurer (dir.), *La crise de l'apprentissage en Afrique francophone subsaharienne. Regards croisés sur la didactique des langues et les pratiques enseignantes.* 2018.

Vol. 3 – Kaouthar Ben Abdallah et Mohamed Embarki, *Éducation et formation en contexte plurilingue maghrébin. Problématiques entre didactique et politique linguistique éducative.* 2020.

Vol. 4 – Maria Helena Araújo e Sá & Carla Maria Ataíde Maciel (eds.), *Interculturalidade e plurilinguismo nos discursos e práticas de educação e formação. Contextos pós-coloniais de língua portuguesa.* 2021.

Vol. 9 – Haydée Silva (dir.), *Regards sur le jeu en didactique des langues et des cultures. Penser, concevoir, évaluer, former.* 2022.

Vol. 10 – Jean-Marc Mangiante et Chantal Parpette (dir.), *État de la recherche en FOS et en FOU.* 2022.

La recherche en mouvement

Vol. 2 – Jue Wang Szilas, *Apprendre des langues distantes en eTandem. Une étude de cas dans un dispositif universitaire sino-francophone.* 2020.

Vol. 5 – Pierre Demers, *Elements of Second and Foreign Languages Teaching to Indigenous Learners of Canada. Theories, Strategies and Practices.* 2021.

Vol. 6 – Francisco Lorenzo, Virginia de Alba Quiñones, Olga Cruz-Moya (eds.), *El español académico en L2 y LE. Perspectivas desde la educación bilingüe.* 2022.

Vol. 7 – Zehra Gabillon, *Apprentissage de langues additionnelles dans un cadre scolaire plurilingue. Langues autochtones, étrangères, régionales et patrimoniales.* 2022.

Vol. 8 – Marie-Anne Châteaureynaud, *Sociodidactique du plurilinguisme et de l'altérité inclusive. Des langues régionales aux langues des migrants.* 2022.

Vol. 11 – Rita Carol, *Enseigner une matière scolaire dans une langue étrangère. Des théories aux pratiques.* 2022.

Vol. 12 – Zehra Gabillon, *Learning additional languages in plurilingual school settings. Autochthonous, foreign, regional and heritage languages.* 2022.

Vol. 13 – Marie-Anne Chateaureynaud and Peter John (eds.), *LSP Teacher Training Summer School. The TRAILs project.* 2023.

www.peterlang.com

Printed in Great Britain
by Amazon

32566341R00155